Strategy-Technology Alignment: Deriving Business Value from ICT

By

Paul Griffiths

Published by Academic Conferences and Publishing International

Strategy-Technology Alignment: Deriving Business Value from ICT Projects

Second Printing 2012

First published August 2011 by Academic Conferences and Publishing International Ltd, Reading, UK info@academic-publishing.org

ISBN: 978-1-908272-11-9

Printed by Lightning Source POD

Contents

About the Editor

Dr Paul Griffiths BSc, MEng, DBA, A.Dip.C

Dr Paul Griffiths has been advising global companies on how to use ICT for over 20 years. He has advised corporate leaders on how to steer their organisations towards environmental sustainability and manage their intangibles. He has assisted business leaders to reflect on ethics and corporate responsibility.

Paul is a partner with The Birchman Group global management consulting firm headquartered in the UK; he is President of the Professional Association for the Environment in Chile (AEPA in Spanish); he is Visiting Faculty at Henley Business School, University of Reading; and Affiliate Professor at the Catholic University (Lima, Peru).

Paul has consulted for global companies on business transformation, including Zurich Financial Services, Allianz-AGF, BHP-Billiton, Kinross, Mercedes Benz, Nabisco, Chrysler, Cadbury-Schweppes, Coca-Cola, Pirelli, Nestle, Colgate, Fonterra, ENDESA, Aguas Barcelona, Varta, Copec, Arcor, Masisa and Orica. He has written market reports for *Lafferty World Card Intelligence* and *Business Monitor International*.

Paul holds a DBA (Doctorate in Business Administration) from Brunel University and a Master's degree in engineering from Sheffield University, both in the UK. He was a Humphrey Fellow (Fulbright Commission) at the University of Minnesota. He is a prolific writer and a renowned speaker at conferences and seminars.

List of Contributors

Frederic Adam; *University College Cork, Ireland*

Maria Alaranta; *Turku Centre for Computer Science, Finland*

Tom Biss; *University of Plymouth, UK*

Sven Carlsson; *Lund University, Lund, Sweden*

Fergal Carton; *University College Cork, Ireland*

Julie Dawson; *University of Lincoln, UK*

Ibrahim Elbeltagi; *Plymouth Business School, UK*

Linda Frygell; *Lund University, Lund, Sweden*

Jonas Hedman; *Lund University, Lund, Sweden*

Robbert in 't Hout; *Delft University of Technology, The Netherlands*

Mojisola Olugbode; *University of Plymouth, UK*

Jonathan Owens; *University of Lincoln, UK*

Pieter Schrijnen; *Delft University of Technology, The Netherlands*

Matthew Simmons; *Beale and Cole Building Services Limited, UK*

Jos Vrancken; *Delft University of Technology, The Netherlands*

Carla Wilkin; *Monash University, Victoria, Australia*

Foreword

This book represents the accumulation of many years of experience and also a decade of academic research.

Aligning Strategy and Technology is the object of many organisations, but few have ever managed to achieve this with any noteworthy degree of success.

Paul Griffiths has been involved in such organisations and has made a major contribution to both strategic thinking and the planning and implementation of these technological achievements.

Paul has combined his experience and knowledge into a hybrid book which both discusses the theory of strategic technology alignment and also provides case study descriptions of how this has been done in practice. The case studies used are examples which have been written by leading researchers in the field.

I have pleasure in highly recommending this book to academics who need a solid text for teaching, to researchers who require a base line from which to conduct further research ant to practitioners who wish to keep up to date with the latest thinking in the field.

Dan Remenyi
Henley Business School
October 2012

Introduction

In the late 1980s Union Fenosa of Spain, a large electric utility, decided it would try and get some payback on the tens of millions of US dollars it had paid Andersen Consulting to develop its information systems. It decided to do so by setting up a consulting firm aimed at utilities that would customise Union Fenosa's state-of-the-art systems to the specific needs of those organisations.

In the early 1990s I was employed by Union Fenosa to start their consulting business in Latin America under the brand name *Ibersis*. Because we had a large contract in Uruguay, it was decided that this company should be set up in Montevideo. The business model was that Ibersis would recruit young and bright professionals (e.g., engineers, accountants), give them a consulting skills training, and then send them to on-the-job training for a few months in key business areas (e.g., distribution, generation, customer service) at Union Fenosa in Spain. After this experience the consultants would be ready to send to the Group's consulting Clients around the world for a significant daily rate.

In 1992 we entered a new service area that opened up a huge growth potential. I could easily say that I had a vision that transformed Ibersis radically, but I would be deceiving both the reader and myself. The truth of the story is that I had found an opportunity to place a few plant-maintenance consultants at utilities in the region so I needed to have them taken in the trainee programme at Union Fenosa. In those days the company owned and operated two nuclear power stations, so the ideal thing would be to have them placed there where, I imagined, they would learn the leading practices in plant maintenance.

The issue was that when I called my friends and bosses Santiago Roura and Javier Lopez-Costa in Madrid to obtain these placements I found them non-committal and rather difficult to persuade. However, I noticed that every time I called them about that initiative, they kept mentioning in an as-a-matter-of-fact way that a German software company they were working with in Eastern Europe had approached them to see if we could develop together the Latin American market, and would I meet them to assess the potential for this. I was really not very interested in the German software, but I realised that if I did not respond to this request I would not make much progress with the three plant-maintenance positions that were my focus at the time. So I decided to catch a flight to Madrid and go and meet Jürgen Nitzche, the head of the company for southern Europe, and Hans-Werner Hector, one of the four founders of the company. I came out of that meeting with an action plan to jointly tackle Latin America, and went straight to Roura's office - with this action plan I was sure he would now listen more carefully to my plant-maintenance petition. I flew back to Montevideo the following day, happy that I had secured the three positions. I had also committed to sending another four young professionals to work at the German software company´s Madrid office to learn how to deploy the software solution.

In the first few months of 1993 we developed our action plan with the Germans, starting in Buenos Aires. We held a prospective Clients meeting at the *Club Alemán* on Avenida Corrientes, where we had close to 100 business leaders in an IT meeting, something unheard of at the time. The term *Enterprise Resource Planning* and its acronym *ERP* had not been coined yet, so it was quite difficult to explain what this new software was about. Only the term *integration* of all business functions in the organisation seemed to get some traction. Nevertheless, Nitsche and Hector spoke about the marvels of the company and its software, and I presented on how it should be implemented.

One thing came after the other and we eventually managed to secure our first three projects in Buenos Aires (at the local operations of Mercedes Benz, Deutshe Bank and EDENOR, a recently privatised electric utility). Then came Varta in Colombia, IANSA in Chile, Chrysler and Pirelli in Venezuela, Pirelli in Brazil... By the end of 1994 SAP had taken off in the whole region, and despite of having over 200 consultants generating unprecedented fees, we could not meet the demand. The market unravelled in an explosive way. The rest is history and Ibersis became one of the great success stories in the global consulting world.

Opulence never lasts for long, especially in the volatile technology world. In May 2005 I received a call from the head of SAP America (meaning North America) saying that they had now taken over the Latin American market from SAP Spain, and that their intention was to work with the Big-6 consulting firms and not with unknown firms like Ibersis. After I got over the initial shock, I got back onto a plane, this time to Philadelphia, to meet Bruce Smith. That was one of the toughest meetings in my professional career. Smith was a hard-nosed American who had been persuaded by someone that we were not adequate partners. But I managed to get some concessions and agreement on certain market niches where we could continue operating. But our fate was drawn – the Big-6 firms started taking an ever larger share of the game and we had continuous poaching of our expert staff by these large latecomers. Eventually I also caved in and 11-months after having been approached by Dave Lewis, the man at Price Waterhouse who oversaw the SAP practice in Latin America, after several meeting with Tim Leonard, then head of Management Consulting at Price Waterhouse in South America, and a final interview with the legendary global leader of the Price Waterhouse SAP practice, Chris Evert, I jumped ship. This was not common in those days, and a bit traumatic for me in relation to my friends at Iberisis and Union Fenosa.

I continued as a Partner at Price Waterhouse (later Pricewaterhouse-Coopers) for several years until the management consulting arm was acquired by IBM. However, by the late nineties I was worried that our elder partners, then approximately 55 years old, for some of whom I had deep professional respect, were being shunted aside. I did not want that to happen to me in years to come, so I decided to enrol on a doctoral programme – if the organisation did not have room for someone with my experience, at least I would make sure that I would have alternative paths to direct my career.

After some three years of searching and evaluating alternatives, I decided to enrol on the doctoral programme at Henley Management College. After lunch on the second day of my induction course I was walking down the corridor to my next lecture and walked past the bar area that was packed with people watching the large-screen television. I thought to myself what a curious place that people crowd around a television set early afternoon on a Tuesday. When that lecture finished I went back to the Commons area to find out that the Twin Towers in Manhattan had been felled. September 11. That was the date I inserted myself in the academic world. I finished my doctorate in ICT evaluation in close to record time – not due to brilliance, mind you, but simply that I was self-funding my fees - by early 2005, and have not left research and part-time academia ever since.

As I was approaching the end of my doctorate I decided I wanted to bring my consulting work closer to the realm of my research, and found a company called Birchman, then based in Reading but that has subsequently moved to London, that was precisely in that space. I contacted the heads of the organisation and shortly afterwards we agreed on a plan to start up and develop the firm in Latin America – so that is what I have been doing for the past five years.

That summarises what I intend to compress into this book: Over twenty years' experience as a management consultant helping practitioners get value from their ICT investments, and over 10 years as a part-time researcher in the field. The former should help me keep the content relevant, while the latter should ensure that I stay rigorous.

I believe this book fills an important gap in the literature, both for practicing senior managers participating in significant ICT investment decisions, and for young academics attempting to develop theory in this field. The purpose of the book is to present a theory of *Market Power as a Driver of ICT Investments* developed for the banking industry in Chile, and extend it to other industrial sectors and other geographies.

Chapter 1 will propose a method for building theory from case study analysis. It is not my intention to say that this is the only way to build theory. Nor am I saying this method should be followed rigidly; that would be naive and contradictory to the idea of *scientific anarchy* for which I have deep sympathy:

> *The idea of a method that contains firm, unchanging, and absolutely binding principles for conducting the business of science meets considerable difficulty when confronted with the results of historical research. We find, then, that there is not a single rule, however plausible, and however grounded in epistemology, that is not violated at some time or other...such violations are not accidental events...they are necessary for progress. Feyerabend (2002 [1975], p.14)*

All methods are troublesome, but some are needed and occasionally even useful[1]. Methods are not ends, they are only means, and should be

[1] I am borrowing from Box-Jenkins' characterisation of models in social sciences.

adapted to fulfil the real ends of a research that are to explain, or even predict, a phenomenon. The method I present has worked for me in the ICT evaluation space and in some other management fields, and I offer it as a starting point and guide for young researchers who wish to enter the exciting world of theory building.

Chapter 2 describes a research project based on the prior methodology that proposes a theory of converting ICT investments into value. It was developed by analysing six banks in the Chilean market. The theory has the merit of moving away from the traditional input-output model of ICT evaluation that has proven to be highly erratic. It does this by introducing a *process* construct that explains *how* the input affects the output, and it subtends this process box using a well established theory. Crowston & Treacy (1986) suggest *Market Power* or *Transaction Cost Economics* as potential routes to underpin the process construct. Interestingly, transaction costs economics, although developed strongly in the last 30 years through the work of Oliver Williamson and others, has its roots in the work of Commons and Coarse in the early 1930s. Coincidently, market power theory was formalised in 1932 by an economist called Edward Chamberlin.

I went with Market Power for two reasons:

The impact of ICT on organisational structure through the application of transaction costs economics has been substantially researched. ICT reduced the costs of transaction which led to changes in the "make vs. buy" equation (vertical integration) and the redefinition of organisational boundaries. It has led some thinkers to propose the advent of Meta-Capitalism (Grady Means and Schneider). Much of this research takes the form of supply chain management and e-business. Far less research has been done into ICT and its impact on Market Power – so in my decision there was a drive for originality.

I am motivated by the role of ICT in revenue enhancement. As can be seen in Roach (1991), financial services organisations have really put too much focus on cost reduction and therefore put their long term survival at risk. There is already substantial research in the role of ICT in cost *avoidance* (a better term than cost *reduction*) as most academics and practitioners in this field will be able to witness.

This chapter ends by proposing the Theory of Market Power ICT Investments for Value Creation and presenting the Value-Builder ICT Investment Decision Model.

Chapter 3 closes Part I by describing how I have selected a series of published case studies to map onto the *Theory of Market Power ICT Investments for Value Creation* and attempt to extend its validity to other industries and other geographies.

Chapters 4 to 10 each include a case study and its review. The cases have been classified into *Efficiency driven* and *Market Power driven* ICT investments. The former are included in Part II and the latter in Part III.

Chapter 11 generates a discussion through mapping the case studies onto the theory presented in Chapter 3 with an aim at elucidating new insights and extending the theory to industrial sectors other than banking, and geographies other than Chile.

Chapter 12 arrives at an extended theory and Chapter 13 includes reflections on the process.

How to read this book:

Academics are recommended to read it from cover to cover. Practitioners may opt to skip Chapter 1 entirely, and skim through the initial pages of Chapter 2 – the key concepts of Chapter 2 that will be referred to throughout the rest of the book are in section 2.4 and 2.5, which should be read in detail. Chapter 4 to 10 are fundamental in that they present the case studies, but they can be read in a different order to that presented, without an impact on understanding of the rest of the book.

PART I
Theory Building

Chapter 1

Theory-Building through Comparative Analysis

1.1 Chapter Overview

ICT evaluation is not backed by a comprehensive body of theory. The little theory that exists is fragmented and derived from other fields of study.

Without more theory ICT evaluation is unlikely to mature. This chapter discusses an approach to theory development which is of practical use to ICT researchers. This approach draws on empirical evidence and integrates this evidence with established theory from other sources. It is effectively a data driven hybrid method which employs comparative case analysis techniques.

The approach to theory building described in this chapter reflects the research experience of the author.

1.2 Introduction

A question which is now raised frequently is *Do we actually a need theory of ICT evaluation? Does general evaluation theory not actually suffice?* IS Management academics may readily jump to the conclusion that we obviously do. But when we reflect on how little ICT evaluation is actually done then this question becomes much more challenging and a very pertinent one. On a philosophical level we recognise that ICT evaluation is an important and perhaps endurable or even intractable organisational problem. But, as part of the IS research agenda, is it important that IS evaluation be addressed? And, if so, how much energy should be expended on this topic?

There is of course a tension between what academics do and feel about ICT management and what happens in practice. As pointed out by Benbasat & Zmud, (1999, p.11)

> *for IS research to be more relevant, it is important that authors develop frames of reference which are intuitively meaningful to practitioners ....*

There is also the fact that ICT people whether they are academics, practitioners or consultants tend to place much more importance on their field than do other academics, practitioners and consultants. Even within the field, business practitioners tend to disregard theory. They appear to go from problems to solutions, without much rigorous analysis and little reference to theory[2]. To make things worse, many management techniques or initiatives have been discredited as "the latest management fad", or they may be perceived as potentially good ideas that have been applied to the wrong problems. Solutions that have been applied without taking full account of context and therefore have led to disappointing outcomes. The challenge, therefore, is not only to generate theory that is relevant and possible to implement, but also to clearly define it's circumstance-contingency.

Evaluation of technology is not a new area of practice or research. Notwithstanding the considerable attention it has been given by researchers over the last twenty years, there are surprisingly few generally accepted theories or even frameworks to help practitioners solve the problems that arise in their day to day interactions with technology investment decisions.

This chapter provides a view on the generation of theory on the basis of empirical work, which is the discovery or the development of theory from systematically obtained and analysed evidence. The advantages of

---

[2] In this respect it is interesting to recall the wisdom of Keynes (1936) who pointed out 'The ideas of economists and political philosophers, both when they are right and when they are wrong, are more powerful than is commonly understood. Indeed the world is ruled by little else. Practical men, who believe themselves to be quite exempt from any intellectual influence, are usually the slaves of some defunct economist.'

theories developed in this way, as opposed to those generated through speculation and reformulation of others' speculations, is that the "*theory derived must fit the situation being researched, and must work when put into use*" (Glaser & Strauss, 1967). The theory is developed from the evidence, rather than the theory defining the type of evidence to be collected as in theory testing exercise (Layder, 1993, p.20). However, the method proposed here moves away from the 'pure induction' stance of the traditional grounded theory method by the adoption of a conceptual framework from a synthesis of prior literature and practitioner knowledge.

1.3 The shortcomings of traditional Input-Output Models

The relatively modest success achieved to date in assessing the value of ICT arises from several shortcomings in prevalent research models and business practices. One of these shortcomings arises from the lack of accepted causal models. Current research has, in general, used simple bi-variate correlation analysis to link ICT expenditures to bottom line indicators but has failed to explain *how* and *why* ICT directly affects performance (Griffiths, 2005; McKeen & Smith, 1996). Figure 1.1 typifies this simple approach of trying to correlate one input variable (or even more than one input variable) with a single measure of success.

Figure 1.1: Input-Output Model

Clearly such simple approaches to understanding the value of ICT in organisations is incomplete. As was stated by Bannister (2001, p. 41):

> *Overall, the result of this type of input/output focused research into IT value using the tools of econometrics are less than satisfactory. The data is problematic, the appropriateness of the methodology debatable, the theoretical models open to challenge and the conclusions either weak or intuitively suspect. To cap the problem, the research even throws up conflicting evidence.*

There is an emerging view that studies based on multi-variable process perspectives hold the key to the problem of ICT investment evaluation (Bannister, 2001; Ginzberg,1979, cited by Crowston & Treacy, 1986). So to avoid the shortcomings indicated above from applying the simple bivariate model, this book proposes applying a three-construct model where the intervening construct would explain 'how' ICT investments would impact performance (see Figure 1.2). In other words, it would reveal the 'process' by which ICT investments affect performance and it is thus called 'process box'.

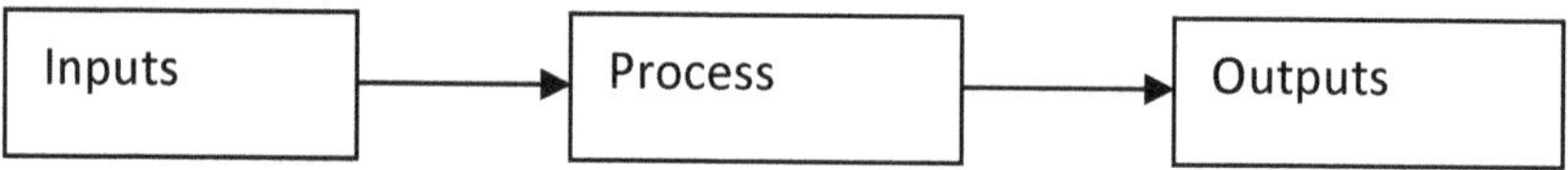

Figure 1.2: Three-construct Model

Based on the work by Crowston & Treacy (1986) on revealing the value of the new technology through understanding 'how' the resulting information will be used, it is proposed that a theory is applied to underpin the process box.

The first step is that the *process theory* should clarify which inputs and outputs are important and needs to offer methods to measure them. Secondly, by explicitly including the processes, the impacts of ICT will be examined in detail. Thirdly, and most importantly, the researcher can discover the contingencies that allow systems to affect firm performance, and prescribe the features of systems that will be useful to particular firms.

With this three-construct model as its foundation stone, this chapter moves on to the process of generating theory.

1.4 What is theory?

Weber (2003, p.iv) points out that:

> *a theory is an account that is intended to explain or predict some phenomena that we perceive in the world.*

Christensen & Raynor (2003, p.68) stress the prediction role of theory and are thus more restrictive in their definition; however, when they describe why good theories are valuable, they say that

> *First, they help us make predictions...Second, sound theories help us interpret the present, to understand what is happening and why.*

Considering that interpret has its roots in the Latin *interpretari,* which means explain (The Concise Oxford Dictionary, Sixth Edition, Eighth Impression, 1979), it can safely be assumed that the definitions are coincident. This book therefore adopts the broader conception: explain or predict.

Reflecting on this characterisation of *account* and *phenomena*: Does it carry an implicit epistemological and ontological position? It is believed that this is not necessarily so. On what a positivist and a post-positivist, or an external realist and an idealist, would differ is in their conception of the fundamental constructs: *things* and *properties of things.*

Rather surprisingly, Weber (2003) puts little explicit emphasis on causation and the importance of rising above mere correlations. He defines *account* of the phenomena as:

> *the explanation of the laws that are hypothesized to relate them – laws that specify the relationship between the values of different properties of a single thing, or laws that specify the relationship between the values of properties of different things. (p.v)*

According to Christensen & Raynor (2003) the construction of a theory requires three steps. It begins with a description of the phenomenon to be understood. It then classifies aspects of the phenomenon into categories. And finally, it formulates a hypothesis of what causes the phenomenon to happen and sometimes why (Figure 1.3).

As a final reflection on theory formulation, we need to differentiate two terms, substantive theory and general theory. The theory we are talking about here is substantive (developed for the study of one small area of investigation and from one specific population). It therefore does not have the explanatory power of a general theory. But the real merit of a substantive theory is that it can directly or specifically address the issues of the population from which it was developed.

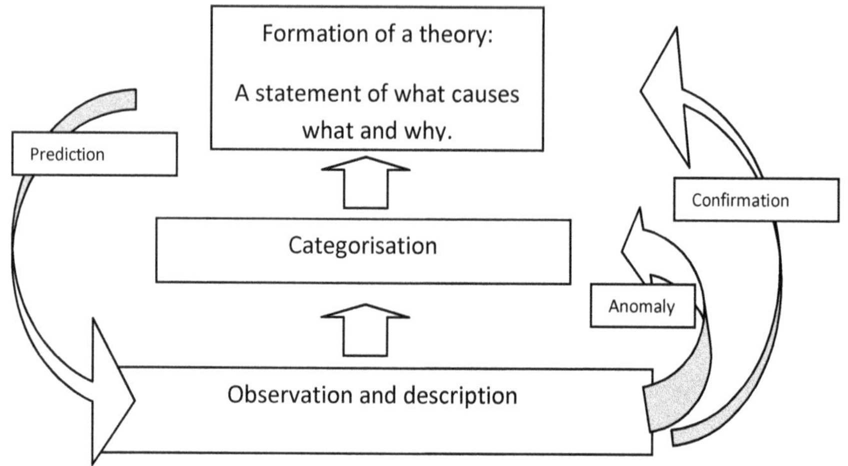

Figure 1.3: Formulating a Theory (Christensen and Raynor, 2003)

And, of course, the greater the variations considered in the theoretical sampling[3], the greater will be its explanatory power and its applicability in case-to-case generalisations (Strauss & Corbin, 1998, p.267). It needs to be remembered that we are studying concepts and their relationships, and manifestations of these concepts may emerge many times in a multiple case study. If our concepts are abstract enough, they are likely to be applicable to other organisations (Strauss & Corbin, 1998, p.284).

1.5 The importance of the selection of cases

According to Hamel (1993, p. 38) a central idea is to *"locate the global in the local"* thus making the careful selection of the research site a highly important decision. Case study research should rely on theoretical sampling where the cases may be chosen to fill theoretical categories and provide examples of *"polar type"* (Eisenhardt, 1989, p. 537).

---

[3] Theoretical sampling may be defined as the process by which the researcher, after previous analysis, seeks samples of population, events, activities guided by his or her emerging (if still rudimentary) theory. This sampling is directly linked to an analysis of the basic categories and distinctions of the emergent theory. The process of sampling, and therefore evidence collection, is guided by the emerging theory (Layder, 1993; p.138; Glaser & Strauss, 1967; p.45).

> *With only a limited number of sites, consider purposeful selection, rather than relying on the idiosyncrasies of chance. The same logic applies to selecting informants and observations, (Light et al., 1990, cited by Maxwell, 1996, p.71).*

Qualitative samples tend to be purposive rather than random, (Kuzel, 1992 and Morse, 1989, cited by Miles and Huberman, 1994, p.27) and it is also important to remember that the selection of an appropriate population controls extraneous variation and helps to define the limits for generalising the findings (Eisenhardt, 1989).

In terms of number of cases to select, Giddens (1984, cited by Hamel, 1993, p.34) says that:

> *...the traditional small-scale community researches of fieldwork anthropology are not in themselves generalising studies. But they can easily become such if carried out in some numbers, so that judgement of the typicality can justifiably be made.*

While there is no ideal number of cases, a number between 4 and 10 often provides adequate evidence. With a small number of cases it is more difficult to generate theory, and its empirical grounding is likely to be less convincing. With more than 10 cases, it becomes difficult to cope with the complexity, volume and the number of variables likely to be present in the evidence (Eisenhardt, 1989).

1.6 Unit of analysis

With respect to selecting the unit of analysis, assessment of the value of information technology can occur at any of six levels of analysis: from the individual level to the economy level, passing through Project, Division, Organisation, Industry (McKeen & Smith, 1996). Based on that there is rigorous research to support that ICT's impact is difficult to capture at the aggregate and industry level (OECD. 2003, p.81), these macro levels of analysis are not recommended for ICT evaluation. Because the impact of an ICT investment depends largely on its alignment with strategy (Griffiths, 2005) and that in qualitative research the unit of analysis does not need to be reduced to its simplest form but may include the complexity of 'whole' situations (Easterby-Smith *et al.*, 2002), organisation level would usually be the most appropriate. However, there may be specific problems where the more micro individual project or division levels are adequate.

In the selection of the cases it is important to keep in mind the need to diminish the effects of extraneous factors or noise in the environment (Eisenhardt, 1989; Remenyi *et al.*, 1998). For example, by taking all organisations from the same country the introduction of noise due to national cultural and macro-economy performance differences would be avoided.

Within that target group of companies, the researcher would benefit by including some extreme or *polar* cases in terms of business strategies and of the use of information technology. In other words, the cases are to be selected with a view at extending the development of emerging categories, properties, hypotheses and the integration of the theory (Eisenhardt, 1989; Griffiths, 2005; Layder, 1993). Additionally, practical considerations such as the following will influence the final selection of the cases:

(a) entry should be relatively easy;
(b) the site should present the possibility of collecting pertinent evidence;
(c) trust should be able to be established with informants; and
(d) evidence quality and credibility of the research should be assured.

1.7 Preparing for fieldwork

In case-study research interviews, despite their limitations as we shall see later, are usually the most relevant source of evidence. This is due to the fact that they are an appropriate means of collecting *highly complex and sensitive information* (Hair *et al.,* 2003, p.142) and when the objective is to obtain insight through the informants' interpretation of human affairs (Yin, 1994, p.85). Most interviews in case studies are semi-structured ones (Scholtz & Tietje, 2002, pp.13-14; Yin, 1994, p.84-85).

The reason for applying semi-structured in-depth interviews, as opposed to open ended ones is to retain some control over the type and quantity of evidence supplied (Miles & Huberman, 1994, p.17). Focused Interviews are recommended as a method for corroborating certain concepts as they emerge, and interpretations of events. They are narrower in scope than the semi-structured ones (Yin, 1994, p.85). Because interview evidence are verbal reports and therefore need to be corroborated by other types of evidence (Bickman & Rog, 1998, p.247), the research design is to contemplate the analysis of multiple documentary sources, including meeting memorandums, strategy plans, project charters and annual reports. A critical aspect of this is imposing a framework or structure on the evidence that will allow the researcher to catalogue the themes and concepts.

With this framework the researcher is then ready to bring together the theoretical concepts that emerged from the literature (represented in the model of departure), with the case-specific concept that emerged from analysing the Annual Reports and preliminary interviews, on an interview guide. The questions should start from general background (on the company and the informant), then move on to business strategy, and finally move onto the ICT evaluation issue object of the study. Based on experience, it is most important to leave a final section of the interview for open discussion where the informant is encouraged to comment on an issue of his or her specific interest in relation to ICT evaluation; some of the most insightful concepts emerge from this section of the interview.

> *Data reduction refers to the process of selecting, focusing, simplifying, abstracting, and transforming the data that appear in written-up field notes or transcriptions"*

Reduction is followed by evidence *display* which, in addition to extended text, would take the form of matrices, graphs, charts and networks (Miles & Huberman, 1994, pp.10-11). After having an early version of the interview guide, the researcher should try to imagine how she wants to display the evidence, and check that this is coherent with the evidence that is going to emerge from the interviews.

Once the researcher is satisfied with the interview guide, preparation should be finalised by planning the meetings themselves and when to use techniques such as *the silent probe*, *overt encouragement*, *request for elaboration and clarification*, and *repetition*. Again, although much of the literature found in this area applies more to survey interviews, some useful and applicable advice can be found (Churchill & Iacobucci, 2002; Trochim, 2001).

1.8 Comparative analysis as a theory-building process

Theory building is about creation as well as discovery; or, to use Weick's (1995) terms, about authoring as well as interpreting. As such it depends much on the creativity or imagination of the researcher. Almost by definition there are no rules to secure results in this endeavour. In the final analysis, it depends on the researcher's personal qualities; on her natural curiosity; on his interpretation of the evidence which in turn will be dependent on the researcher's values and philosophical stance and context; and, to a certain extent, providence. However, I do believe that creativity can be triggered by method, and I will now describe a method that has worked for me.

Concepts are the building blocks of theory (Strauss & Corbin, 1998), so the research process consists of identifying concepts, analysing their differences and similarities through comparison, and finally integrating them into a theory by defining relationships between them. In line with this, the method I propose for building theory essentially consists of questions followed by comparisons, which in turn lead to further questions. This approach is materialised in a process that goes from theoretical model of departure, to evidence collection, to analysis, to comparison with theory, to conceptualisation, to theoretical sampling, and back to evidence collection and a new cycle (see figure 1.4). It has similarities with the grounded theory approach of Glaser & Strauss (1967) – particularly in that it promotes theory which is grounded on empirical evidence - but differs from it in two fundamental ways: that it builds on prior knowledge, and that it carefully questions the evidence before disregarding any accepted theory.

Building on prior knowledge means that it is not pure induction. On the continuum between purely inductive and purely deductive, positivist research, this method is off-centre towards induction. It adheres to Glaser & Strauss' remarkable contributions in democratising theory-building, but I do not believe we should disregard the work of our predecessors. I know that there is a cost in this, and that we may be losing opportunities by not starting from a green-field, but I believe the benefits off-set the costs.

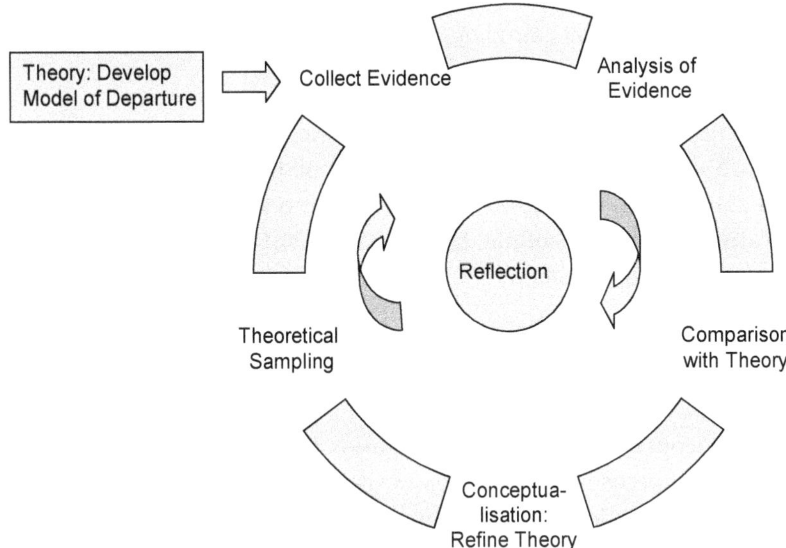

Figure 1.4: Theory-building Process

We modestly abide by Newton's expression that *If I have seen further, it is because I have stood on the shoulders of giants*. Starting from scratch has its attraction, but it is not pragmatic in times when research projects are ever more constrained for time and budgets.

Grounded theory is a "progress in small steps" approach. It will not lead to quantum leaps in knowledge. It is empiricist in that it assumes that if theory and evidence are in disagreement, it is the theory that is "wrong" and needs changing or dumping. But it ignores the fact that if theory and evidence disagree, it could actually mean that the evidence is contaminated by our present set of accepted knowledge (i.e., paradigms). It ignores that evidence is distorted or tinted by the lens through which we observe it. It does not give space for the "counterinduction" concept (Feyerabend, 1975). The empiricist approach of grounded theory is necessary for progress, but it needs to be followed or preceded by non-empiricist work that questions the evidence. That makes us aware of our tacit assumptions, and helps us scrutinise our accepted theories through comparison rather than through analysis.

I shall not describe each of the stages in the theory-building process indicated in figure 1.4, in this chapter. However, I will analyse sampling, in particular theoretical sampling, which is a critical factor in the development of theory.

The sampling strategy needs to respond to the research question, and because we are concerned with theory-building, it is theoretical rather than statistical sampling. In other words, the focus is not on the representativeness of the sample, but on its ability to identify similarities and differences across cases.

Theoretical sampling is about selecting sources of evidence on the basis of the concepts that emerge in the research, as they emerge. It is based on the idea of making comparisons with an aim at detecting variations in these concepts and at making categories denser in terms of their properties and dimensions. The focus of theoretical sampling is on incidents and events; people, organisations and places are means to study those incidents and events. Rather than being pre-determined from the beginning, theoretical sampling evolves during the research process.

Theoretical sampling is important when exploring new areas because it enables the researcher to choose those avenues that render the greatest theoretical returns. It is cumulative; each event sampled builds from and adds to previous evidence; and it becomes more specific with time and progress. It should be worked out carefully in order not to waste time on unproductive detours, but on the other hand it cannot be too rigid, as this limits creativity. It should be directed by the logic and aim at each stage of the research project. In the early stages

> *it is crucial to maintain a balance between systematically gathered data that will enable the development of categories (Strauss & Corbin, 1998)*

and flexibility that allows events and interviews to flow openly. During relational and variational sampling the researcher looks for dimensional variations and differences in concepts, and links between concepts. Discriminate sampling and selective coding come in the final phases when integrating concepts for articulating the theory, validating the relationships amongst concepts, and filling in categories for further refinement. Sensitivity usually grows as the research progresses, and this enables the researcher to better understand what concepts to look for and where to find them. When more sensitivity has developed, the researcher can legitimately return to the evidence and re-analyse it, meaning that evidence collection and analysis is not a linear process but an interactive one (Layder, 1998; Remenyi *et al.*, 1998).

Finally, the question is, up to when should the researcher continue sampling? It is until she has reached theoretical saturation, and she will know when she has arrived there when:

(a) No new relevant evidence seems to arise for all categories;
(b) Categories are dense in terms of their properties and variation of dimensions; and
(c) When relationships between categories are validated by evidence.

(Strauss & Corbin, 1998, p.201-213).

Once the researcher has enticed four to ten organisations into volunteering as case studies, it is quite a common short-coming for her to go out and interview informants in all or several of them in parallel. By doing so the researcher forfeits the opportunity of using the conceptualisations that emerge from one case, to guide evidence collection in the subsequent ones. My experience is that it is more productive to start off with evidence collection and analysis in two organisations (rather than one, to allow for comparison) and then do the remaining ones in succession, as a means of exploiting theoretical sampling (and the research process in general) at its full potential. It is also good practice to leave one or two cases out for the theory building phase, and using them to corroborate or refine the theory at a later stage.

A further reflection is that, although one is aware of the interplay between philosophical ideas and the methodologies to apply when doing empirical research work, it is quite common for these two levels of thinking to move on different, parallel planes. On one hand, it is difficult to "land" abstract philosophical ideas in order to make them of use to solve practical problems, and on the other we get so involved in the process of empirical work (evidence gathering and analysis) that we do not take a step back and see how our findings can be related to higher level philosophical positions.

1.9 The interview as a source of evidence

Through interviews we obtain the interpretations of our informants on the things and events of the phenomenon we want to study. But there are many other issues at stake in an interview. It is the attitude of the informant towards an interview (people have different ideas on what is expected of them in an interview, of the time they should devote to it, of whether they are doing it as a favour or whether the organisation is imposing it on the individual; on the informants opinion on the value of the research for her and her organisation). And there are political issues such as how will what the informant is saying affect her career in the organisation.

And there are marketing aspects such as what image of herself, of the Division, of the Company, of the Profession, of the Industry, does the informant want to convey, or rivalry across Divisions within an organisation (e.g., I have been asked more than once what other people in their organisation had responded to a particular question).

Alvesson & Sköldberg (2000, p.193) put it graphically when they say that:

> *How interviewees appear or represent reality in specific interview situations has less to do with how they, or reality, really are (or how they perceive a reality out there); rather, it is about the way they temporarily develop a form of subjectivity, and how they represent reality in relation to the local discursive context created by the interview.*

The researcher has to try to see through these things and take them into account at the time of interpretation, analysis and reflection. But also,

> *it is important to raise the perspective and not be too limited by observed behaviours or interview accounts, but to consider these in terms of the broader context (Alvesson & Sköldberg, 2000, p.270).*

Interviews can become too much of an evidence extraction exercise or, applying Potter's (1997, p.149, cited by Alvesson & Sköldberg, 2000, p. 206) terminology, *as a machinery for harvesting data from respondents*. An effective interview should move beyond this and become integrated into the action/interaction of the organisation. If this is achieved, the interview becomes an interaction in its own right (Alvesson & Sköldberg, 2000, p.206). But this is difficult to achieve and may need the researcher becoming deeply familiar with the organisation before the interview. It probably means spending a significant amount of time in the informant organisation. It is also more difficult to do in highly structured or semi-structured interviews where one follows a script. It is more feasible to do in a focused interview when the researcher is highly conversant on the issue in discussion and the informants open up in a discussion from which they believe they are getting value in the form of expert advice.

In line with this, I recommend not relying entirely on interviews for evidence collection, and suggest some form of collaborative thinking (Remenyi, 2005) or participant-observation as the method to obtain empirical material of non-trivial nature (at least as a complement to interviews).

1.10 Discussion on the strengths of this approach.

As opposed to quantitative theory testing research projects, where so much emphasis is put on generalisability and are as a consequence method-driven, the research method proposed here is very much defined by the concepts that emerge during the research process.

It is understandable that if I have been effective in conveying these ideas, the reader will now have doubts as to what it would mean if quantitative testing of his theory falsified it. What will an anomaly mean? Will it mean the theory needs reviewing, or will it mean that the evidence is contaminated?

Going further, Alvesson & Sköldberg (2000, p.274) ask themselves how do you know if the project has been successful? If you do not allow empirical evidence to provide a basis for assessing research, then the evaluation of theories and of ideas becomes considerably more difficult. Worse, if excessive focus is given to

> *linguistics and [on] the textualisation of social and material conditions*

it can easily lead to *freedom projects* which are the result of armchair constructions which would be problematic to put into practice.

> *The very definition of meaningful research makes it impossible to lay down any simple or unambiguous rules for evaluation of the research in question.*

And these two issues (putting the findings into practice, and being able to evaluate the research) are important factors in my opinion. So my compromise is that we should not take empirical evidence on face value; we should question it and try to understand the underlying paradigms in their definition and perception. But once we have done this, we accept that empirical evidence (qualitative and quantitative) is valid for testing theory. This is like a virtuous spiral that leads to ever more clear understanding and explanation (knowledge).

1.11 Conclusions

There are different approaches to building theory from empirical evidence. However, I believe that one of the most powerful means of doing so is through the comparative method which involves comparing groups of both maximum and minimum similarity, because of its coverage of many diverse properties of the groups studied. These exercises in comparison enable developing categories, properties and hypotheses as they emerge from the collection and analysis of evidence (Layder, 1993, pp.137-139; Glaser & Strauss, 1967, pp.21-31). The multiple-case-study method as a means of doing comparative analyses for addressing the *why?* and *how?* questions about contemporary events over which the researcher has little or no control (Eisenhardt, 1989; Remenyi *et al.*, 1998; Yin, 1994) is tackled in considerable depth.

The use of several sources of evidence is proposed in order to triangulate information, but interviews are especially relevant, due to that they are an appropriate means of collecting *highly complex and sensitive information* (Hair *et al.*, 2003, p.142), particularly when the objective is to obtain insight through the informants interpretation of human affairs (Yin, 1994, p.85). However, I argue that over-reliance on interviews can be a weakness as there are many external factors at stake in an interview which introduce limitations. Overcoming these limitations requires the researcher to move beyond the interview as an evidence extraction exercise, to one where the interview becomes integrated into the action/interaction of the organization (Alvesson & Sköldberg, 2000, p. 206; Potter, 1997, p.149).

Further, this chapter articulates some reflections on representativeness or generalisability, as being not so much a function of the group or case under investigation, as it is of the object of the study (Hamel, 1993).

Therefore the selection of the cases to analyse must not be done at random, but observing closely the object of the study, and it is the researcher's responsibility to try to understand what it is that the cases might fail to represent (Yin, 1994).

As a final reflection, I question myself for having called this methodology as theory-building, as opposed to theory testing. As I reflect on the process as it develops, I find this labelling loses strength in the sense that this research approach does both theory building and theory testing, as almost a continuous process of switching from one mode to the other. It departs from a conceptual framework which is compared to evidence (in a theory testing mode) and then goes on to conceptualise (theory building) ending up with the model and theory, and then goes to testing findings through corroboration of the theory with the final one or two cases, once it is considered that theoretical saturation is achieved.

Chapter 2

Market Power as a Driver for ICT Investment Decisions

This chapter describes a piece of research in the strategy-technology alignment space. It specifically addresses the question How can managers in financial services organisations (FSOs) use ICT investments to improve performance through the attainment of Market Power?

Applying the methodology described in Chapter 1 to six cases from the Chilean banking sector, the conceptual underpinning of the study draws from the industrial economics theory of market power; the value discipline of market leaders; and the 'Managing by Maxims' process of ICT planning.

Based on the literature and grounded on the findings of the empirical work, it proposes the following theoretical conjecture: Banks that operate in a *customer intimacy* or *product leadership* value discipline will only convert into value those ICT investments which enable them to increase their Market Power.

2.1 Introduction and Research Question

The objective of this chapter is to derive a theory that will help financial services organisations in deploying information and communications technology (ICT)[4] for value creation. With this objective in mind, the concept of Market Power is applied to developing guidelines for practitioners in their decision making in the ICT investment space. This is achieved by addressing the following research question:

---

[4] To all practical purposes in relation to this research, the acronyms ICT and IT are equivalent and will be used interchangeably.

How can managers in financial services organisations (FSOs) use ICT investments to create improved performance through the attainment of Market Power?

This research is approached in a theory building mode. In a general sense, it pursues the construction of theory through empirical work (Glaser & Strauss, 1967; Layder, 1993). The research strategy is multiple case studies (Yin, 1994) and the methods applied are primarily qualitative.

2.2 Converting ICT Investments into Value

2.2.1 The Literature

A characteristic of ICT is that it is *an interdisciplinary field straddling other disciplines* (Webster & Watson, 2002), and as a consequence the ICT evaluation literature is overlapping and highly dispersed. So, how can we understand the way information technology investments create value in this complex environment? According to Read *et al.* (2001, p. 97)[5]:

> *At its simplest level, value is created by generating revenues from the delivery of products and services to customers that exceed the cost of the delivery process.*

So, in essence, the impact of information technology on value creation in any organisation can happen either through increasing revenues or through reducing costs, and thus enhancing operating profits. This section provides conceptual order along the four perspectives through which cost reduction and revenue enhancement ICT investments were analysed in the literature review, as is summarised in table 2.1.

The first of these perspectives, which can be called the *inadequacy of measurement tools*, addresses the relationship between ICT investments and productivity. Although the link between ICT investments and firm

---

[5] This definition is based on economics; there are many other approaches to defining value (from the strategy and organisation behaviour literature; marketing; labour economics; ...). See Payne & Holt (2001) for a literature review on different approaches to value.

performance still needs to be researched, there is evidence to support that the productivity paradox of information technology can be explained by the output measurement limitations in a service economy, and by the limitations in change management in ICT projects. In other words, that present accounting practices are inadequate to measure productivity in the information economy (Brynjolfsson, 1993; Haynes & Thompson, 2000; Bannister & Remenyi, 1999; OECD, 2003), and that the benefits from ICT can take several years to show results on the bottom-line due to limitations in learning how to do business in the post-ICT investment environment (Brynjolfsson, 1993; Peppard, 2001; Haynes & Thompson, 2000; OECD, 2003).

The second perspective, which is referred to as the *portfolio effect* tackles the fact that different ICT Investments achieve fundamentally different systems objectives. These are usually described under four headings as infrastructure, transactional, informational and strategic. These management objectives lead to an ICT infrastructure and transactional, informational, and strategic systems which, together, form the organisation's ICT investment portfolio. Each of the four value creation categories has its own value proposition driven by a different risk and returns profile, and therefore should have its own investment decision criteria (Weill & Broadbent, 1998; Ross & Beath, 2002). But moving to these more sophisticated ICT investment criteria surfaces the limitations of the traditional accounting based tools for supporting business case quantification. Information technology decision-makers need to adopt and adapt tools from other disciplines that give more flexibility for estimating risk and can give value to investment deferral options. However, much research needs to be done before these tools are available for practitioners (Davis, 2002; Benaroch & Kauffman, 1999; Taudes *et al.*, 2000).

The third perspective, which is the *change facilitator* factor, refers to ICT investments and Change Management. ICT implementations can result in radical changes on how work is performed, and therefore stakeholder management needs to be handled with care. Leaders need to go beyond what multiple stakeholders say about the intended information systems implementations and attempt to understand their deeper values and beliefs (communicative action vs. deep structures) as a means of anticipating and reducing resistance to changing the way people work and their use of the new ICT tools (Heracleous & Barrett, 2001). Although ICT

Usage is key to enabling ICT investment returns, there is a notorious lack of accumulation of knowledge in this area. This shortcoming is attributed to the absence of standardised measures which, in turn, derives from the absence of accepted underlying theories (Trice & Treacy, 1986). Finally, there is research to suggest that in order to realise value from ICT investments, these need to be accompanied by complementary investments in changing the organisation, in training, and in infrastructure (McConnell, 1997; Keen, 1991; OECD, 2003).

The fourth perspective, referred to here as the *competitive advantage,* is ICT investments to create a distinct competitive edge. Although there is some evidence that information technology investments have a positive effect on long-term firm performance (Bharadwaj *et al.*, 1999), it appears that it is ICT capability (more than investment) that has a positive effect on the bottom line. Thus, firms should not merely invest in ICT, but also focus on developing their ICT capabilities (Bharadwaj, 2000; Santhanam & Hartono, 2003). What is not well understood are the underlying mechanisms through which rational information technology investments and strong ICT capability lead to superior performance. The main reason for this is that most research efforts have measured the direct relationship between some independent variable related to information technology and performance, without paying attention to intervening variables. An alternative conceptualisation is to have a two-stage model that examines the effect of ICT on intermediate process variables, which in turn are associated with higher level performance variables (McKeen & Smith, 1996; Trice & Treacy, 1986; Crowston & Treacy, 1986).

An additional finding in terms of ICT investments and competitive advantage is that firms that use ICT investments to pursue a cost leadership strategy achieve only a temporary competitive advantage and forfeit the benefits of their ICT investments to their Clients (Hitt & Brynjolfsson, 1996; OECD, 2003).

Considering that it is questionable that ICT investments to pursue a cost leadership strategy convert into value, and that financial services organisations have put excessive focus on cost reduction as opposed to pursuing strategies for growth (Roach, 1991), this study puts emphasis on revenue enhancement. It also puts special emphasis on shedding light on the underlying mechanisms through which ICT investments lead to superior performance. This it does by drawing from theory in Strategy and Industrial Organisation.

Table 2.1: Summary of Literature

Perspective	Most relevant issues	Key papers
Inadequacy of measurement tools	Productivity paradox of IT can be explained by: Output measurement limitations in a service economy The benefits from ICT can take several years to show results	Brynjolfsson, 1993 Haynes & Thompson, 2000 Bannister & Remenyi, 1999 OECD, 2003
Portfolio effect	ICT portfolio of infrastructure, transactional, informational and strategic systems. Each has its own value proposition driven by a different risk and returns profile. need to move away from traditional accounting based tools for supporting business case quantification.	Weill & Broadbent, 1998 Ross & Beath, 2002 Prahalad & Krishnan, 2002 Davis, 2002 Benaroch & Kauffman, 1999
Change Facilitator	Stakeholder management needs to be handled with care Notorious lack of accumulation of knowledge on ICT usage Complementary investments in changing the organization, in training, in infrastructure	Heracleous & Barrett, 2001 Trice & Treacy, 1986 McConnell, 1997 Keen, 1991 OECD, 2003
Competitive advantage	ICT capability (more than investment) has a positive effect on the bottom line. Must understand the underlying mechanisms through which rational information technology investments and strong ICT capability lead to superior performance. Quantity of ICT usage and availability of ICT competencies are not enough. A clear mission is a pre-requisite for any ICT based transformation. ICT investments to pursue a cost leadership strategy achieve only a temporary advantage. Sustained advantage comes from the ICT platform, not from specific ICT applications.	Bharadwaj et al., 1999 Bharadwaj, 2000 Santhanam & Hartono, 2003 McKeen & Smith, 1996 Trice & Treacy, 1986 Scott Morton, 1991 Hitt & Brynjolfsson, 1996 McConnell, 1997 Keen, 1991

2.2.2 Synthesis: Model of Departure

Based on McKeen & Smith (1996), Crowston & Treacy (1986) and Trice & Treacy (1986), this research adopts the three construct model shown in figure 2.1 with a robust theory underpinning the process box:

According to Crowston & Treacy (1986), the industrial economics theory of market power - or monopolisation theory - provides a basis for understanding the effects of ICT on prices, market share and revenues. Chamberlain (1932, cited by Backhouse, 2002) defined monopoly or market power as the ability of a firm to control price through altering supply, and he defined 'pure' competition as competition in which monopoly elements are absent. He argued that the reason why real-world competition diverges from pure competition is that firms in practice experience some degree of monopoly power. Markets are both competitive (firms compete with each other) and monopolistic (firms have control over the price of the goods they sell). In this context, Chamberlain (1932) analysed market structure in terms of two dimensions: the number of firms in an industry and the degree to which each one produces a differentiated product. Product differentiation means that each firm has a degree of monopoly power in that it can raise its prices without losing all its customers (Backhouse, 2002, pp.205-206; Maurice & Smithson, 1988, p.408).

From this perspective, ICT investments operate on prices, market share and revenues through product differentiation and/or by reducing the amount of searching by customers (Crowston & Treacy, 1986). This can be represented as shown in Figure 2.1.

2.2.3 Some Critical Issues

Before exploring market power in depth there are some critical issues to be addressed including *How far should financial organisations go on Product/Service differentiation?* Being the financial services industry highly competitive, if the firm conforms to the strategies of others it will find itself approaching perfect competition where economic rents[6] ap-

---

[6] Economists refer to the opportunity cost of capital as 'normal return'. Any return over and above the 'normal return' is called 'economic rent', 'economic profit' or 'pure profit' (Maurice & Smithson, 1988, p.352)

proach zero. Therefore it needs to differentiate as much as possible. On the other hand, being the industry sensitive to public trust and highly regulated, institutional forces put pressure on the individual firms to conform mainstream strategies under the argument that a firm that is similar to others avoids legitimacy challenges.

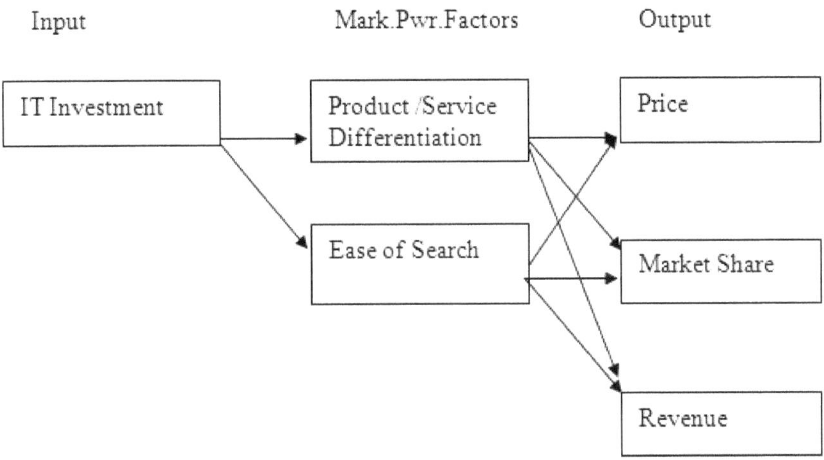

Figure 2.1. Effect of Market Power (based on Crowston & Treacy, 1986)

By analysing the tension between forces to differentiate and forces to conform, Deephouse (1999) has found evidence to support his strategic balance proposition: "Moderate amounts of strategic similarity increase performance". From the results of Deephouse's (1999) tests, it appears that the relationship between *performance* (dependent variable) and *strategic deviation* (independent variable) is quadratic and has the shape of an inverted "U". Performance will maximise at a *strategic balance point* where the increased benefits of more differentiation equals the cost of increased non-conformity as demonstrated in Figure 2.2.

Returning to the model being proposed, and assuming that product/service differentiation is a materialisation of strategic positioning, it appears that *strategic balance* acts as a moderator between *product differentiation* and *performance*. In a similar way, it can be shown that *security* is a moderator between *ease of search* and *performance.* This is depicted in Figure 2.3.

Performance
Strategic Balance
Point
Strategic Deviation

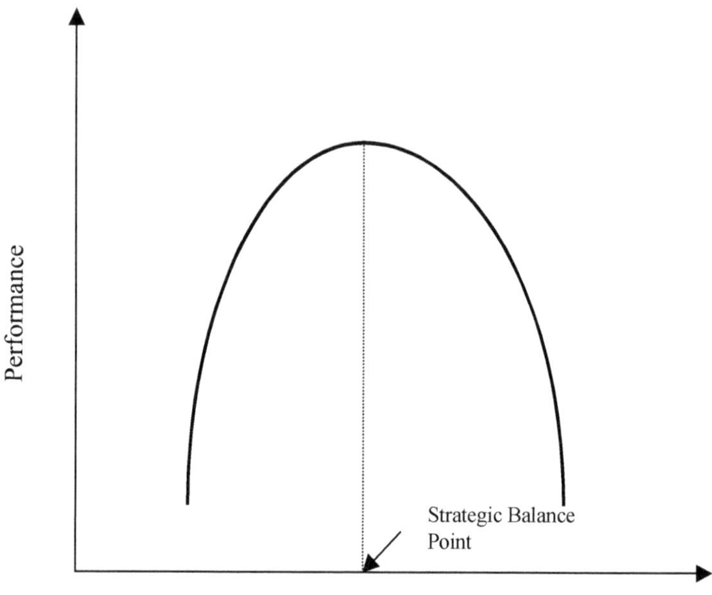

Figure 2.2: There is an optimal level of Strategic Deviation (Deephouse, 1999).

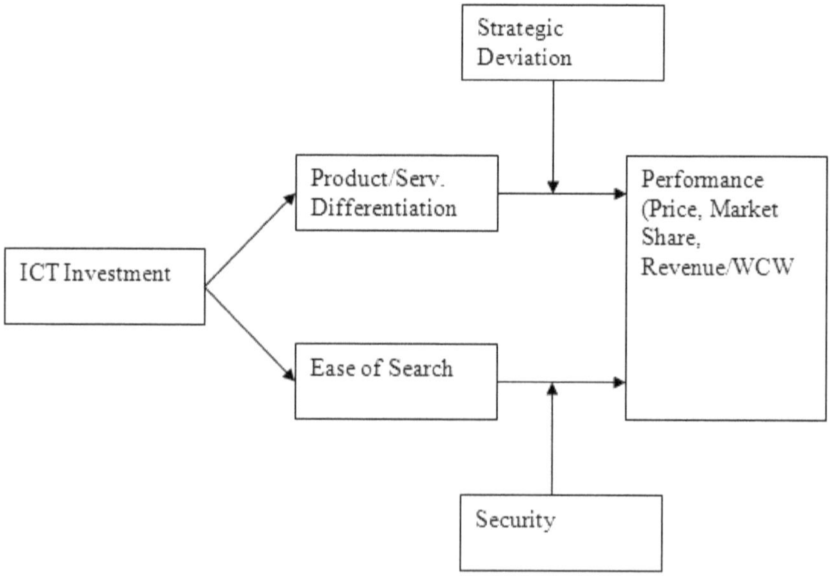

Strategic
Deviation
Product/Serv.
Differentiation
Performance
(Price, Market
Share,
Revenue/WCW
ICT Investment
Ease of Search
Security

Figure 2.3: Effect of Market Power Moderated by Strategic Balance and Security

The model described in figure 2.3 represents, therefore, the conceptual framework that is applied as a theoretical underpinning for the field-work in this research.

2.3 Methodology

2.3.1 Research Strategy[7]

The research strategy adopted is the construction of theory on the basis of empirical work, which is the discovery of theory from systematically obtained and analysed evidence. As explained in Chapter 1, although the research design capitalises on some of the advantages of the grounded theory approach, it differs from early ideas on this strategy (Glaser & Strauss, 1967, p.45) in that it is not purely inductive. It capitalises on existing literature and practitioner-based knowledge to develop a conceptual framework of departure, in line with more recent writings which admit adopting *a priori* constructs (Leonard & McAdam, 2002, p.51; Strauss & Corbin, 1990). Because this research focuses mainly on managerial and organisational issues, as opposed to purely technological ones, qualitative research methods become particularly useful (Myers, 1997, p. 241). The study is fundamentally qualitative, but quantitative tools are also applied when judged appropriate (Yin, 1994; Layder, 1993; Bryman,1989 cited by Bannister, 2001).

The approach is interpretive which has the advantage for a study of this nature, that it is holistic and not reductionist, and therefore allows for the examination of more complicated situations (Remenyi *et al.,* 1998). Because the resource limitations and time constraints for this study were stringent, a cross sectional as opposed to a longitudinal approach was followed. However, because ICT decision-making is a process that varies over time, a historical dimension was found relevant and included in the analysis of each case (i.e., a summary of the history of the organisation; a summary of each informant's career; and the historical role of ICT in the organisation) (Layder, 1993).

---

[7] Strategy is understood here as the manner in which particular methods and technique are brought together in the research so as to produce the most efficient means of collecting empirical evidence (Layder, 1993, p.2), and analysing it.

Because this is case-study research where the objective is to study a phenomenon in its context (Easterby-Smith *et al.*, 2002; McGrath, 1982; Yin, 1994), it is essential to describe the context of the cases. A deep description and analysis of the Chilean banking system from a strategy perspective is given in Griffiths (2005).

2.3.2 Unit of Analysis and Selection of the Cases

Two possible levels of analysis were considered: Project and Company. After considerable reflection it became clear that this research should be done at company level.

According to Hamel (1993, p.38) a central idea is to *"locate the global in the local"* thus making the careful selection of the research site the most critical decision in the analytic process. Case study research should rely on theoretical sampling where the cases may be chosen to fill theoretical categories and provide examples of *"polar type"* (Eisenhardt, 1989, p. 537).

Qualitative samples tend to be *purposive* rather than random, as qualitative researchers usually work with small samples (Kuzel, 1992; Light *et al.*, 1990, cited by Maxwell, 1996, p.71; Morse, 1989, cited by Miles and Huberman, 1994, p.27). According to Glaser & Strauss (1967), in the service of generating theory the researcher must select comparison groups according to their theoretical relevance

> *in furthering the development of emerging categories, properties, hypotheses and the integration of the theory.*

Six banks enrolled as volunteers for this study: Bank Boston (subsequently acquired by Banco Itau of Brazil and adopted its acquirer's name), Banco de Chile, Banco Santander Santiago, BancoEstado, BCI and Banco Security. These six banks were among the twelve largest banks in Chile and jointly represented over 80 percent of the assets of the Chilean Banking System at the time of evidence collection in 2004.

It was decided early on to use the evidence from four cases to develop the theory, and then consult the evidence from the remaining two case studies to confirm the theoretical conjectures.

The four cases selected, and the rationale for their selection, were the following:

Banco de Chile: It was a locally owned, private sector bank; it was the second largest bank in the market; it was a universal bank with products for all market segments; it cultivated a *customer intimacy* value discipline; it had a long tradition in the Chilean business community; it was going through a major technology-enabled business transformation; its leadership was moving towards an *enabling* view of technology.

Banco Santander-Santiago: It was a multinational bank; it was the largest bank in Chile; it was a universal bank with products and services for all market segments; in prior years it had operated on an *operational excellence* value discipline, but appeared to be questioning that model; it had a clear utility approach to technology.

Banco Security: It was a locally owned private sector bank; it was mid size; it had a niche approach to the market, focusing on enterprise banking and high income individuals, with a *customer intimacy* value discipline; it was a fast follower on technology.

BancoEstado: It was a state owned bank, which had a social mission of making banking services accessible to all Chileans, aside from the need to be profitable; as such, it operated with a two-pronged value discipline of *customer intimacy* and *operational excellence*; it served all market segments, but was particularly active in the micro-business segment; it relied heavily on, and had a *dependent* view of, technology.

These four banks belonged to different strategic groups according to the analysis done by Griffiths (2005). The remaining two banks, BankBoston and BCI, belonged to the same strategic groups as Banco Security and Banco de Chile, respectively.

2.3.3 Evidence Collection and Analysis

Several sources were used in order to triangulate information, but interviews were the main one. Different types of interviews were used, namely semi-structured and focused ones (Scholtz & Tietje, 2002, pp.13-14; Yin, 1994, p.84-85):

a. **Semi-structured Interviews**: It was decided to apply semi-structured in-depth interviews, as opposed to open ended ones, because this is a multiple case study and otherwise there is a risk of collecting a wealth of information from individually valuable interviews that are then difficult to generalise from (Miles & Huberman, 1994, p.17). An interview guide was developed on all aspects of the research question, and the conceptual framework indicated above. This type of interview was held only with the informants of the case-study banks.
b. **Focused Interviews**: These are applied as a method to corroborate certain facts and interpretations of events. They were narrower in scope than the semi-structured ones of the previous paragraph, and were open-ended in structure (Yin, 1994, p.85). These interviews were held with outside observers or with informants of the case-study banks who were not part of the core interviewee group designated by each bank.

Because interview evidence are verbal reports and therefore need to be corroborated by other types of evidence (Bickman & Rog, 1998, p.247), the research design contemplated the analysis of multiple documentary sources, including meeting memorandums, strategy plans, project charters and annual reports. A critical aspect of this is imposing a framework or structure on the evidence that will allow the researcher to catalogue the themes and concepts.

The holders of the following positions were to be interviewed: the Managing Director, the Operations (& ICT) Manager, the Planning Manager and the Market Managers. In addition, each interviewee was asked whom else in the organisation they thought should also be interviewed, and why.

In terms of rigour in the collection and analysis of evidence in the case-study method, it is important to minimise the introduction of subjectivity, and therefore bias, by both the informants and the researcher. The recommendations given by Hamel (1993) were applied for this purpose.

2.3.4 Tests for Validity

The quality of case-study research is judged on the basis of four tests: *construct validity, internal validity, external validity* and *reliability* (Yin,

1994; Remenyi *et al.,* 1998). Particular attention was given in this research to construct validity, internal validity and reliability. Because the intention was to rely on an analytical generalisation to generalise from the cases studied to a broader theory of converting ICT investments into value, rather than doing a statistical generalisation from a sample to a population, external validity was not critical in this research (Yin, 1994, p.36; Remenyi *et al.*, 1998, p.180).

2.4 Theory of Market Power ICT Investments for Value Creation

2.4.1 Process of Development of the Theory

In general terms, it can be said that I was made aware of the particular problem tackled in this research, by my experience as a practitioner. However, the way it was framed and the way the research question was stated were clearly influenced by my epistemological and ontological position, and my theoretical starting point.

In the early stages of this research a substantial amount of reading was done on theory of strategy-technology alignment, on market power, and on other theories that underpin this research. As a result I was able to articulate the idea that organisations have over-emphasised the drive towards cost-reduction, and would probably get better returns on their ICT investments if they focused on revenue enhancement. Also that Market Power could be used to support ICT investments for growth by applying it to underpin the mentioned process box in figure 2.2.

From there the theory and model developed through creativity triggered by a method essentially based on questions followed by comparisons (which, in turn, lead to further questions and so on). This approach was materialised in a process that went from evidence collection, to analysis, to comparison with theory, to conceptualisation, to theoretical sampling, and back to evidence collection and a new cycle, as depicted in figure 2.4. Some of the key concepts that emerged from this process were 'Strategic Positioning' (with its three categories), 'View of ICT' (i.e., enabler, dependent, utility, none), 'Change Management', 'Outsourcing', 'e-Banking', 'Digital Signature', 'E-Invoicing', 'ICT Investment' (classified into efficiency driven or market-power driven projects), 'Differentiation', 'Ease of Search', 'Strategic Deviation', 'Security', 'Performance', 'Value Proposition' (with its three categories), 'Customer Value' (with its 7 properties), 'Personal Banking', 'Enterprise Banking', 'Micro-credit', Porter's Five Forces, 'Core Processes' for delivering value, 'Size', 'Product Range', 'Target Market', 'Ownership' (i.e., local private, multinational, state), 'Barriers to Entry'; 'Competitive advantage' (i.e., none, parity, temporary, sustainable).

In the final analysis, after much reflection, 'ICT Investment' (project) emerged as the core category. It classifies projects in market power driven and efficiency driven ones. It emerged gradually as a result of the development of the taxonomy of ICT projects in the synthesis of the cross-case analysis. This development was relatively complex because relationships with 'Strategic Positioning', 'ICT Planning', 'Differentiation', 'Ease of Search', and 'Performance', had to be analysed.

In terms of relationships, one of the most significant relationships that emerged was that between 'Strategic Positioning' (classified along value disciplines) and 'ICT Investment' (classified between market power driven and efficiency driven). It later emerged that the 'ICT Planning' (classified by view of ICT) had a significant influence on that relationship. A dialectic analysis took place to define if this concept was a mediator or moderator; after much reflection it was included as a mediator to operationalise the alignment of 'ICT Investment' initiatives with 'Strategic Positioning.'

The model of departure did not explain why some banks appeared to be successful on efficiency-driven projects, and others were not. It was this that led to including the 'Strategic Positioning' and 'ICT Planning' constructs in the model, which appears to have explained the issue.

The result of this process will be presented in the following sections in the form of a theory and model.

2.4.2 Theory of Building Value Through ICT Investments for Market Power

Grounded on the theoretical and empirical work described in the preceding sections of this summary, I proposed the following theoretical conjecture: Banks that operate in a customer intimacy or product leadership value discipline, will only convert into value those ICT investments which enable them to increase their Market Power.

By value discipline I referred to “the three desirable ways in which companies can combine operating models and value propositions to be the best in their markets”, as defined by Treacy & Wiersema (1995, p.xii). The third value discipline, not mentioned in the theoretical proposition, is operational excellence.

Another key definition is what we understand by ICT, which can be described as a widely applicable technology whose main contribution lies in enabling new methods and processes when combined with other complementary investments such as new work systems, organisational restructurings, or redesigning processes. This definition is borrowed from Sanchez & Albertin (2004).

Finally, Market Power is defined as the capacity of an organisation to increase its prices without losing all its Clients. In banks, Market Power can take two forms: differentiation of products and services, or ease of search.

This theory categorises ICT investments into Market Power driven initiatives, and non Market Power driven ones. Prominent among the non Market Power ICT investments are the efficiency-driven initiatives. A corollary of this theory is that banks that adopt a customer intimacy or a product leadership value discipline will not convert efficiency-driven ICT investments into value.

This theory categorises banks according to the value discipline they adopt. Another corollary of this theory is that only banks that adopt an operational excellence value discipline have a chance of converting efficiency-driven ICT investments into value, provided they invest heavily on change management.

2.5 The Value-Builder ICT Investment Decision Model

2.5.1 Completion of the Model

Having elaborated the cases, developed the cross-case analysis, and enunciated the theory, I am now in a position to fulfil the objective of this chapter: tackle the question of *How can managers at financial services organisations use ICT investments to create Market Power?* I shall address this question by proposing what I have called the “The Value-Builder ICT Investment Decision Model.”

Based on the literature I developed the model represented in figure 2.4 for ICT investment decision-making. But, of what use is a model if we do not define a context in which its application is valid? Precisely, defining in what context this model is applicable is the most important contribution of the empirical work done with the Chilean banks.

As mentioned in the "Theory of Building Value through ICT Investments for Market Power" (Section 2.4.2), the fieldwork allowed me to identify restrictions in its applicability which must also be translated to the model. The theory categorises banks according to their value discipline, and has limited its applicability to customer intimacy and product leadership banks. This has led me to include 'Strategic Positioning' as a construct in the model, which defines the context of ICT investment decisions.

As emerged in the case-studies and in the cross-case analysis, in order to have agreement across the management team on ICT investment decision criteria, there must be an ICT planning process in the bank. This ICT planning process should link strategy and technology investment decisions, and should define the organisation's vision of the role of technology, which is closely connected with the value discipline adopted (Weill & Broadbent, 1998; Treacy & Wiersema, 1995). ICT investment decisions must, therefore, fit into the ICT plan which therefore defines the setting for ICT investment decisions. This is materialised in the model by including ICT Planning as another construct in the model.

The previous considerations led me to propose the following model (figure 2.4) for ICT investment decisions, which I have called the "Value-Builder ICT Investment Decision Model":

The Strategic Positioning construct is defined as the value discipline of the organisation, and its state is determined through the application of Treacy & Wiersema's (1995) three-value disciplines model.

The ICT Planning construct represents the ICT guidelines of the organisations. Its state is defined through the application of Weill & Broadbent's (1998) 'Managing by Maxims' methodology.

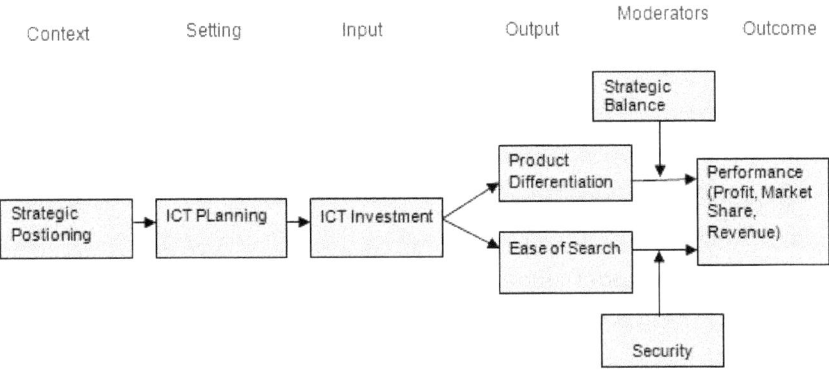

Figure 2.4. The Value Builder ICT Investment Decision Model

The ICT Investment construct represents the individual ICT initiative, with its descriptive characteristics such as objectives, functionality, processes it is aimed to support, technology, and amount of investment required.

The remaining constructs have been characterised above.

Chapter 3

Approach for Extending the Theory

The remainder of this book will attempt to extend the applicability of the *Theory of Building Value Through ICT Investments for Market Power* presented in Chapter 2 to industrial sectors other than banking, and to geographies other than Chile. It will do so by analysing a series of ICT projects on the basis of published case studies.

The prior theory categorises ICT projects into *Efficiency-driven* and *Market-Power-driven*. These two types of ICT investments are characterised in table 3.1.

Table 3.1: Characterisation of ICT Investments

	Efficiency Driven	**Market Power Driven**
Objectives	Back office efficiency; cost reduction	Solve client problem; help front line staff
Trigger	Severe transaction limitation; lack controls; operational risks	Competitive disadvantage (catch-up) Strategic opportunity (market, product)
Outcome	Increase throughput; improve controls; improve cost structure; downsize	Increase market power, mainly through differentiation of product or service; occasionally ease of search
Impact on Industry and competitiveness	Small impact on industry structure; if so, though entry barriers based on scale: Temporary competitive advantage	Eliminate barriers to sub-segment or increase rivalry. Usually impacts competitiveness: Catch-up; temporary or sustainable competitive advantage
Output	If operational excellence bank, impacts performance through market share of profit; if customer intimacy, no impact on performance	If customer intimate or product leadership, improves performance through market share which then translates into profitability

	Efficiency Driven	**Market Power Driven**
Leadership	Usually led by back-office units: Operation, IT, risk, finance, controlling; scarce involvement of client/market facing units	Always led by the business unit that needs the tool to meet its goals
Size	Usually large, affecting many people in the organization.	Relatively small, located in client facing units
Change Management	Requires specific CM front because impacts many people, leads to downsizing, and are led by relatively small teams	Do not require specific CM effort, because led by business unit manager, just requires training small teams on use of a tool which they are all eagerly awaiting

The case studies have been selected amongst those published in the Electronic Journal of Information Systems Evaluation (www.ejise.com), in the Proceedings of the European Conference on Information Technology Evaluation (ECITE), and the Proceedings of the European Conference on Information Management and Evaluation (ECIME). These sources focus on publishing research on, precisely, ICT evaluation and thus most of the case studies found in them tend to analyse business transformation processes based on the implementation of ICT solutions.

The cases were neither selected for the elegance of their narrative, nor for the consistency of their methodology, nor for the simplicity of their insights, although they may have some or all of these virtues, as will become clear in the case reviews of each chapter. They are selected in view of their potential to help extend the theory to other industrial sectors and to other geographies – that is what theoretical sampling is about.

In a first analysis the situations described in the case studies are categorised into *Efficiency-driven* and *Market-Power-driven* ICT investments on the basis of the criteria given in Table 3.1. The selected cases are described by their titles and authors in table 3.2. Those included in Part II analyse projects categorised as *Efficiency-driven*, while those in Part III refer to *Market-Power-driven* initiatives.

Each of Chapters 4 to 11 deal with one case study and their content has the same structure broken down into four sections:

- An overview
- The published case study

- Summary on a page using Toulmin's argument structure
- Case Study Review

The overview highlights the key issues that the case study brings to this research. The second section presents the case study as it was published. The third one compresses the case study author's arguments down to the bone marrow by deconstructing the narrative into *Data, Claim, Warrant* and *Backing* and presenting the authors arguments according to Toulmin's structure.

Finally, the last section does a review of the case study. I profess deep consideration for research case writers, particularly those that use qualitative methods, because I know through personal experience the pressure they are subject to. Their research projects have very low budgets, their deadlines are demanding, they have to interact with informants who are protective of their own time; and when the time comes for publishing their work, editors insist on keeping their papers short. It has always stricken me as asymmetrical to put the same demands on length for a qualitative as for a quantitative piece of work. The density of content and meaning in numbers, plus the tacit rules that connect them, can speak thousands of words; and reducing a piece of qualitative work where findings, method, reflections, discourse, language, figures and text are an integral part of the product, can kill its *soul* . Brevity is highly commendable, but not when it compromises clarity[8]. So the qualitative researcher is permanently agonizing to decide what to leave out of his work. Nothing easier, therefore, than to critique a piece of qualitative work by saying it should have included this, or should have tackled the other. I will refrain from this at all cost. The critique I include in the case reviews is limited to methodology discrepancies and to expose the issues that will be used in Part IV to map the case onto the *Theory of Building Value Through ICT Investments for Market Power* with an aim at extending it.

---

[8] "In my view, aiming at simplicity and lucidity is a moral duty of all intellectuals: lack of clarity is a sin, and pretentiousness is a crime. (Brevity is also important, in view of the publication explosion, but it is of lesser urgency, and it sometimes is incompatible with clarity.)" Popper, K. (1979 [1972]) *Objective Knowledge: An Evolutionary Approach,* Oxford University Press: Great Clarendon Street, Oxford; p.44

Table 3.2 Description of Cases included in Parts II and III

PART/Chapter	Title	Authors	Source
PART II Chapter 4	Evaluating Success in Post-Merger IS Integration: A Case Study	Alaranta, M (2005)	eJISE, Vol.8 Issue 3, pp.143-150
PART II Chapter 5	The Influence of Net Benefits on Collective, Innovative, Configural System Use: A Case Study of Small-to-Medium Enterprises)	Wilkin, C. (2009)	Ejise, Vol.12 Issue 2, pp.187-198
PART II Chapter 6	Towards a Model for Determining the Scope of ICT Integration in the Enterprise: The Case of Enterprise Resource Planning (ERP)	Carton, F & Adam, F. (2010)	eJISE, Vol.13 Issue 1, pp. 17-26
PART II Chapter 7	The Fundamental Challenge: Human and Organisational Factors in an ERP Implementation	Dawson, J & Owens, J. (2007)	ECIME 2007 pp.121-130
PART III Chapter 8	The Effect of Information Systems on Firm Performance and Profitability Using a Case Study Approach	Olugbode, M., Elbeltagi, I., Simmons M. & Biss T. (2008)	eJISE, Vol 11 Issue 1, pp. 11-16
PART III Chapter 9	Evaluation of a CRM System Implementation in China	Carlsson, S. Frygell, L. & Hedman, J. (2005)	ECITE 2005 pp. 129-136
PART III Chapter 10	Wiki-Based Knowledge Management in a Transport Consultancy, a Case Study	In 't Hout, R., Vrancken, J. & Schrijnen, P. (2010)	eJISE Vol. 13 Issue 2, pp. 133-142.

So we now shall move onto Parts II and III where these case study analyses will be developed.

PART II:
Efficiency Driven ICT Investments

Chapter 4

Defining Post-Merger IS Integration Success in a Manufacturing Outfit (Finland)

The case study that follows describes the IS integration aspect of a merger of operations in a manufacturing context. It is generally accepted that IS integration is a vital success factor in mergers in the more information intensive industries such as financial services, but this case will demonstrate its importance in a manufacturing environment as well.

There are surprisingly scarce tools and models for guiding the CIO and other senior managers in the process of anticipating the problems in IS integration in this kind of situation. In most cases the process is tackled in an *ad hoc* way, and reaching acceptable levels of information integration is slow and cumbersome. This is particularly troublesome in mergers where, as in the company described in this case study, the purpose of the merger is to achieve economies of scale and operational excellence. How can you possibly merge and streamline the processes of the two combining units if you do not have the information workflows to support this?

This paper makes an interesting contribution by distilling a framework from the literature that sheds light on the multi-faceted aspect of IS post-integration evaluation. It then applies this framework to analyse the outcome of IS integration at the company X merger. Is the outcome a foolproof formula for applying thoughtlessly in every merger situation? Clearly not; the author shows us that each case will require a specific weighing of the four components of the proposed framework. But at least it gives managers somewhere to start their integration thinking and planning.

Evaluating Success in Post-merger IS Integration: A Case Study

Maria Alaranta
Turku Centre for Computer Science, Lemminkaisenkatu, Finland

Abstract: Despite the importance of post-merger IS integration to the success of the whole merger, post-merger IS integration literature remains scarce. This paper attempts to synthesise the often implicit or vague definitions of post-merger IS integration success with those provided in the vast body of literature on IS evaluation. As a result, four categories of success issues for post-merger IS integration are proposed: User satisfaction with the integrated software's system and information quality as well as its use; Efficient and effective IS integration management; Efficient IS staff integration; and IS ability to support the underlying motives of the merger.

Keywords: IS Integration, Mergers, Acquisitions, M&A, Success, IS Evaluation

Originally published in the Electronic Journal of IS Evaluation, Volume 8, Issue 3, pp.143-150.

4.1 Introduction

Today, the number of mergers and acquisitions exceeds even the records of the merger wave in the 1980s, and consequently, more and more firms are facing the challenges of post-merger integration of such things as their operations, personnel, cultures and information systems. Post-merger integration is a gradual and interactive process, in which the individuals from two or more organisations learn to co-operate in the transfer of strategic capabilities. The importance of post-merger integration is derived from the fact that value creation can only begin when the organisations begin to work towards the purpose of the acquisition. In other words, integration is the source of value creation. Besides this, faulty integration is a significant cause of merger failures (Habeck et al. 2000; Haspeslagh – Jemison 1991; Shrivastava 1986), and mergers and acquisitions frequently miscarry. (See e.g. Shrivastava 1986; Thach – Nyman 2001 etc.)

Furthermore, since information systems (IS) are of the utmost importance in the operation of (large) business, a merger or acquisition may not succeed if information systems planning is inappropriate. Furthermore, potential counter-synergies can be concealed in information systems. (I/S Analyzer 1989; Franck 1990)

All this makes post-merger integration of enterprise systems both a challenging task, and an interesting topic for academic studies. Consequently, several authors recognise the importance of IT in post-merger integration (See e.g. Franck 1990; I/S Analyzer 1989). Nevertheless, after reviewing the 567 mergers and acquisitions (M&A) related articles published in 65 core journals in the 1990s, Parvinen concludes that "- *-post-integration management - - enjoy[s] conspicuously little attention*" (Parvinen 2003). Consequently, the literature covering post-merger integration of the IS is also scarce. We examined the titles of the 567 articles on M&A reviewed by Parvinen (2003), and found 18 titles that had some reference to the post-merger integration phase. Out of these, 16 abstracts were found, and only one of them (i.e. McKiernan – Merali 1995) contained the words "Information Systems" or the equivalent. Similarly, e.g. Merali-McKiernan (1993), Stylianou et al. (1996), Mehta-Hirschheim (2004) and McKiernan-Merali (1995) note that the literature on post-merger IS issues is sparse, and furthermore, it has been claimed that the research has been case-specific and anecdotal in nature, and has appeared in practitioners' rather than academic journals.

On the other hand, information systems success is an ambiguous, multifaceted phenomenon that can be addressed with various measures. In practice, there are nearly as many measures as there are studies. IS success has often been defined as a result or outcome, or a favourable result or outcome. Already defining how this outcome should be characterised, however, or for whom the result should be favourable, is ambiguous. Furthermore, there may exist complicated contextual effects on what is considered favourable or satisfactory (Saarinen 1996, 104-105). Similarly, addressing post-merger IS integration is likely to be equally challenging.

So determining IS success in general is problematic, and so is finding reliable measures for it. Hence, the measures used are often surrogate and criticised for lacking strong theoretical underpinnings. One of the roots of these problems is the fact that IS investments often have corporate-wide, intangible and long-lasting effects. Because of this, quantitative measures and economic evaluation tend to be difficult to obtain and easy to manipulate. (Saarinen 1996, 105. See also: Brynjolfsson – Hitt 1998, 51-52; DeLone-McLean 1992, 61; Goodhue 1995, 1827, Kortteinen et al. 1995, 175 etc.) In fact, "There are no generally acceptable measures available to quantitatively and objectively assess an information systems' success. Researchers have, therefore, developed surrogate measures based on subjective evaluation approaches." (Saarinen 1996, 116) Attempts to address post-merger success bear out these challenges. Furthermore, the complex and multi-faceted nature of merger processes makes this task even more challenging.

This paper attempts to explore the various aspects of post-merger IS integration success. In order to reach this aim, IS evaluation and post-merger IS integration success are discussed, and a case study is conducted to illustrate the discussion.

The expected results of this study include an in-depth understanding of the multi-faceted concept of success in post-merger IS integration.

4.2 Addressing success in post-merger IS integration

As explained in Section 1, the literature on post-merger IS integration is scarce. Furthermore, much of this scarce literature does not define post-merger IS integration success, e.g. Buck-Lew et al. (1992), Merali-McKiernan (1993), McKiernan-Merali (1995), Weber-Pliskin 1996, Giacomazzi et al. (1997), I/S Analyzer 1989, Bentley 2002, Mehta-Hirschheim (2004).

At best, post-merger IS integration success is addressed implicitly, stating that IS integration is expected to be carried out within a predefined timeframe, and without disrupting the work of employees or inconveniencing customers (I/S Analyzer 1989, 2; Merali – McKiernan 1993, 111; Kubilus 1991, 34). Problems such as the cost of ineffective integration, ignoring information quality issues in merger planning, the loss of IS expertise and failure to evaluate the alignment of the IS integration with the achievement of corporate and acquisition objectives, are quoted (e.g. Merali-McKiernan 1993, Cossey 1991).

Merali and McKiernan (1993) claim that IS integration processes are typically not formally evaluated, and both executives and academics frequently evaluate acquisition performance and acquisition strategies on monetary criteria in the short-term right after the acquisition. Examples of this include e.g. Cossey (1991), Weber and Pliskin (1996) and Goodwin (1999), who all suggest cost-savings (economies of scale) and synergies (reducing or exploiting redundant capacity) as benefits obtainable from post-merger IS integration.

On the other hand, Cossey (1991) states that, first, any system can be scored on functionality and value to the business, and secondly, systems success depends on the users' perceptions of them. Main and Short (1989) see increased partnership between the IS and general managers as a key result of post-merger IS integration. This partnership includes (1) alignment of the firms' business strategies and IT, (2) better understanding of line managers' information requirements and readiness to manage IS locally, and (3) better determination of future systems needs. (Main – Short 1989, 470-471)

Perhaps the most comprehensive definition of post-merger IS integration success found in the literature was first presented by Stylianou, Jeffries and Robbins (1996), and then further refined by Robbins and Stylianou (1999). Robbins and Stylianou (1999) suggest the following components of success in post-merger IS integration:

- The ability to exploit opportunities arising from the merger,
- The ability to avoid problems stemming from the merger,
- End-user satisfaction with the integration process and integrated system,
- Improved IS capabilities that help support the underlying motives for the merger, and
- Efficiency and effectiveness of resource utilisation during the integration process.

Robbins and Stylianou (1999) elaborate the construct "Improved IS capabilities" further by claiming that successful IS integration can generate a wide range of positive outcomes that support the merger goals. These include:

- enhancing the firm's competitive position,
- shaping or enabling business strategies,
- integrating IS planning with organisational planning,
- contributing to overall organisational financial performance,

- providing integration of related technologies across organisational units, providing corporate-wide information accessibility,
- providing good quality (accurate, useful, timely information),
- managing its own financial performance,
- operating systems efficiently by ensuring system availability, reliability and responsiveness,
- developing systems efficiently and effectively,
- providing adequate end-user support,
- recruiting and maintaining a technically and managerially competent staff, and
- identifying and assimilating new technologies.

The list above provided by Robbins and Stylianou (1999) illustrated the complex and multi-faceted nature of success in post-merger IS integration.

This list, however, as well as all the other literature quoted earlier in this section fails to make use of the vast body of IS evaluation literature.

In brief, the IS evaluation literature started moving from technical measures such as system response times towards a more user and organisation oriented view, with the surge of the first user- satisfaction measures, such as the User Information Satisfaction (UIS) instrument by Ives et al. (1983). The UIS is a measure of user satisfaction and hence it is subjective, and addresses IS success indirectly. Being one of the best known tools, it offers a standardised measure (results can be compared across different organisations, systems and points of measurement). On the other hand, it has been criticised for such things as insufficient definition of key concepts, weak theoretical underpinnings and a narrow approach. A step towards more sophisticated measurement tools is, for example, the End-User Computing Satisfaction instrument by Doll – Torkzadeh (1988) that includes the constructs of Content, Accuracy, Format, Ease of Use, and Timeliness of the information. Thereafter, attempts such as the Task-Technology Fit model by Goodhue (1995) or the four Main dimensions of IS success (development process, use process, quality of the IS, and impact on the organisation) by Saarinen (1996) aimed at providing a more comprehensive and multi-faceted view of IS success.

In their seminal review of the IS evaluation literature, Smithson and Hirschheim (1998) divide the IS evaluation criteria into Efficiency Zone (doing things right), Effectiveness Zone (doing the right thing), and Understanding Zone. This model, however, does not provide actual success measures and constructs. One of the contributions of the Effectiveness Zone literature is that measuring IS success is context-bound, and different systems and situations require different evaluations (e.g. Smithson-Hirschheim 1998). In post-merger IS integration, for example, a partial integration of operational IS is likely to have very different goals – and hence very different success measures – from a full consolidation of strategic IS. Therefore, it is only feasible to attempt to define central categories of post-merger IS integration success issues and perhaps give examples of these issues The relative importance of these categories and their contents must then be decided upon for each evaluation situation individually.

Another seminal literature review was carried out by DeLone and McLean (1992). This condenses IS evaluation literature into an IS Success Model. In a revised version of their model (2003), they also present a set of six categories. First, system quality, information quality, and service quality affect both user satisfaction and use & intended use. These, in turn, are interrelated and yield net benefits. Finally, these net benefits also affect user satisfaction and use & intended use. In the following, the DeLone-McLean (2003) model is discussed with respect to the post-merger IS integration literature and modified to suit this domain.

- System quality: The importance of system quality in post-merger IS integration was noted by Robbins-Stylianou (1999) and Cossey (1991), and Merali and McKiernan (1993) state that integration should not disrupt the work of employees nor inconvenience customers.
- Information quality: The integrated system may provide corporate-wide information accessibility (Robbins-Stylianou 1999), and it should provide accurate, useful and timely information (Robbins-Stylianou 1999, and Cossey 1991).
- Service quality: The integrated IS departments should operate systems efficiently, develop new systems efficiently and effectively, provide integration of related technologies across organ-

isational units, provide adequate end-user support and manage their own financial performance (Robbins-Stylianou 1999).

- Use, intended use: This construct was not mentioned in the post-merger IS integration literature reviewed.
- User satisfaction: The importance of user satisfaction with the integrated system was noted by Robbins-Stylianou (1999) and Cossey (1991). This construct, however, is not without problems in the context of post-merger IS integration. For example, in some cases users are asked to change their well-functioning systems for others, which is likely to cause frustrations, as the adoption of a new system is always troublesome but does not necessarily bring benefits at the level of the individual user. Also, systems integration may translate into more co-ordinated systems that dictate the users' work processes more than before, and this may be considered a drawback by individual users.
- Net benefits: The integrated system is expected to support the underlying motives of the merger. These include enhancing the firm's competitive position (Robbins-Stylianou 1999; Cossey 1991), as well as shaping or enabling business strategies and integrating IS planning with organisational planning (Robbins-Stylianou 1999). Furthermore, post-merger IS integration may contribute towards overall organisational financial performance by providing possibilities for cost-savings and synergies (Robbins-Stylianou 1999, Merali-Mc-Kiernan 1993, Cossey 1991, Weber-Pliskin 1996, Goodwin 1999).

The above list shows that, while the DeLone-McLean (2003) model offers a valuable insight into the components of post-merger IS integration success, it does have some shortcomings. First, the use or intended use was not found to be an important issue in the post-merger IS integration literature. This could perhaps be because this construct has been widely criticised for such reasons as the amount of use is a meaningful measure of success only when the use is voluntary, more time in use does not necessarily give better results. Secondly, the construct *net benefits* seems to be too general and simplistic effectively to embrace the full richness of the phenomenon. Also DeLone and McLean (2003) admit that, in some studies, finer granulation may be necessary. Furthermore, the post-merger IS integration literature provides some further benefits that do not correspond to the DeLone-McLean (2003) model.

First, issues such as the ability to exploit opportunities arising from the merger, and the ability to avoid problems stemming from the merger (Robbins-Stylianou 1999) are too ambiguous to be classified, and they may be related to practically all the categories above, depending on the particular opportunities and problems. Besides this, other issues include:

- Efficiency and effectiveness of resource utilisation during the integration process (time, money, personnel) (Robbins-Stylianou 1999, I/S Analyzer 1989, Kubilus 1991)
- Recruiting and maintaining a technically and managerially competent staff (Robbins-Stylianou 1999, Merali-Mc-Kiernan 1993)
- The learning opportunity to manage better future IS integrations (Merali-Mc-Kiernan 1993)

To sum up the post-merger IS integration discussion, and to make effective use of the IS evaluation research to support it, four components of post-merger IS integration are proposed: User satisfaction with the integrated software's system and information quality; Efficient and effective IS integration processes; Efficient IS staff integration; and IS ability to support the underlying motives of the merger. These, as well as the issues pertaining to these categories, are presented in Table 4.1.

The post-merger IS integration success components presented in Table 4.1 are illustrated in a case study in the following Sections.

4.3 Methodological choices

The empirical evidence for this paper was collected as a case study on IS integration in Company X, a manufacturing company that gained its current form through a joint venture of Group A and Corporation B in 1999. A case study was chosen to enable the in-depth understanding of different aspects of post-merger IS integration. The selected case is interesting in this context as Company X chose to pursue deep IS integration in order to co-ordinate better the production capacity between the factories, and to enable better financial reporting. On the other hand, the implementation process has been somewhat complicated, and different problems have been reported in different factories.

Table 4.1: Components of post-merger information systems integration success

Post-merger IS integration success component	Issues
User satisfaction with the integrated software's system and information quality as well as its use	Not disrupting the work of employees, not inconveniencing customers, corporate-wide information accessibility; accurate, useful and timely information
Efficient and effective IS integration management	Efficient and effective use of resources (time, cost and personnel) during the integration processes, effective management policies with regard to project management, change management, outsourcing, etc.
Efficient IS staff integration	Avoiding the loss of key IS people and their expertise; Recruiting technically and managerially competent IS staff; Avoiding problems like: Reduced commitment and disloyalty, Reduced productivity, Motivational problems, Dissatisfaction, frustration, confusion and stress, Dysfunctional behaviour and sabotage, People refusing assignments, Increased absenteeism, Health problems, Power struggles
IS ability to support the underlying motives of the merger	For example, cost-cutting and exploiting redundancies in the IS function; supporting synergies in production by e.g. better co-ordination of production capacity; supporting new, integrated R&D function; supporting vertical integration and visibility with the supplier/client acquired, etc.

The data for the study come mainly from interviews, and was complemented with a short questionnaire, observation and documents. The data were collected both during the pilot phase (Factory F1) and during the actual implementation (the system was implemented in three more factories). The pilot implementation started January 1, 2003, and semi-structured interviews conducted with 11 interviewees in April 2003. The new enterprise system (ES) was implemented in three more factories on January 1, 2004, and six interviewees gave their opinions in May 2004. The interviewees adequately cover various actors and management levels that were involved in the ES integration processes studied. They included the integration project manager, representatives of top management, user support, users of different levels and the software vendor. With some key interviewees such as the implementation project manager, several interviews were carried out.

A short questionnaire was directed to the end-users in April 2003 and May 2004. Thirty-three and 168 responses were received in 2003 and 2004 respectively. The questionnaire was based on the Motwani et al. (2002) framework on change management in ERP implementation, and

Saarinen's (1996) instrument for evaluating information system success, choosing and modifying suitable constructs of each of these. The role of the questionnaire in this study was to provide an efficient way to collect the users' perceptions and opinions to complement the data from the interviews; that is to say, there was no causal model to be tested. The data were completed by observation, and internal company reports. The raw data from the interview transcripts, responses to the questionnaire, field notes and internal company reports were first collected into a case study database consisting of an organised folder structure, and thereafter the data were analyzed according to the classes suggested by the theory. (See: Yin 1984, Yin 1993)

4.4 Case: company x

Research environment

The empirical evidence for this paper was collected from the enterprise systems (ES) integration in Company X, a manufacturing company that gained its current form in 1999 through a joint venture between Group A and Corporation B, in which one of Corporation B's factories (Factory F1) became part of Company X. Company X chose to pursue deep IS integration in order to better co-ordinate the production capacity between the factories, and to enable better financial reporting.

The production function asked for information systems integration as soon as the decision to go ahead with the merger was made. Tailored software was chosen, as it was thought to better support the new company structure. Implementing the new system started on January 1, 2003, three years after the merger took place. The new information system consists of sales applications, manufacturing applications, inventory and supply applications, cost accounting and financial reporting. However, accounting functions such as accounts receivable and payable, asset accounting, book-keeping etc., as well as human resource management applications, are not run in the new, integrated system because Group A administers them centrally.

According to the deal, the vendor delivered the software three years after Company X was formed. During this first phase, it was implemented only at Factory F1. Three other factories implemented the software the following year, and implementation at a fifth factory was postponed by one year because of problems with software quality.

Findings: post-merger IS integration success in Company x

User satisfaction with the integrated software's system and information quality

One year after the first installation and five months after the installation in the other factories, the operative functions were using the system, but its use was not trouble-free. The system was up and running and, as one interviewee put it: "*Despite all the trouble there has not been any order that we wouldn't have been able to deliver*". The end-users, however, were highly dissatisfied with the system and its usage. One of the interviewees commented: "We have reached a satisfactory level of know-how in using the system. However, the system has not fulfilled the hopes and expectations we had [with regard to quality]." The results of the end-user survey supported this view: 61% of the respondents felt that the system was slow, and only 11% almost or totally agreed that the system was fast (N=168). Furthermore, only 26% of the respondents totally or almost agreed that the system was being used successfully whereas 47% held the opposite view (N=167).

Efficient and effective IS integration management

In Company X, post-merger IS integration took a relatively long time since the new enterprise was programmed from scratch. Before the merger, both factories were using proprietary enterprise systems, tailored by different domestic software vendors. Neither of these systems, however, was thought to have the properties necessary to support the new company, and there were no new versions available of either software. Consequently, Company X chose to develop a tailored integrated system in order to gain a strategic competitive advantage. Due to the time required for programming new software from scratch, Company X could only start implementing the new system on January 1, 2003, three years after the merger took place. This time span, however, was planned and accepted by the decision makers.

As explained before, economies of scale were sought in production, not in the IS function. In fact, the IS integration turned out to be a significant investment for Company X. The budget for this investment was exceeded by 10-15%.

Implementation was carried out within the planned timeframe with the exception of the fact that in the fifth factory it had to be delayed. The implementation team was relatively small, and hence, their time was consumed in training and solving daily problems. There was therefore insufficient time to test the critical software modules that were to be used in that factory, as their quality did not meet the expectations of Company X. Finally, the quality of these modules was not thought to be up to standard, and the implementation was postponed.

As the implementation team was occupied with daily issues, not enough time was left for strategic planning and efficient managing of the software vendor. No formal project management tools or techniques were used, as only major steps such as go-live dates were formally tracked. Managing the vendor relationship was complicated despite the close relationship with the vendor. A database for communicating with the vendor was only established more than six months after first implementation. On top of this, their first formal and extensive evaluation of the project was a side project of this study, and only the project manager initiated the second evaluation.

With regard to users' perceptions on managing the change, 49% of the respondents totally or almost disagreed with the statement that the implementation and the change related to it were well managed, whereas 20% totally or almost agreed, and 25% were indifferent (6% didn't know, N=166). Also related to this, the interviewees frequently reported that user involvement in the requirements engineering phase was not sufficient. On the other hand, the interviewees emphasised the efforts made with user training, and the users were pleased with the quality of the user support. Moreover, the changes required in different factories were different. The project manager claims that these differences have been taken into account during IS integration, as the individual sites have been allowed to maintain their particular features, as long as the system and the overall merger goals permit it.

Efficient IS staff integration

In the case of Company X, none of the typical merger-related problems stemming from lay-offs, such as corruption of morals, stress and losing key IS workers was encountered, as there was no need for staff reduction. Instead, a few extra people were recruited to participate in the extensive end-user training programmes.

According to the first plans, the new system was only meant to be implemented in the pilot Factory F1, and an implementation project manager was appointed from Factory F1. Later on, it was decided that this software was to be used to run the whole company, and the implementation project manager now faced a larger-scale, more complex implementation project than he had originally accepted. Besides the project manager, the implementation team consisted of IS professionals from both Factory F1 and other factories belonging to Company X, and the team was supported by Group A's IS department. Issues such as the lack of formal project management and problems with managing the vendor, showed that the implementation team needed more support and expertise in these areas, at least at the beginning of the project.

IS ability to support the underlying motives of the merger

The motive for this merger was the fact that machinery was getting old both in Group A's factories and in Factory F1, and heavy investments were required. This, in turn, would have created a huge over-capacity in the market, and therefore Group A and Corporation B decided on the joint venture. Related to this, and in order better to co-ordinate the production between the different factories, Company X pursued full consolidation of the enterprise systems. That is to say, synergies were sought in production, not in the IS function. Despite the bugs, the system supported the operations, and clear benefits such as better control and co-ordination of resources between the factories were realised.

Furthermore, when Company X was formed, the management of the company concluded that Factory F1 – that used to belong to Corporation B – had more efficient processes. Hence, they decided to implement these processes in the other factories. Before starting to implement the new software, however, these attempts met with little success. This illustrates the reactive and proactive roles of IS integration. First, IS integration has a reactive role in the sense that it follows the overall post-merger integration strategy. On the other hand, it has a proactive role in the sense that it is used to implement changes in company processes.

4.5 Summary and concluding remarks

Sections 1 and 2 of this paper show that, first, post-merger IS integration literature is scarce and secondly, most of this literature does not define success in post-merger IS integration at all. The definitions provided are often implicit or vague, the only exception being the papers by Stylianou et al. (1996) and Robbins-Stylianoi (1999). Furthermore, none of this literature manages to exploit the vast body of literature on IS evaluation.

Much of the IS evaluation literature is summed up in the DeLone-McLean models (1992, 2003). This paper compares the success issues proposed by the post-merger IS integration literature with those presented in the DeLone-McLean model (2003). As a result, four categories of success issues for post-merger IS integration are proposed: User satisfaction with the integrated software's system and information quality as well as its use; Efficient and effective IS integration management; Efficient IS staff integration; and IS ability to support the underlying motives of the merger.

Issues pertaining to each of these categories were observed in the illustrative case study presented in this paper. The case study also demonstrates some of the complex interrelationships between the success issues and categories. For example, an insufficient number of IS personnel combined with somewhat inefficient IS integration management aggravated the system quality problems as observed by the users. Furthermore, low system quality caused dissatisfaction among the users, however, the system functions well enough to support the new processes and the coordination of production capacity between different factories – i.e. the underlying merger goals.

Further studies are recommended, first to study these interrelationships in more detail, and secondly to provide more comprehensive lists of success issues related to different types of merger goals.

4.6 References

Bentley, Ross (2002) IT key to integration success. Computer weekly, 1/31, p.32

Brynjolfsson, Erik, Hitt, Lorin M. (1998) Beyond the Productivity Paradox. Communications of ACM, Vol. 41, No.8, p. 49 - 55

Buck-Lew, Maylun, Wardle, Caroline E. , Pliskin, Nava (1992) Accounting for information technology in corporate acquisitions. Information & Management, Vol. 22, p. 363 – 369

Buono, Anthony B, Bowditch, James L, Lewis, John W III (1985) When Cultures Collide:

Cossey, Bob (1991) Systems assessment in acquired subsidiaries. Accountancy, Vol. 107 No 1169, p. 98 – 99

DeLone, W.H. , McLean, E.R. (1992) In Information Systems Success: The Quest for the Dependent Variable. Information Systems Research, Vol.3, No.1, p. 60 – 95

DeLone, W.H., McLean, E.R. (2003) The DeLone and McLean Model of Information Systems Success: A Ten-Year Update. Journal of Management Information Systems, Vol 19, No 4, pp. 9 - 30

Doll, William J., Torkzadeh, Gholamreza (1988) The Measurement of End-User Computing Satisfaction. MIS Quarterly, June, p. 258 – 274

Franck, Guillaume (1990) Mergers and Acquisitions: Competitive Advantage and Cultural Fit. EMJ, Vol. 8, No. 1, p. 40 – 43

Giacomazzi Franco, Panella Carlo, Pernici Barbara, Sansoni Marco (1997) Information Systems Integration in Mergers and Acquisitions: A normative model. Information & Management, Vol. 32, p. 289-302

Goodhue, Dale L. (1995) Understanding User Evaluations of Information Systems. Management Science, Vol. 41, No. 12, p. 1827 – 1844

Goodwin, Candice (1999) Merging IT. Accountancy International, Vol. 124, No, 1271, p. 37-38

Haspeslagh Philippe C , Jemison David B. (1991) Managing Acquisitions – Creating Value Through Corporate Renewal The Free Press: New York, USA

Habeck Max M, Kröger Fritz, Träm Michael R (2000) After the merger – seven rules for successful post-merger integration Pearson Education: Edinburgh Gate, GB

I/S Analyzer (1989) Dealing with mergers and acquisitions. I/S Analyzer, Vol 27, No 3, p. 1 – 12

Ives, Blake - Olson, Margrethe H. - Baroudi, Jack J. (1983) The measurement of user information satisfaction. Communications of the ACM, Oct 1983, Vol. 26 Issue 10, p785, 9p

Kortteinen, B. – Nurminen, M.I. – Reijonen, P. – Torvinen, V.(1995) Improving IS Deployment through Evaluation: Application of the ONION Model. 3rd European Conference on the Evaluation of IT, Bath University, p. 175 – 181

Kubilus, Norbert J (1991) Acquired and Abandoned. Journal of Information Strategy: The Executive's Journal, Vol. 7, No 2, p. 33 – 40

Main, Thomas J. – Short, James E. (1989) Managing the Merger: Building Partnership Through IT Planning at the New Baxter. MIS Quarterly, Vol. 13, No.4, p.469 – 484

McKiernan, Peter – Merali, Yasmin (1995) Integrating Information Systems After a Merger. Long Range Planning, Vol. 28 No 4, p. 54 – 62

Mehta, Manjari – Hirschheim, Rudy (2004) A Framework for Assessing IT Integration Decision-Making in Mergers and Acquisitions. Proceedings of the Hawaii International Conference on Systems Sciences.

Merali, Yasmin – McKiernan, Peter (1993) The strategic positioning of information systems in post-acquisition management. Journal of Strategic Information Systems, Vol. 2, No 2, p.105 – 124

Motwani, Jaideep – Mirchandani, Dinesh – Madan, Manu – Gunasekaran, A. (2002) Successful implementation of ERP projects: Evidence from two case studies. International Journal of Production Economics, Vol. 75, p. 83 - 96

Parvinen, Petri M.T. (2003) Towards a governance perspective to mergers and acquisitions. Unpublished doctoral thesis, Helsinki University of Technology. Helsinki

Robbins, Stephanie S. – Stylianou, Antonis C. (1999) Post-Merger systems integration: the impact on IS capabilities. Information & Management, Vol. 36 p.205 - 212

Saarinen, Timo (1996) An expanded instrument for evaluating information system success. Information & Management, Vol. 31 p. 103 – 118

Smithson, S - Hirschheim, R.A. (1998) Analysing information systems evaluation: Another look at an old problem. European Journal of Information Systems, Vol.7, No.3, p.158-174

Shrivastava, Paul (1986) Postmerger integration. The Journal of Business Strategy Vol. 7, No. 1, p. 65-76

Stylianou, Antonis C. – Jeffries, Carol J. – Robbins, Stephanie S. (1996) Corporate mergers and the problems of IS integration. Information & Management, Vol. 31, p.203 – 213

Thach, Liz – Nyman, Mark (2001) Leading in Limbo Land: the role of a leader during merger and acquisition transition. Leadership & Organization Development Journal, Vol. 22, No. 4, p. 146 – 150

Weber, Yaakov – Pliskin, Nava (1996) The effects of information systems integration and organizational culture on a firm's effectiveness. Information & Management, Vol. 30, p. 81-90

Yin, Robert K. (1984) Case Study Research – Design and Methods. SAGE PUBLICATIONS, CA, USA

Yin, Robert K. (1993) Applications of Case Study Research. SAGE PUBLICATIONS INC: Newbury Park, California, USA

4.7 Summary on a Page, using Toulmin's Argument structure

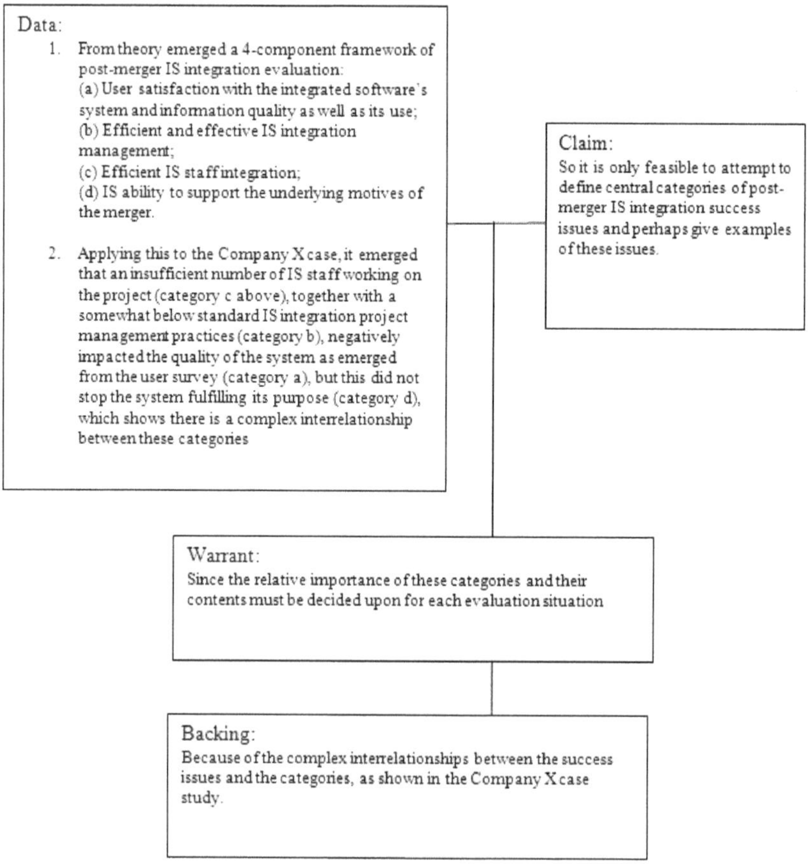

Data:

1. From theory emerged a 4-component framework of post-merger IS integration evaluation:
   (a) User satisfaction with the integrated software's system and information quality as well as its use;
   (b) Efficient and effective IS integration management;
   (c) Efficient IS staff integration;
   (d) IS ability to support the underlying motives of the merger.
2. Applying this to the Company X case, it emerged that an insufficient number of IS staff working on the project (category c above), together with a somewhat below standard IS integration project management practices (category b), negatively impacted the quality of the system as emerged from the user survey (category a), but this did not stop the system fulfilling its purpose (category d), which shows there is a complex interrelationship between these categories

Claim:
So it is only feasible to attempt to define central categories of post-merger IS integration success issues and perhaps give examples of these issues.

Warrant:
Since the relative importance of these categories and their contents must be decided upon for each evaluation situation

Backing:
Because of the complex interrelationships between the success issues and the categories, as shown in the Company X case study.

4.8 Case Study Review

Date of Review:	29JAN11
My Reference: ISBN: Other Reference:	IM.257.
Title/Document:	*Evaluating Success in Post-merger IS Integration: A Case study,* The Electronic Journal Information Systems Evaluation, Volume 8, Issue 3, pp.143-150, available on line at www.ejise.com
Author/Date:	Aralanta, M. (2005)
Source:	EJISE
Theme:	An exploration of various aspects of post-merger IS integration success.
Purpose of Paper:	Shed light on the multi-faceted characteristic of post-merger IT integration success, and propose a framework for its evaluation
Classification/Philosophy	Basic research/Positivist (deductive)
Hypotheses/Research Question:	As a result of the literature review, it proposes four components of post-merger IS integration: (a) User satisfaction with the integrated software's system and information quality as well as its use; (b) Efficient and effective IS integration management; (c) Efficient IS staff integration; (d) IS ability to support the underlying motives of the merger. The paper then illustrates (the author obviously could not bring herself to say 'tests') this through a case study.
Methodology:	Does a deep literature review, and then develops a

	single case study that combines qualitative and quantitative methods. It is essentially qualitative, based on semi-structured interviews, complemented by a survey of users to understand their satisfaction with the system. The Case: Company X is a manufacturing company that has emerged in 2000 as a joint venture between Group A and Corporation B; factory F1 of Corporation B was transferred to the JV and became the pilot plant. The driver for the merger was that the two companies operated in a mature market that required high investments due to obsolescence, which risked creating over-capacity. As part of this JV it was decided to perform a deep enterprise system (ES) integration in order to better co-ordinate production capacity between plants and enable financial reporting. Defying the by then prevailing trend towards standard ERP packages, the company opted for a tailor made system that was thought to better support the new company structure. Going live with this ES happened three years later as planned, and its functionality consisted of sales applications, manufacturing applications, inventory and supply applications, cost accounting and financial reporting. Financials such as A/R, A/P, AM, GL were not included as these services were given by Group A. There was a budget overrun of 10-15% and the ES had significant quality problems (bugs) due to that the project team downplayed the importance of testing. Evidence collection: The main source of evidence was semi-structured interviews. Eleven were conducted when the pilot plant went live in January 2003, and six more when three other plants went live on the system a year later. They included the integration project manager, representatives of senior management, user support, users of different levels, and the soft-

	ware vendor. Interviews were complimented with analysis of internal documents and a survey. The short questionnaire based on instruments for change management and information systems implementation success, was sent out in April 2003 (33 responses) and May 2004 (168 responses). It was aimed at capturing users' perceptions, and not to test a causal model. Analysis: The evidence of all sources was placed in a case study database consisting of an organised folder structure, and later analysed according to the four classes suggested by the theory.
Results:	Aralanta, based on work by Smithson & Hirschheim (1998) arrives at the foundation stone of her post – implementation IS valuation proposition: It is only feasible to attempt to define central categories of post-merger IS integration success issues and perhaps give examples of these issues. The relative importance of these categories and their contents must then be decided upon for each evaluation situation. There are complex interrelationships between the success issues and the categories. For example, an insufficient number of IS staff working on the project (category c above), together with a somewhat below standard IS integration project management practices (category b), negatively impacted the quality of the system as emerged from the user survey (category a), but this did not stop the system fulfilling its purpose (category d).
Managerial Implications:	It appears that user training was reasonably effective (the users did not complain about their knowledge of the system; actually it appears to emerge from the survey that they perceive themselves as knowledgeable of its functioning.) However, it is obvious from the survey that their expectations of the system were

	let down. On the other hand, the ES appeared to meet its functionality ("...there has not been any order that we would not have been able to deliver.") Yes, there were system quality problems (bugs) due to opting for a tailor-made ES and to doing insufficient tests, but users can be persuaded to be patient in the early stages of deployment of the system. The impression one gets from here is that the organisation invested enough on one aspect of change management (i.e., training) but overlooked other key dimensions such as stakeholder management and expectations management. After an organisation's 3-year effort in developing and implementing an efficiency-driven ES solution, user expectations can become unrealistically high, making change management critical for integration success.
Limitations / Future Research:	Observing the summary of Results (above) that "It is only feasible to attempt to define central categories of post-merger IS integration success issues" and that "There are complex interrelationships between the success issues and the categories," one concludes that the framework offered here for post-merger IS integration has too many "degrees of freedom" to be of practical use in problem solving. Future research needs to be performed with an aim at reducing these degrees of freedom.
Critique and Learning:	The author does a competent literature review and arrives at a rational framework for understanding the multi-faceted aspect of IS post-integration evaluation. But what are the managerial implications of this? What, if any, are the theoretical implications of the empirical findings? What should we extract from this work? How will it help us in future evaluations? The fact that after a detailed analysis of the case study the reader finds it hard to respond to these questions makes a good piece of work lose relevance.

	Lessons learned: **Reflections**: Where do you draw the line between case specific research and anecdotal information? Determining IS success is problematic, as is finding reliable measures for it. The problem is that ICT is not an end in itself, but only an enabler; so it is not ICT that succeeds or does not succeed, it is whatever it enables. If there is a measure of ICT success, it is an indirect one, in terms of metrics of the enabled phenomenon. Both executives and academics usually evaluate acquisition performance and acquisition strategies in terms of monetary criteria such as cost savings (economies of scale) and synergies (reducing or exploiting redundant capacity) as benefits obtainable from post-merger IS integration. This research reports a case of efficiency driven ICT project, aimed at coordinating plant capacity and avoiding over-capacity in the market. As indicated in section 4.4 the project was led and carried mostly by IT – this is typical of an efficiency driven ICT project, and requires significant effort in change management.

Chapter 5

Collective Use of a Hotel Management Core System (Australia)

This case study brings two interesting issues onto the discussion table. The first is that the unit of analysis is not an organisation but an application, in this case a hotel management core system. The other issue is that its business environment is small and medium business as the application is aimed at small to medium sized hotels.

The case does a review of the literature on *use* as a measure of an information system's success. It moves away from the traditional individual use of a system to focus on its collective use.

Because the IS tool analysed is targeted on SME hotels it covers all the functionality of these organisations, from back office accounting to operational house-keeping management to the customer facing functions such as checking-in or checking-out. So how do you classify these projects in terms of *efficiency-driven* or *market-power-driven* as characterised in table 3.1?

The Influence of net Benefits on Collective, Innovative, Configural System use: a Case Study of Small-to-Medium Enterprises

Carla Wilkin
Monash University, Victoria, Australia

Abstract: In today's business world, Small-to-Medium enterprises (SMEs) increasingly join their larger counterparts regarding the use of Information Technology (IT) and Information Systems (IS) as fundamental to business operations. For SMEs, investment in packaged software that has not been customized to individual enterprise needs, allows ready access to much of the IT function enjoyed by their larger counterparts. However, given these systems are not exclusively tailored to the enterprise and further given the collective nature of the work-place in these enterprises, the likelihood increases for work-arounds and unexpected usage to occur to manage enterprise needs. Studies that explore system use typically focus on individual use. Using an interpretive case study approach, this study considers users of a common system in individually owned SMEs to explore evidence of collective, innovative, configural (CIC) use, the causes of this and its impact on fellow workers. Results provide insight into the role of systems as dynamic business tools and show that despite impacts on financial and operational reporting, CIC use occurs for reasons of operational efficiency and also out of frustration with system functionality. This provides some insight into attitudes concerning Use and Net Benefits in the IS Success Model, which in turn informs system evolution.

Keywords: collective use, work-arounds, innovative use, configural use, small-to-medium enterprises, net benefits.

Originally published in the Electronic Journal of IS Evaluation, Volume 12 Issue 2, pp 187-198.

5.1 Introduction

In the past investment in Information Technology (IT) was regarded as a business opportunity wherein an enterprise could gain competitive advantage or even create barriers to entry for competitors in the marketplace. Today investment in IT is seen as an essential tool for operating enterprises. Much has been written about the management of IT systems in large enterprises (Brown and Magill, 1994; Xue et al., 2008). Here the focus has been on system use at the individual level (Doll and

Torzadeh, 1991; Szajna, 1993) and at the corporate/strategic level (Earl, 1993). In these contexts systems are normally used as a means to achieve a goal. However, instances arise that result in the normal functioning of the system becoming an impediment to ready achievement of desired goals. The dynamic environments in which these systems are deployed highlight the impossibility of designing "systems which are appropriate for all users and all situations" (MacLean et al., 1990, p175). This motivates innovation in the way the systems are used. Slappendel (1996, p108) define innovation as "the process through which new ideas, objects and practices are created, developed or reinvented". Such innovative use in the ebb and flow of work-place interactions, when linked with dependence on the cooperative input of individuals, affects strategic reporting and record-keeping functions.

Given use relates to the user's view of IT quality (Ozkan, 2006), understanding use in all its forms is important in progressing a more positive approach to system design (Avital et al., 2006). Adding to this complexity is the fact that collectives, such as groups (Dennis et al., 2001; Easley et al., 2003), organizations (Devaraj and Kohli, 2003), even nations (Dedrick et al., 2003), use systems. Moreover, members of these collectives may use the system more or less frequently and for different purposes, but there can be stable patterns in their use. This is referred to as configural use. However, despite system usage (Barkin and Dickson, 1977) being reviewed over many years, research suggests we still know little about it (DeLone and McLean, 2003). Consequently there have been calls to deepen insights into IT artifacts through conceptualization of systems in new ways (Burton-Jones and Gallivan, 2007). The objective of this paper is to respond to this call by illustrating what evidence exists of collective, innovative, configural (CIC) use in Small-to-Medium Enterprises (SMEs), its causes and how it impacts fellow workers. This understanding would provide insight into the constructs Intention to Use and Net Benefits in the IS Success Model (DeLone and McLean, 2003).

Like their larger counterparts, the benefits afforded to SMEs by IT systems necessitate new structures and processes. However, these are mediated by the close and inter-dependent working relationships in these enterprises. In this research an interpretive case study approach was used to understand CIC use in SMEs. This offers insight into human interpretations concerning IT systems (something that is fundamental in appreciating IT use, particularly given its users who evaluate the fit between their tasks and software packages (Mathieson and Ryan, 1997)) and the processes that are intrinsically linked to their conception of work in these enterprises (Smith et al., 2007).

The importance of SMEs to the success of a country's national economy (Johnston and Loader, 2003) makes them a relevant research environment. For example, in Australia there are estimated to be around 130,000 SMEs. The annual turnover is between $2-250 million; they pay around 15% of total tax collected; and contribute a further 12% of total tax through the withholding payments (Australian Taxation Office, 2008). Likewise in China they account for 60% of industrial output and employ about 75% of the workforce (The American Embassy in China, 2002), whilst another study of SMEs in 62 countries found that their share of total employment was well over 40%, with reports of 86% in Chile, Greece and Thailand (Beck et al., 2004).

In reporting on this study of CIC system use in SMEs, the paper is structured as follows. After outlining the literature regarding system use, the research questions are posed. Following this the methodology is outlined and findings that revealed institutionalized CIC system use at a number of SMEs are reported. The paper then concludes with comments about future research and the place of this study in the context of IT research.

5.2 Literature review

5.2.1 Use

Barkin and Dickson (1977 p1) first defined use as occurring when "the output from the information system is included in the Human Processing System of a decision maker". DeLone and McLean's (1992, pp64-80) later definition of use as the "recipient consumption of the output of an information system" is no less helpful as it is really only significant for voluntary use. Better clarification was provided by Burton-Jones and Straub (2006) who, in drawing upon this and work by Szajna (1993), and Subramani (2004), defined system use as an activity with three elements wherein an individual user employs one or more features of a system to perform a task. At an operational level an individual user can use the system in one of two ways, exploitatively (the routine execution of duties) and exploratively (the search for and use of innovative means to achieve results) (March, 1991). Whilst exploitative use is consistently concerned with the normal operations of an enterprise, often the deepest engagement is at the exploratory level. Therein innovation achieves outcomes not realizable with normal use, but which facilitate more immediate results like improved customer satisfaction.

The investigation reported on in this paper considered innovative behavior as far more challenging because:

- for operational users, innovation is usually the result of past frustration about lack of desired or timely outcomes;
- for manager/owner users, it may affect the integrity of data for decision-making; and
- for system developers, it may indicate system deficiencies.

Through its study this research aims to extend understanding about the consequences and drivers of the interplay between Net Benefits, Intention to Use and Use as detailed in the IS Success Model (DeLone and McLean, 2003).

5.2.2 Innovative use

Given the ubiquity of IT and growth of off-the-shelf software packages that are less individualized to work-place requirements, the likelihood increases for innovations to become agreed and accepted ways of getting information into and out of an IT system. IT offers SMEs efficiencies in managing customers, financial record keeping and accountability for staff performance. Yet SMEs exhibit differences from their larger counterparts. In large organizations use is characteristically hierarchically segmented. In contrast in SMEs owner/managers use the systems for operational as well as reporting functions. Thus, for SMEs the extent of collective and cooperative system use is different and accordingly so too are the opportunities for an enterprise to accept and practise divergences from normal system use. Consequently the opportunity for agreed innovation increases (Slappendel, 1996).

In exploring users' innovations the investigation was not concerned with work-arounds that may be a 'one off' response by an employee who has yet to master system functionality. Rather it sought to identify innovative use that has been hierarchically institutionalized as an acceptable/required way to handle a circumstance of system use. Investigation that explores the types, role and outcomes of such innovation offers rich opportunities to understand systems as dynamic tools that can be contextualized to their work-place.

Innovative use involves non-compliant user behaviors (Koopman and Hoffman, 2003), typically ad hoc strategies used to handle immediate and confronting problems (Gasser, 1986, p216). Here it offers a means to identify system dysfunctionality (Ciborra, 2002; Devaraj and Kohli, 2003) and even argue for system evolution (Zhang et al., 2005). For example, Diconsiglio (2008) investigated nurses working-around the barcodes on patients' arm bands when these codes could not be scanned because they were damaged. Here, given administering medication to patients is time critical, some nurses worked-around the problem by scanning duplicate wristbands, which they kept on their arms as a backup; others simply carried pre-scanned pills. Similarly, the malfunction of an email system was overcome by locking the F9 key on the keyboard into a down position (Sharky, 2007). Both are examples of users dealing with a lack of system functionality in exploratory ways; however they differ from this investigation because there is no collective agreement across hierarchical levels to accept the practice as the normal way to achieve an outcome.

Whilst it is acknowledged that exploitative use should be valued as normal use of IT, it is important to focus on users' exploratory use of systems to advance literature about the inner workings and dynamics of IT use (Ciborra, 2002; Ferneley and Sobreperez, 2006) and the IS Success Model. This offers insight into the reasons for such acceptance in a co-operative/collective environment.

5.2.3 Collective use

Although system use has long been studied at the individual level (Davis et al., 1989), it is not the only way that system use occurs. Often groups of users work together, interacting in their use of a system to produce outputs that have been collectively generated and upon which they are collectively reliant. Indeed earlier research by Cross et al. (2002) found that workers relied on social networks rather than the internet or databases to find necessary information. This aspect of system use has largely been ignored and in contrast to the economic theory of collective action, which focuses on the provision of public goods, together with other collective consumption (Coase, 1937), collective use focuses more on the actual IS usage practices by workers in organizations, which can be driven by a number of factors including customer service. Arguably this area warrants further investigation and SMEs offer a rich environment in which to conduct such research.

In exploring this it is important to understand the distinction between individual and collective constructs. Morgeson and Hofmann (1999) define an individual as a person and a collective as an interdependent group of individuals with a collective goal direction. Further, in a multi-level construct, the system can be used differently at different levels: this becomes a collective when interaction occurs and interdependencies arise because two or more (entities) are mutually dependent on each other (Karsten, 2003).

Collective use, therefore, is more than social or task-related interaction among members of the collective. Collaboration, communication and coordination are essential components of any interdependency and constitute evidence of collective use (Burton-Jones and Gallivan, 2007). Further, they argued that collective use may take one of two forms: shared and configural. Shared constructs occur when individual use emerges at the collective level as homogeneous use among collective members. Configural constructs occur when members of the collective use a system more or less frequently and for different purposes, but there is a stable pattern to their use.

All of these theoretical constructs have relevance to IT use in SMEs where the workforce is not merely a group of individuals who use a system. Instead SMEs characteristically have several levels of users, with some members switching between functions. For example, some utilize the system operationally, like front office staff in accommodation enterprises: alternatively owners/managers use the system operationally when dealing with customer transactions, but switch to analysis/financial functions for reporting. With the tendency towards off-the-shelf systems, the likelihood increases for agreed innovative use to work-around the lack of system functionality to achieve desired outputs. This relates to research by Sussman and Seigal (2003) who found that usefulness could be the mediating influence for workers in the knowledge adoption process. As a result it is hypothesized that collective use should exist, and when expected levels of agreed commonality of use are present, then that use should be both collective and configural. This impacts customer service and in turn customer service may impact use.

5.2.4 Customer service and SMEs

A focus on customer service is often regarded as the best method to progress an enterprise (Rorholm, 2008) with twofold benefits. Firstly, research has shown that increased customer satisfaction is beneficial to an organization's productivity (Kwak, 2003; Rorholm, 2008); and secondly a focus on consistent customer service will create a point of difference between the enterprise and its competitors (Business Wire, 2009). With their limited marketing budgets, SMEs are very aware that costs associated with attracting customers are higher than those associated with retaining customers (Kwak, 2003; Rorholm, 2008); and that investment in the development of quality customer service relationships will improve customer loyalty, retention and in turn profitability (Ennew and Binks, 1996; Vandenbosch and Dawar, 2002). Thus, the relationship between customers and front-line service providers is regarded as more significant for SMEs than for larger organizations (Batt, 2000).

Secondly SMEs are less likely to use consultants or research and development to extend the functionality of IT systems (Miles, 2008). Budgetary constraints may be part of the reason. A separate comparative study of IT management of SMEs in Canada and the USA found that the robust exchange of information between managers and others in the organization was reflected in the organization's ability to use IT innovatively in operational and strategic ways (Montazemi, 2006). Similarly, Miles (2008) reported that project management and on-the-job innovation are common ways of achieving service innovation.

Thirdly, SMEs tend to take a less strategic view of the enterprise and are more reactive to immediate needs than longer term goals (Rangone, 1999; Sexton and van Auken, 1982). In fact, a business plan is a necessity for larger enterprises given their size and consequently the formal demands of financial providers and/or shareholders. For SMEs these financial undertakings are often backed by personal guarantees, so many owners opt for the ad hoc option of thoughts about the enterprise, which are sometimes not written and certainly not backed with strict budget accountability (Brailsford, 1995). As such, SMEs may watch the gross returns carefully, but not the detail (Brailsford, 1995). These factors all ultimately impact customer service and thus the individuals concerned as well as the organization as a whole. Moreover, they impact IS Success.

5.2.5 IS evaluation

In attempting to structure the myriad of variables associated with the diversity of information systems, DeLone and McLean (1992) argued that there was little relevance in calculating input variables like user participation or level of IT investment with respect to information systems, if the dependent or output variable, IS Success or MIS Effectiveness, could not be calculated with similar accuracy. Herein IS success is "a value judgement made by an individual, from the point of some stakeholder" (Seddon, 1997 p83). Since DeLone and McLean's 1992 paper there has been much debate around the components of the IS Success Model and their operationalization (DeLone and McLean, 2003). However, the end of their model, which is concerned with Intention to Use, Use, User Satisfaction and Net Benefits has been least understood.

Given this background, from an IS evaluation perspective, it seems pertinent to ask:

- What evidence is there of CIC use in SMEs?
- What causes this type of use to occur?
- How does it impact fellow workers?

Answers to these questions provide deeper understanding about CIC use and offers some insight into its effect on the related components of the IS Success Model.

5.3 Research method and context

5.3.1 Methodology

As already mentioned, an interpretive case study approach (Walsham, 1995) was used to understand the evidence of CIC use in SMEs, the causes that give rise to such use, and how it impacts fellow workers. This method has been used in a significant number of studies that cover a range of topics and issues (for example, Orlikowski and Baroudi, 1991; Carey, 2008). Given the relevance of the method in exploring social issues (Walsham, 1995) and the "how" and "why" questions where a researcher wants to investigate events or actions in real-life contexts and has little control over these events (Yin, 2003), it was relevant in this study in investigating evidence, causes and impacts of CIC use across a variety of SMEs. Here the method facilitates drawing out the subtleties of human interactions with a system, something that is only possible with rich data.

Accepting Yin's (2003) stance on case studies, evidence of use in this case study came from documents (in this case training manuals); interviews; direct observation; and physical artefacts (such as house-keeping lists and check-out reports). The focus was on capturing participants' interpretations as accurately as possible, whilst also allowing the normal social exchanges that occur in interviews to take place. Moreover, by positioning as an outside observer, any perception of having a personal stake in the results was removed.

Participants were motivated because their concerns about operationalizing aspects of the system (Walsham, 1995) were appreciated. For each interview detailed notes were taken so that a conceptual understanding of system use could evolve (Corbin and Strauss, 1990). Further, as the interviews progressed the questions were refined and new ones added to clarify emerging understanding. To improve validity, results from the initial analysis were shared with a senior independent expert of the system. Collaboration was felt to be effective because participants expressed their own ideas, yet challenged those of other people: their opinions developed understanding about system use; and moreover most commented that they benefited from the process (which was in line with Levina and Vaast, 2008).

5.3.2 Research context: enterprises, system and participants

This study investigated SME tourist accommodation enterprises that are individually owned and operated, but are part of marketing groups called Beta and Omega. These SMEs were chosen because the author had practical familiarity with the context and because they operate in a dynamic environment. Both marketing groups are key players in one sector of the Australian tourism industry. Whilst neither Beta nor Omega mandate a particular transaction processing system, approximately 65% of enterprises have installed the same system, although each installation operates entirely independently, with no central server. This commonly used system is the focus of this study into collective IS use.

For Beta and Omega, the transaction processing system is the operational core, managing accommodation bookings, financial recording keeping and business reporting. Use is characteristically routine and structured. Further, activities that occur within the system are reported to accounting systems with financial information used, for example, to prepare daily banking. This system has been in use within the Beta and Omega groups for over 16 years, with multiple releases.

Participants in the study included front-office staff (operational level users) and site managers/owners (operational and managerial users). Most were confident users as they had at least 5 years' relevant experience in actual use of this system (many in excess of 10 years). The training provided to users varied, but included a combination of: what was provided at the time of installation; on-demand pre-booked telephone support; and refresher courses at annual conferences. Training was generally accessed by owner/managers, with front-office or operational level staff trained by their superiors. The remainder of users' knowledge was acquired on site as they experimented – usually by executing actual transactions, but sometimes by using the system in training mode.

Over a lengthy period, observations and interviews with 12 managerial and 25 operational users provided evidence of CIC use in the chosen SMEs. Interactions that occurred with participants took place in a friendly, collegial manner and were aided by copious notes, which facilitated the refinement of questions in revisits. These revisits played an important role in clarifying understanding and enabled investigation of use that had not been fully appreciated in the first visit.

Participants were spread across 14 locations that were geographically dispersed and operationally different with respect to enterprise size, nature of bookings and managerial control. This meant that any common instances of innovative use were particularly interesting.

5.4 Case study findings

Five main areas were identified where there was consistent evidence of users' CIC use with functionality of the transaction processing system to manage various circumstances (see Table 5.1). Explanations for the innovations varied, but were all driven by operational imperatives. Some said:

> *"We could not let staff know about the discounted rates given to wholesalers (up to 50%) because otherwise our full fee customers could learn of it and want a cheaper rate"; or*
>
> *"Late check outs are painful and not worth the effort in managing cleaning staff, but at off-peak times they keep a lot of customers very keen to return for weekends so we manage"; or*
>
> *"Group bookings (a receptionist) are the commonest cause of front office error. One receptionist does one party and another does the next, so on one invoice you have credits for amounts paid and balance owing with that customer refusing to see how you can have this rolling balance until all have paid. Splitting this into separate bookings was the best thing we ever did"; or*
>
> *"I (an owner) got really upset one day when a receptionist had again failed to charge a customer for half their account because they had moved units and she had overlooked the second account for this part of the stay. The customer had to be contacted and it was all very uncomfortable so I resolved to find a way around this. The office manager and I worked out a solution and we all agreed to use it".*

In Table 5.1 (see below), six types of CIC use are reported. Each was identified at more than one site. Moreover, each had the same motivation, being operationally driven to please customers despite implications for managerial reporting/analysis.

By their very nature, once an enterprise started to manage a circumstance of functionality like those outlined above in a manner that differed from the normal functionality, it had to be collectively used in the organization or customer and staff problems were bound to arise.

Table 5.1: Examples of CIC use in the transaction processing system and categorized implications for the enterprise

Functionality	Description of the functionality	User of the functionality	Problem	Collective, innovative, configural (CIC) use	Generalized implications/results (see Table 2 for practical consequences)
Pricing	Some bookings customer buys holiday from wholesaler; the enterprise needs to claim this payment less commission from wholesaler	Front office staff	The enterprise does not want the customer or office staff to know the amount of commission and any discounts	Automatic pricing is overridden with the customer's receipt showing the amount owing as $0. Customer is pleased they have paid the wholesaler and have the receipt showing that no money is owed	When these payments are claimed they are banked without being entered into the reservation part of the transaction processing system. Thus occupancy is known, cash flow is inaccurate and returns per room are understated
	Customer may request a late check-out for an extra charge	Front office staff in conjunction with Owner/ Mangers	This functionality is not available as part of the standard package	The late check-out fee is debited to the customer's account by adding a miscellaneous charge	Inconsistencies may occur in the treatment of customers. The system does not recognize this when printing check-out reports (and in producing cleaning rosters)
Yield Management	Rooms can be priced according to demand with increased prices in periods of demand	Owner/ Manager	Front office staff ignore price fluctuations when taking telephone reservations because they check availability not pricing	The enterprise is obliged to honor the quoted price and consequently needs to override the higher price when checking the customer in	Loss of revenue
Check-out	On the customer's departure date the system expects everyone to check-out by the normal time'	Front office staff	Cleaning rosters are generated at the start of each day. These detail the rooms to be cleaned	Details regarding late check-outs need to be manually recorded on the roster to prevent cleaners disturbing customers	Customer complaints would occur without manual intervention
Group Booking	A number of accounts can be linked together on a single invoice	Front office staff	Members of groups often wish to settle their accounts separately and demand separate receipts to record this	The enterprise actively ignores the group booking functionality and records the bookings as a series of individual entries i.e., Smith 1, Smith 2, Smith 3 etc.	Information about the value of group bookings is lost
Caravan Storage	When a customer stores a car or van onsite between visits, the system handles this with separate accounts	Front office staff	The customer wants one account rather than multiple accounts	Group functionality enables the customer's individual accounts to be linked to one master account for payment	Information about group bookings is distorted

* All examples are in common use by at least one work-place.

For each reported example, the system was collectively used at different, but yet integrated, vertical levels at two or more enterprises within Beta and/or Omega. Interactions between users at the relevant enterprises were ongoing as they grappled with the ramifications of system use. For example, owners/managers were aware of the implications of each use for analytical/reporting functions, but sanctioned those listed as being the best operational alternatives (see Table 5.2). This gave us insights into how interdependencies-in-use affected performance (Burton-Jones and Gallivan, 2007). As the reported examples are concerned with individual uses that emerge at a collective level in distinct outputs, it is argued, in Burton-Jones and Gallivan's (2007, p668) terms, that configural, collective system use had been observed, with glints of innovation (Slappendel, 1996).

5.5 Insights from the case study

There are several notable outcomes arising from this case study. Firstly, there was variation in use of the common transaction processing system across different enterprises within Beta and Omega. This variation exists despite the well established nature of the system. Furthermore, evidence of both innovative and normal use was found. For example, looking at use of the group booking functionality, it was found that users in some SMEs used the functionality in innovative ways, whilst users in other SMEs opted to neglect the functionality altogether. Both represent work-arounds, but only one is innovative in nature.

Secondly, with respect to pricing functionality, a number of instances of user innovation were evident. Notably, it appears that some enterprises have been slow to adopt new approaches to market opportunities (such as wholesaler packages). In part some owners agreed that this failure was due to an inability to innovate around constraints of the system to handle the necessary transactions. Not only does this appear to impact negatively on the current operation of the enterprise, but it also hinders the ability of the enterprise to take advantage of new market opportunities because enterprises were unwilling to access new business opportunities when they perceived difficulties in operationalizing the system to accommodate the variation.

Table 5.2: Implications for the enterprises from the CIC use

Collective, innovative, configural (CIC) use (from Table 5.1)	Specific implications for managerial analysis/financial reporting (comments from the sites investigated)
Automatic pricing is overridden with the customer's receipt showing the amount owing as $0. Customers are happy because they have already paid the wholesaler and have the receipt showing that no money is owed.	For confidentiality, payments from the wholesaler are confirmed against client records, but the amounts are not credited into that part of the system (so staff cannot read them). Instead the cheques are entered into the MYOB file and banked. This means that analysis in that category of accommodation is accurate with respect to occupancy, but returns per unit are understated. We made $50,000 per year from this so the effort and misreporting were significant.
The late check-out fee is debited to the customer's account by adding a miscellaneous charge	In charging the customer, some staff fail to read the notes in the IT file and consequently wrongly charge the customer or don't charge them at all. For a "walk up" booking requesting a late checkout, at times staff fail to add a note in housekeeping that will warn the house keeper about a later clean. At $10 per time charge does seem much, but you have to realize that you wouldn't have the rest of the booking otherwise ($200-$500).
The enterprise is obliged to honor the quoted price and consequently needs to override the higher price when checking the customer in	Manually over-riding a price in the system means that the price remains fixed and if the guest adds extra people or nights, the system will not alter the price. This means that staff have to remember to manually recalculate the bill or we lose money. Manual recalculation can produce errors and argument; and undue time spent at check-in. The loss of income per booking was usually not great ($20), but the angst and errors were not good for customer service at first point of contact.
Details regarding late check-outs need to be manually recorded on the roster to prevent cleaners disturbing customers	My guests are not happy if we do not offer this in off-peak times; and are not happy if they pay for being undisturbed and we overlook this and a cleaner knocks on the door. It costs management a lot of attention to detail.
In this situation the enterprise actively ignores the group booking functionality instead recording the bookings as a series of individual bookings i.e., Smith 1, Smith 2, Smith 3 etc.	Income per accommodation type is accurate, but in looking at sources of bookings, the role of groups is seriously under estimated. They are a major source of business for long weekends and Easter, but you only know this from the initial phone contact and by talking to guests. This affects marketing initiatives.
Group functionality enables the customer's individual accounts to be linked to one master account for payment	Group bookings as a source of business are misreported (this time upwards). We put up with it because it means that no one overlooks charging the guests for some of their stay and that used to cost us at least several hundred dollars per slip-up.

Thirdly, looking at use of the yield management functionalities, users in some enterprises used the system functionality faithfully. Others used the system ineffectively with obvious immediate negative effects on task performance as was the case when customers were quoted a price different from that in the system and manual overriding of the pricing functionality was the method used to manage this disparity. The same sorts of problems arose with the innovation created to handle the late check-out of customers. Here, once again, collective understanding and agreement were essential in managing this lack of functionality so that the customer was not affected.

Finally, where there was a consistent pattern in the examples of innovative use, these were typically performed at the front counter to manage customer transactions quickly and efficiently and/or to maximize customer satisfaction with the booking process. Delays, lack of clarity in the process and the production of incomprehensible invoices are not conducive to customer satisfaction (Yu, 2001). This pattern of using customer-friendly outputs had considerable impact on the reporting of data for both administrative and financial management records (see Table 5.2). Yet managers actively countenanced such outcomes.

Given the culture of service apparent in this case study, the decision to favor CIC use of the transaction processing system to ensure customer satisfaction is understandable. Moreover, in light of the fact that SMEs tend to take a less strategic view, their focus upon the immediacy of customer service (Appiah-Adu and Singh, 1998) explains the willingness by staff to collectively adopt innovative use as routine practice (configural use), despite the negative impacts on other reporting aspects of the enterprise function.

Results show that the SMEs who used the system in an innovative manner were among the more successful ones in their groups. As entrepreneurship has long been a characteristic of successful SMEs (Brailsford, 1995; Sheehan, 2006), this flexible attitude to IT use is unsurprising (the attitude to wholesaler packages is an example of this).

So in answer to the research question concerning what evidence was there of CIC use in SMEs, the support is clear: it occurs in a multitude of ways (see Table 5.1). In line with Slappendel (1996) there was evidence of agreed innovation. Moreover, this study has shown that in contrast to

Gasser (1986), innovative use does not always involve ad hoc strategies. In fact these innovations can assume collective understanding and agreement amongst staff, such that they become common place so that customers are not affected. Understanding this type of use is important given it has managerial and thus organizational impacts. Moreover, capturing such deep understanding is important in system evolution. Yet, as with this case, system developers do not appear to be immersing themselves in the environments in which these systems are used to gather such deep insight which can enrich future versions of systems.

As for what causes this type of use, it would certainly seem to be driven by a desire to offer better customer service. Given customer service is seen as important for progressing an enterprise (Rorholm, 2008), this is perhaps unsurprising. However, those who used the system in this manner were operational users acting with management's agreement (again see Table 5.1). With respect to affects, given CIC use impacts financial, marketing and analytical reporting, owner/managers typically bear the ramifications. However, there are also individual impacts with flow-on consequences to fellow workers when they are directed by management to use the system in certain ways (see Table 5.2). Thus, there has been some conscious choices made about Net Benefits that could be gained from Use. Accuracy in reporting functions has been sacrificed to customer service: or in other words, environmental factors have directly affected Intention to Use, Use and Net Benefits.

Whilst the findings are insightful, there are caveats with the approach. Firstly, although multiple users were examined within the SMEs, these users were drawn from only two accommodation marketing groups (Beta and Omega). Secondly, given that approximately 65% of enterprises in these marketing groups used the same system, the focus was on users of one system. Thirdly, use of the system was mandatory in the enterprises studied. None of these caveats substantially detract from the findings reported in this paper. Instead they offer avenues for future research.

5.6 Future research directions

A logical extension to this study would be to take these understandings about CIC use and interdependencies-in-use and frame them as a set of specific questions in a survey administered to a wider audience. Despite this investigation being carried out solely in Australia, the nature of the work environment and the relationship between users in SMEs within this service sector is likely to be quite universal. Therefore, replication of the study in other countries/other cultures should provide interesting data, allowing the study to evolve whilst still being executed within the existing methodological framework thereby making comparisons to support or reject the regularity of such practices in SMEs.

Reflecting on these findings in the context of DeLone and McLean's (2003) framework for conceptualizing the IS function, it is the components Intention to Use, Use (beyond Individual Use) and Net Benefits whose performance have been less understood. The proposed extension to this study (see above) would facilitate some understanding of these components through a practical study of users in their work environment. Moreover, by focusing on SMEs, there is the opportunity to talk with different types of users who are comfortable engaging with one another in the use of a common system, who share common frustrations with system functionality and who are likely to seek their own solutions rather than engaging consultants. Given that the literature to date has focused on larger organizations with more structured hierarchies and work demands, such an approach would be particularly informative.

Finally, this study raises interesting questions about the link between willingness to be innovative in system use and formal business planning in SMEs. Entrepreneurial skills have long been regarded as an advantage in the successful operation of SMEs and this study provides some thoughtful insights beyond the usual examples related to niche manufacturing or retail. Comparing the occurrence of innovative collective IT system use in SMEs with that in larger enterprises in the same service sector would be a further worthwhile extension.

5.7 Conclusion

This research has attempted to investigate, using an interpretive case study approach, evidence of CIC use in SMEs, its causes and how it impacts fellow workers. In doing so, valuable insights are offered into use that occurs due to frustration with system functionality.

Further, with results demonstrating that SMEs can indeed be innovative in their use of IT, there is merit in investigating this to expand current understanding about system use beyond individual use. Like Venkatesh et al. (2008), this work goes beyond system use as a measure of IT functionality and sees use in terms of task performance and as a consequence of interaction in the context of the system, the task, the user(s) and their environment. The CIC use was accepted as the chosen preferred option from a choice between a happy customer and tidy reporting information. Realization that this Net Benefit (customer service) was better than normal exploitive use was what created the innovative intention to use and consequent use, with these attitudes and uses becoming the norm. Herein there is clear evidence of the role of environmental factors (customers and the demand for good service) directly affecting Intention to Use and Use through the influence of Net Benefits that is outside the functionality of the system itself. Thus, this study has extended understanding of the central components of the IS Success Model (DeLone and McLean, 2003). Indeed the case study may suggest that in a workplace where close and inter-dependent working relationships are present, Net Benefits may influence Intention to Use and Use more than User Satisfaction.

Finally, this study shows that SMEs can indeed be collectively innovative in their adoption of IT systems. Given the impossibility of designing systems to suit all users in all situations, this is perhaps unsurprising. In this study, like Slappendel (1996), innovation was facilitated by communication between an organization and its environment. Further, given their critical role in the success of national economies, SMEs provided a rich source of data for conceptualizing understanding about interdependencies in CIC system use. Systematic understanding of such use is fruitful for achieving better insights that can feed in to evolution of packaged software applications and increase system longevity.

5.8 References

(The) American Embassy in China (2002) China's small and medium enterprises: Room to grow with WTO. Retrieved January 11, 2009, from www.usembassy-china.org.cn/econ/smes2002.html.

Appiah-Adu, K., and S. Singh (1998) Customer orientation and performance: A study of SMEs. *Management Decision*, Vol. 36, No. 6, pp385-394.

Avital, M.K. Lyytinen, R. Boland, B. Butler, D. Dougherty, M. Fineout, W. Jansen, N. Levina, W. Rifkin, and J. Venable (2006) Design with a positive lens: An Affirmative Approach to Designing Information and Organizations, *Communications of AIS*, Vol. 18, pp519-545.

Australian Taxation Office (2008) Compliance program 2008-09, http://www.ato.gov.au/corporate/content.asp?doc=/content/00155156.htm&page=38&H38&mnu=42758&mfp=001

Barkin, S.R., and G.W. Dickson (1977) An investigation of information system utilization. *Information and Management*, Vol. 1, No. 1, pp35-45.

Batt, R. (2000) Strategic segmentation in front-line services: matching customers, employees and human resource systems. *International Journal of Human Resource Management*, Vol. 11, No. 3, pp540-561.

Brailsford, T.J. (1995) Small business plans, budgets and performance measures. *Businessdate*, Vol. 3, No. 3, pp1-5.

Beck, T., A. Demirguc-Kunt, and R. Levine (2004) SMEs, growth, and poverty: cross-country evidence, available at: www.worldbank.org/research/projects/sme/Beck-SMEs_Growth_and_Poverty.pdf.

Brown, C.V., and S.L. Magill (1994) Alignment of the IS function with the enterprise: Toward a model of antecedents. *MIS Quarterly*, Vol. 18, No. 4, pp371-403.

Burton-Jones, A., and M.J. Gallivan (2007) Toward a Deeper Understanding of System Usage in Organizations: A Multi-level Perspective, *MIS Quarterly*, Vol. 31, No. 4, pp657-679.

Burton-Jones, A., and D.W. Jr Straub (2006) Reconceptualizing system usage: An approach and empirical test. *Information Systems Research*, Vol. 17, No. 3, pp228-246.

Business Wire (2009) TigerDirect named "excellent in customer service". *Business Wire*, New York: Jan 20.

Carey, J. (2008) Role misconceptions and negotiations in small business owner/web developer relationships. *Journal of Management and Organization*, Vol. 14, pp85-99.

Ciborra, C.U. (2002) The labyrinth of information, Oxford: Oxford University Press.

Coase, R. (1937) The Nature of the Firm, *Economica*, Vol. 4, No. 16, pp386–405.

Corbin, J. and A. Strauss (1990) Grounded theory research: Procedures, canons and evaluative criteria. *Qualitative Sociology,* Vol. 13, No. 1, pp3-21.

Cross, R., N. Nohria and A. Parker (2002) Six Myths About Informal Networks -- and How to Overcome Them. *MIT Sloan Management Review*, Vol. 43, No. 3, pp67-75.

Davis, F.D., R.P. Bagozzi, and P.R. Warshaw (1989) User acceptance of computer technology: A comparison of two theoretical models. *Management Science*, (7)2, pp. 982-1003.

Dedrick, J.L., V. Gurbaxani, and K.L. Kraemer (2003) Information Technology and Economic Performance: A Critical Review of the Empirical Evidence, *ACM Computing Surveys,* Vol. 35, No. 1, pp1-28.

DeLone, W.H. and E.R. McLean (1992) Information systems success: The quest for the dependent variable. *Information Systems Research*, Vol. 3, No. 1, pp60-95.

DeLone, W.H., and E.R. McLean (2003) The DeLone and McLean model of information systems success: A ten-year update. *Journal of Management Information Systems*, Vol. 19, No. 4, pp9-30.

Dennis, A.R., B.H. Wixom and R.J. Vandenberg (2001) Uderstanding Fit and Appropriation Effects in Group Support Systems via Meta-Analysis, *MIS Quarterly*, Vol. 25, No. 2, pp167-193.

Devaraj, S. and R. Kohli (2003) Performance impacts of information technology: Is actual usage the missing link? *Management Science*, Vol. 49, No. 3, pp273-289.

Diconsiglio, J. (2008) Creative “work-arounds” defeat bar-coding safeguards for meds. *Materials Management in Health Care,* Vol. 17, No. 9, pp26-28.

Doll, W.J. and G. Torzadeh (1991) The measurement of end-user computing satisfaction: Theoretical and methodological issues. *MIS Quarterly,* Vol. 15, No. 1, pp5-10.

Earl, M.J. (1993) Experiences in strategic information systems planning. *MIS Quarterly*, Vol. 17, No. 2, pp1-24.

Easley, R.F., S. Devaraj and J.M. Crant (2003) Relating Collaborative Technology Use to Teamwork Quality and Performance: An Empirical Analysis, *Journal of Management Information Systems*, Vol. 19, No. 4, pp249-270.

Ennew, C.T. and M.R Binks. (1996) The impact of service quality and service characteristics on customer retention: Small businesses and their banks in the UK. *British Journal of Management*, Vol. 7, No.3, pp219-230.

Ferneley, E.H. and P. Sobreperez (2006) Resist, comply or workaround? An examination of different facets of user engagement with information systems. *European Journal of Information Systems*, Vol. 15, No. 4, pp345-356.

Gasser, L. (1986) The integration of computing and routine work. *ACM Transactions on Office Information Systems*, Vol. 4, No. 3, pp205-225.

Johnston, K., and K. Loader (2003) Encouraging SME participation in training: Identifying practical approaches. *Journal of European Industrial Training,* (*27*)6, pp. 273-280.

Karsten, H. (2003) Constructing interdependencies with collaborative information technology. *Computer Supported Cooperative Work*, Vol. 12, pp437-464.

Koopman, P. and R.R. Hoffman (2003) Work-arounds, make-work, and kludges. *IEEE Transaction on Intelligent Systems*, Vol. 18, No. 6, pp70-75.

Kwak, M. (2003) The True Value of a Lost Customer. *MIT Sloan Management Review*, Vol. 44, No. 2, p9.

Levina, N. and E. Vaast (2008) Innovating or doing as told? Status differences and overlapping boundaries in offshore collaboration. *MIS Quarterly,* Vol. 32, No. 2, pp307-332.

MacLean, A., K. Carter, L. Lovstrand, and T. Moran (1990) User tailorable systems: Pressing the issues with buttons. In *Proceedings of CHI '90*, New Orleans, LA.

March, J.G. (1991) Exploration and exploitation in organizational learning. *Organization Science*, Vol. *2,* No. 1, pp71-87.

Mathieson, K. and T. Ryan (1997) Users' Evaluations of Packages: Demonstrations Versus Hands-On Use, *Electronic Journal of Information System Evaluation*, Vol. 1, No. 1.

Miles, I. (2008) Patterns of innovation in service industries. *IBM Systems Journal*, Vol. 47, No. 1, pp115-128.

Montazemi, A.R. (2006) How they manage IT: SMES in Canada and the U.S. *Communications of the ACM*, Vol. 49, No. 12, pp109-112.

Morgeson, F.P. and D.A. Hofmann (1999) The structure and function of collective constructs: Implications for multilevel research and theory development. *Academy of Management Review*, Vol. 24, No. 2, pp249-265.

Orlikowski, W.J. and J.J. Baroudi (1991) Studying Information Technology in Organizations: Research Approaches and Assumptions, *Information Systems Research*, Vol. 2, No. 1, pp1-28.

Ozkan, S. (2006) A Process Capability Approach to Information Systems Effectiveness Evaluation, *Electronic Journal of Information System Evaluation,* Vol. 9, No. 1, pp7-14.

Rangone, A. (1999) A resource based approach to strategy analysis in small-medium enterprises. *Small Business Economics,* Vol. 12, No. 3, pp233-248.

Rorholm, J. (2008) Cater to the customer. *McLatchy-Tribune News.* Washington, Dec 30.

Seddon, P.B. (1997) A respecification and extension of the DeLone and McLean model of IS success. *Information Systems Research,* Vol. 8, No. 3, pp240-253.

Sexton, D.L., and P.M. van Auken (1982) Prevalence of strategic planning in small business. *Journal of Small Business Management*, Vol. 20, No. 3, pp20-26.

Sharky (2007). Shark tank: Work arounds. *Computer World.* June 18. Retrieved 14 January, 2009, from http://blogs.computerworld.com/sharky/20070618.

Sheehan, J. (2006) Understanding Service Sector Innovation. *Communications of the AC,* Vol. 49, No. 7, pp43-48.

Slappendel, C. (1996) Perspectives on Innovation in Organizations. *Organization Studies,* Vol. 17, No. 1, pp107-129.

Smith, H.A., J.D. McKeen and S. Singh, (2007) Developments in Practice XXVIII: Managing Perceptions of IS. *Communications of AIS*, Vol. 20, pp760-773.

Subramani, M. (2004) How do suppliers benefit from information technology use in supply chain relationships. *MIS Quarterly*, Vol. 28, No. 1, pp45-74.

Sussman, S.W. and W.S. Siegal (2003) Informational Influence in Organizations: An Integrated Approach to Knowledge Adoption. *Information Systems Research*, Vol. 14, No. 1, pp47-65.

Szajna, B. (1993) Determining information systems usage: Some issues and examples. *Information and Management*, Vol. 25, No. 3, pp147-154.

Vandenbosch, M. and N. Dawar (2002) Beyond Better Products: Capturing Value in Customer Interactions. *MIT Sloan Management Review*, Vol. 43, No. 4, pp35-42.

Venkatesh, V., S.A. Brown, L.M. Maruping and H. Bala (2008) Predicting Different Conceptualizations of System Use: The Competing Roles Of Behavioral Intention, Facilitating Conditions, And Behavioral Expectation. *MIS Quarterly*, Vol. 32, No. 3, pp483-502.

Walsham, G. (1995) Interpretive case studies in IS research: Nature and method. *European Journal of Information Systems,* Vol. 4, pp74-81.

Xue, Y., H. Liang, W.R. Boulton (2008) Information technology governance in information technology investment decision processes: The impact of investment characteristics, external environment, and internal context. *MIS Quarterly,* Vol. 32, No. 1, pp67-96.

Yin, R.K. (2003) *Case study research: Design and methods* (3rd ed.). Beverly Hills, CA: Sage Publications.

Yu, L. (2001). What Really Makes Customers Happy? *MIT Sloan Management Review*, Vol. 42, No. 4, pp19.

Zhang, P., J. Carey, D. Te'eni and M. Tremaine (2005) Integrating Human-Computer Development into the Systems Development Life Cycle: A Methodology. *Communications of AIS*, Vol. 15, pp512-543.

5.9 Summary on a Page, using Toulmin's Argument structure:

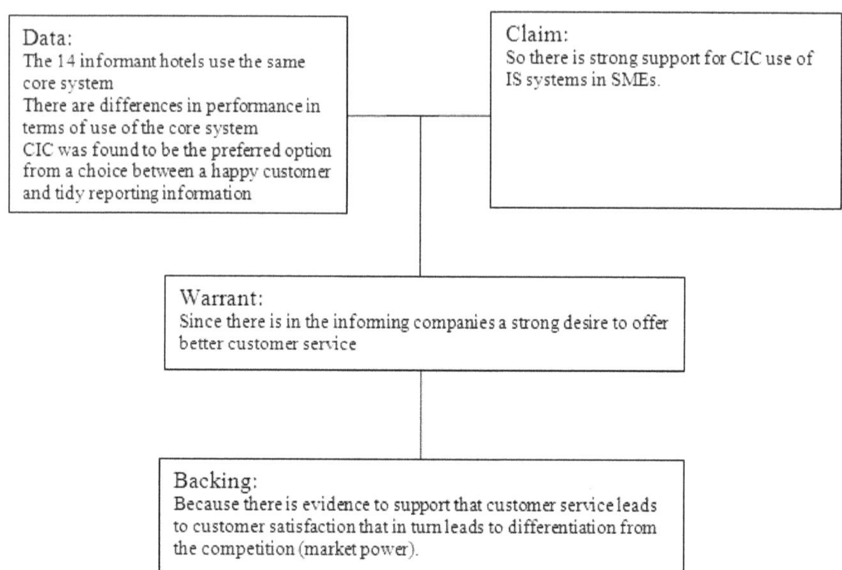

5.10 Case Study Review

Date of Review:	24JAN11
My Reference: ISBN: Other Reference:	IM.253.
Title/Document:	The Influence of Net Benefits on Collective, Innovative, Configural System use: a Case Study of Small-to-Medium Enterprises, The Electronic Journal Information Systems Evaluation, Volume 12, Issue 2, pp.187-198.
Author/Date:	Wilkin, C. (2009)
Source:	EJISE
Theme:	The impact of innovative use of standard IS packages in SMEs; the effect of the system environment in the form of customer satisfaction.
Purpose of Paper:	To present evidence that supports that there is collective, innovative, configural (CIC) use of IS in Small-to-Medium Enterprises; and to shed light on what causes it and how it impacts fellow workers.
Classification/Philosophy	Basic research/Interpretive.
Research Questions:	There are three linked questions: 1. What evidence is there of CIC use in SMEs? 2. What causes this type of use to occur? 3. How does it impact fellow workers?
Methodology:	Case study. Qualitative. The Unit of Analysis is the use of a core Hotel Management application aimed at small hotels. Evidence was collected from documents (e.g., training manuals), interviews, direct observation

	and artefacts (e.g., house-keeping lists and check-out reports). Two types of interviews: semi-structured ones, and focused interviews, the latter for re-visits. The semi-structured interview guide evolved as insights emerged. This is typical of this approach (interpretive) in which collection and analysis of evidence are intertwined. However, there is no mention on how evidence was analysed (coding procedures) or a description of how the insights emerged. There were 37 informants (12 managerial, and 25 operational users) located in 14 different sites. All located in Australia. There is no mention on the period of time in which the evidence collection took place. The outcome of data collection and analysis (case study findings) is presented in two very clear and well thought out tables (linked to each other).
Results:	There was variation in the use of the common transaction system across quite similar organisations operating in the same hotel networks. The application is an efficiency driven system, but with innovation it can also be revenue enhancing. This is a powerful insight. The same application can be one or the other depending on the degree of innovation: this reinforces the role of people in IS projects. *{How does this affect my model?}* In cases where the system proved to have poor or inexistent functionality, collective understanding and agreement were essential in managing this lack of functionality so that the customer was not affected. In the cases where there were consistent patterns of innovative use, these were triggered by front-desk staff to manage customer transactions quickly and efficiently, and/or to maximise customer satisfaction with the booking process. *{Innovation at the front office aimed at customer satisfaction - is this a cause of revenue enhancement in my model?}*

	{Does a CIC culture require less effort in change management? Is it the sharpness of customer facing that throws responsibility for the project on to the users?} The author concludes that "system developers do not appear to be immersing themselves in the environments in which these systems are used to gather such deep insight which can enrich future versions of the system." *{How does this fit with the paper (case study) on agile systems development methods?}*
Managerial Implications:	"Systematic understanding of such [CIC system] use is fruitful for achieving better insights that can feed in to evolution of packaged software applications and increase system longevity."
Limitations / Future Research:	
Critique and Learning:	In the literature on IS evaluation the author adopts DeLone & Mclean (1992) and reasons that it is pointless to define with great precision input variables like 'user participation' and 'IT investment' when the output variables such as IS Success and MIS Effectiveness could not be calculated with similar accuracy. But what is really problematic is to use a simple input-output (black-box) model in IS evaluation; it is by now well understood that an analysis of 'how', 'through what process' the input variables relate to the output is essential. **Lessons learned:** CIC (Collective, Innovative, Configural): The literature review is usefully broken down into five sections: 'Use', 'Innovative use', 'Collective use', 'Customer service and SMEs', 'IS evaluation'. I was interested by the concept of 'collective use' as opposed to simple individual use. Collective: an interdependent group of individuals with a collective goal direction. So collec-

	tive use is more than just social or task oriented interaction; it requires collaboration, communication, and coordination. The author goes on to explain that collective use can take two forms: shared and configural. The latter is the interesting one, as configural constructs occur when members of the collective use a system more or less frequently and for different purposes, "but there is a stable pattern in their use." Shared constructs occur when the collective uses the system in a homogeneous way. With respect to the 'I' in CIC, the author defines innovation not as creative work-arounds to use the system by those who do not know its functionality well, but rather innovative use that has been "hierarchically institutionalised as an acceptable/required way to handle a circumstance of system use." **Customer Service**: It is presented as the best method to progress an organisation with twofold benefits: (a) Increased customer satisfaction is beneficial to an organisation's productivity; and (b) Focus on consistent customer service will create an opportunity for differentiation with the organisation's competitors. The latter is intuitive, however the causal relationship implied by the former requires further explanation. *{I should be able to relate this to the market power constructs in my model}* **SMEs**: They are reluctant to engage consultants, thus less likely to tailor package solutions to their needs and thus stay closer to the standard, which in turn is more likely to lead to implementation success, but will also require more change management. The author gives a robust reference list.

Chapter 6

Better Control at the Cost of Rigidity in Manufacturing (Ireland)

The research paper analysed in this chapter is a multiple case study in that it analyses the impact of implementing ERP systems in two operations in Ireland. The cases are a pharmaceutical company that implemented SAP and an ICT company that implemented Oracle's product. Both cases comprise multinational companies with operations in many parts of the world, but the context of the cases is the operations in Ireland where both have manufacturing plants.

The case study introduces useful insights into the problems that arise in implementing ERP systems in organisations that are not fully centralised. Moreover, it highlights the problems that arise when implementing ERP solutions in organisations whose business model is based precisely on offering innovative products or customised services and thus require decentralisation to make sure the best brains are put to develop new products or to working with the customer to tailor services.

This chapter makes the reader aware of the gaps that emerge between the real-life world of the organisation and how its people work, and the model of the organisation as represented in the configured ERP system.

Towards a Model for Determining the Scope of ICT Integration in the Enterprise: the Case of Enterprise Resource Planning (ERP) Systems

Fergal Carton and Frederic Adam
University College Cork, Ireland

Abstract: The question of integration of information systems (IS) into the planning and execution of operational activities has been the focus for researchers from different constituencies. Organisational theorists recognise the need for integrating mechanisms for co-ordinating the actions of sub-units within an organisation. Centralisation has been seen as a defensive reaction by organisations when placed under increasing external control, and also as a way to improve the efficiency of information processing, at least for routine tasks. In the meantime, researchers have been sceptical about the ability for structured information systems to deal with the complexity of the information flows within the organisation. Frameworks have also been identifying characteristics of the tasks themselves that have a bearing on the amount of information processing required. The real world is complex and moving, thus managers require flexibility in their interpretation of the mixed signals arising from this complexity. However, managers are working in environments where highly integrated information systems blur the distinction between what is real and what is virtual. There is a need for an integration approach allowing organisations to question which areas of activity are worth integrating, and conversely which areas are better left under local control. Where integrated, managers require processes for the maintenance of data integrity (people, tools, procedures). Based on field work involving two multi-national manufacturing companies, this paper proposes a framework for ERP integration, which describes the evolution of functionality gaps as an ongoing and inevitable process that requires management.

Keywords: ERP, enterprise, integration, framework, complexity

Originally published in the Electronic Journal of IS Evaluation, Volume 13 Issue 1 pp. 17-26.

6.1 Introduction

In examining the extent to which information systems (IS) can be integrated into the planning and execution of an organisation's activities, the researcher may draw from rich seams of research from different constituencies. The question of how best to control and co-ordinate the organisation to meet the needs of its customers, while optimising the use of available resources, has tantalised organisational theorists from the earliest days of industrial and economic growth. Key to the concept of control is information, such that goals may be communicated downwards and performance may be measured and communicated upwards. It has been acknowledged by the earliest students of administrative systems that the major cost of implementing control systems of any sort is the investment in human resources to design and maintain the system. Today, advances in data capture, communication and dissemination technologies have allowed designers to integrate the bureaucratic overhead of administration of task monitoring into the activities themselves. However, this very synergy between task and control can have negative side effects in terms of flexibility that are undermining the gains in efficiency. Indeed, the ubiquity of technology in all areas of the enterprise has displaced the question of efficiency towards the administrative aspect of the task and away from the task itself. In this section the two strands of research (organisational and informational) are drawn together to tease out the dimensions of a framework that might permit researchers to situate the adoption of integrated control systems within the broader context of the organisation and its aims.

6.1.1 Integration is a design attribute for organisational rationality

To Mintzberg (1989), organisation means collective action in the pursuit of a common mission. Organisation theory is the body of research that addresses itself to the problem of how to organise (Pugh 1997). How organisations should be controlled, by whom, and to what ends, are *the* fundamental issues for the private sector (Mintzberg 1989). An organisation is *instrumentally* rational if the job gets done, *economically* rational if it gets done at the least cost (Thompson 1967). Thompson (1967) uses the analogy of the ad-hoc organisation of the community in the face of a natural disaster to emphasise that instrumental rationality can be achieved in the face of necessity, but that economic rationality requires more co-ordination and advance knowledge of what resources are required and when. Interestingly, research into how managers actually work suggests a constant mode of crisis management (Mintzberg 1989), denoting the inability to work to a co-ordinated plan because of the contingencies of the moment. It would appear that despite best efforts to control and co-ordinate, managers have to deal with many sorts of unplanned events thrown at them in quick succession and requiring immediate attention.

Organisational attributes are choices about the optimal design of the organisation in view of its aims. Some structural variables considered in organisational theory are specialisation (functional and role), standardisation, formalisation, and centralisation (Inkson et al. 1968). An increasingly important organisational attribute is the incorporation of information systems into ways of working such that task execution and visibility of that performance are instantaneous. The challenge of studying such organisational attributes is that there are underlying interdependencies between these attributes and contextual factors which are difficult to conceptualise. Formalisation of procedures is a step towards standardisation, which itself is a step towards centralisation. Furthermore, business context, culture and managerial capability are additional "softer" attributes of the organisation which will confound generalisations based on any one set of structural variables. In his work on organisational configurations, Henry Mintzberg (1989) suggests that it is the *combination* of basic attributes of an organisation that define its culture, rather than a focus on any one single attribute.

One of the essential dichotomies in the planning and management of routine activities is the trade-off between control and flexibility. With Enterprise Resource Planning (ERP) systems, the interdependence between control and other structuring attributes (such as formalisation, centralisation, specialisation) is configured in the software. As researchers had forewarned, the complexity of the control system made it necessary to invest in specialised skills to design and maintain the system (Child 1973). Without the ability to conceptualise integration as an organisational attribute among others, organisations risk becoming slaves to their self-imposed technostructure.

6.1.2 The use of information technologies for control

Since the earliest days of the application of information technologies to automate manual tasks, the question of integration has intrigued practitioners and academics alike. The potential for the technology to make information flow was understood, but its use in planning and monitoring of performance entailed a trust in the parameters and algorithms in the machine that had hitherto not existed. As far back as 1958, Leavitt &

Whisler suggested that "information technologies" would undermine the decision making role of the middle manager, consigning them instead to jobs that were highly structured. The authors argued that the spread of information technology would be rapid because it would make centralisation much easier, making top executives less dependent on subordinates. In addition, the faster processing of information would shorten the feedback loop that tests the accuracy of original observations and decisions.

There is a relationship between the need to process information and uncertainty deriving from the external business environment. Organisations require "integrating mechanisms" (Galbraith in Pennings, 1983) for co-ordinating the actions of sub-units towards a common objective. Centralisation and standardisation have been seen as a defensive reaction by organisations when placed under increasing external control (Mintzberg 1989), and also as a way to improve the efficiency of information processing, at least for routine tasks (Galbraith 1974). An information system by definition supports the centralisation of control (Markus & Robey 1988). Under conditions of uncertainty, there is a tendency to increase the amount of information sought (Thompson 1967). Earl & Hopwood (in Lucas et al. 1980) refer to the tendency in the MIS area to perceive uncertainty as "threatening rather than inevitable", and, rather than exploiting information for its "educative" (Gorry 1971) potential, information systems professionals tend to design models that mask reality with "assumed certainties".

In parallel to the evolution of the capacity of systems to handle information at speed and in large volumes, the "determinist" consequences of information systems for centralisation has been the subject of much debate (Orlikowski in Knights, D. and Willmott, H. 1988). ERP systems simultaneously centralise ownership of information resources and democratise access to that information, mixing therefore, to an unprecedented extent, centralising and decentralising effects. On the one hand they promote local, cross-functional cooperation and control, breeding skills that are eminently transferable across sub-units. On the other, a best practice model of transaction processing imposes a common standard across the organisation. As Davenport (1998) notes, the real challenges hinges on where to draw the boundary between centralization of control and autonomy of decision making.

Researching the organisational impact of information systems is challenging because the interaction of people with technology in the execution of business processes is so intertwined that it becomes difficult to differentiate organisational from technical factors (Markus et al. 2000). Researchers must differentiate between the symptoms and the cure. Inefficiency and frustration may be the result of poor process design, or incomplete implementation, or a combination of both factors. When the template falls short of actual physical procedures, data quality will inevitably be impacted. Researchers have noted that although ERP systems may be introduced, physical procedures are not always changed, such that a mismatch develops between virtual processes and physical processes (Staehr, Shanks and Seddon in Adam and Sammon, 2004; Lee and Lee 2000).

The literature that provides the theoretical framework for this study of integration unites the themes of organisations and control mechanisms. Organisations require co-ordination mechanisms to transform strategy into operational targets. ERP systems are considered to be an advanced form of control mechanism. Managers are the enactors of this co-ordination, and their decisions are informed by data concerning both performance targets and actual consumption of resources. ERP systems superimpose new patterns on this co-ordination, with an, as yet, poorly researched impact on the quality of decision making.

6.2 The research objective

The objective of this research is to propose a framework which would allow the question of integration to be modelled alongside other related organisational attributes. It was anticipated that some of these attributes, identified already in the literature, such as centralisation, standardisation and specialisation, will figure in the framework. Equally, it was anticipated that other attributes will emerge from the empirical work, which is based around the implementation of ERP in two multinational manufacturing organisations.

The research objective was operationalised into three separate research questions which together yield a picture of the scope of integration in the organisation, and a suggestion for the interdependence between integration and other organisational attributes. Research Question 1 was concerned with discovering the key organisational attributes relating to the implementation of ERP. Research Question 2 was concerned with developing a causality map between these attributes. Research Question 3 drew on the output from Question 1 and 2 to suggest a conceptual framework for the consideration of integration as a set of interdependent organisational attributes. It is envisaged that this framework could be used by managers to evaluate the potential impact of integration on the organisation, as well as a providing a diagnostic tool for the isolation of dysfunctional behaviour and its potential causes.

6.2.1 Profile of the case studies

In this research, two case studies of successful multinational companies (KPC and SIT) are used to explore the impact of integration on the organisation. Both cases studied are multi-national manufacturing organisations with mature ERP implementations. Table 6.1 compares the profiles of the two cases studied.

Table 6.1: Comparison of case study profiles

	Firm A	Firm B
Industry	Pharmaceutical	Data management
Turnover 05 ($bn)	38.72	9.66
Employees	100,000	26,500
WW operations	119	52
Manufacturing sites	80	3
Head Office	London, UK	Boston, USA
ERP System	SAP R/3	Oracle 11.03
Architecture	Single instance	Single instance
Server location	Pennsylvania, USA	Boston, USA
Go-live	Phased 2004	Big-bang 2001

The Key Pharma Company, KPC (real name withheld to allow more detailed reporting), is a leading manufacturer of pharmaceutical products, with a highly successful product portfolio in consumer healthcare, prescriptions drugs and vaccines. With annual sales of nearly €30 billion, and a R&D budget of €5 billion, KPC is in a dominant position in its marketplace. The manufacturing organisation involves more than 20 autonomous plants worldwide. Managing the supply chain to efficiently satisfy demand is extremely complex. With over 30,000 Stock Keeping Units (SKU's) or lines of product, any one of the 600 sources of demand could be ordering 300-600 SKU's each. The case study focuses on the KPC plant in Cork, Ireland, a bulk site which is part of the global Manufacturing and Supply organisation. KPC Cork ships 4,000 batches of goods per year and local managers are proud of their "customer service" record for deliveries, in the context of the complex and sometimes unpredictable scenario described above. KPC Cork was part of the roll-out programme for a new ERP system (based on SAP version 4.0), which involved all the sites in the Manufacturing and Supply organisation. The ERP project had the overall goal of implementing FDA compliant business processes throughout KPC, using the best practice templates that had been designed by KPC around SAP standard functionality. The scope of the ERP project at KPC Cork was the integration of processes in all the main business areas (Production, Finance, Sales, Quality), excluding process control at the manufacturing execution level.

The second case is SIT, a market leader in data management solutions, which sees itself as specialising in helping customers to derive more value from their corporate data. The company is following an aggressive growth path, with 17% growth in consolidated revenue in 2005, which was the year in which the case study was carried out. Revenues have since then continued their upward growth trend, topping $11.2 billion in 2006. SIT Ltd employs over 26,500 people in 52 operations worldwide. Manufacturing is concentrated in three sites, one of which is Cork, Ireland. SIT has evolved into a "solutions" company, delivering not just hardware, but also information "lifecycle" tools and consulting services. A key complexity of such full service offerings is the management of the information flows related to executing a single customer order, which increasingly is constituted of hardware, software and services. Many of these revenue lines are executed by multiple locations, over different time horizons, yet the customer will require a single sales order, single invoice and single goods shipment. SIT implemented a single instance global ERP system in 2001. This big bang implementation addressed user requirements for transaction processing in all back office activities relating to sales order processing, manufacturing, materials planning, distribution and finance. The Oracle based system supports 4,500 users in 52 countries worldwide, 3 of which involve manufacturing operations.

6.3 The research methodology

The premise of this study is that data and process integration are inherent parts of an ERP package. Organisations make considerable assumptions about the level of integration between functions, plants, and headquarters when implementing an ERP system. Although differences exist between the different ERP systems, and these differences will have an impact on the fit with individual business process requirements, it is assumed, as with Gattiker & Goodhue (2005), that the differences are less important than the similarities. The similarities are that all ERP systems are highly integrated at a data level, and all ERP systems use workflow logic to automate the flows of information through the different stages of its transaction process. It is via this data and process integration that different functions can access and transact information relating to the use of common enterprise resources.

Following the Barua et al. (1995) recommendations for evaluating IT investments, Gattiker & Goodhue (2005) selected a fine grained unit of analysis (the plant) and within that the functions examined are close to the operating core of the business (manufacturing planning and control, as well as execution processes). The logic here is that longer lasting transformative benefits on the organisation are more likely to be derived from core value-adding activities of the company, rather than from administrative functions Barua et al. (1995). This research study includes both core operational and support functions, as ERP is inherently an administrative (support function) tool, yet its impact is most felt at the transactional level (operations). The data from interviews regarding ERP impact was classified with respect to organisational parameters, and these parameters had been identified as seed categories from the literature, but other themes also emerged from the analysis of managerial perceptions. The seed categories included themes such as centralisation of responsibility, standardisation of processes and gaps between template process and reality. The emergent attributes include granularity of information, process flexibility and manual manipulation of data.

Business processes were used to analyse findings as an embedded unit of analysis, in order to better identify areas of the organisation where the integration impact was most strongly felt. ERP systems superimpose a process based view of business activity, with integration at data and workflow level. In many cases, these new processes cross traditional functional boundaries, thus it was considered important to be able to view the impact equally from the process level. The definition of processes is closely allied the physical management of resources in the organisation, such as inventory, customer orders, cash, labour or plant capacity. Information flows in a logical and chronological order between different stages of the process as the physical resources are transferred, consumed and transformed through different stages of the supply and demand cycles.

Interviews with managers from both cases were carried out in the period from April 2005 to August 2005 and involved meetings with 76 managers from different functions affected by the implementation of the ERP system. SIT had gone live on their ERP system in October 2001, so these interviews reflect the views of managers using a relatively mature system. Table 6.2 shows a summary of the numbers of managers interviewed, broken down by case and by function.

Table 6.2: Breakdown of interviews by case and by functional area

	SIT			KPC		
Function	Cork	US	Total	Cork	UK	Total
Finance	5	9	14	1	1	2
Manufacturing / Distribution	13	6	19	9	7	16
Sales	4	3	7	1		1
IS	4	2	6	3	3	6
Engineering	2		2	1		1
HR	2		2			
Total	30	20	50	15	11	26

Interviews were carried out using a semi-structured format, and each interview lasted one hour. The interviews were recorded and transcribed, yielding over 400,000 words of raw research material. A robust coding methodology was applied to reduce the data and avoid paralysis by data analysis (Yin 2003). Observations from the transcripts were extracted to a matrix structured by research question, yielding a total of 3,202 observations. Cell entries were either abridged versions of the original quote, summarised to capture the issue raised. Using hyperlink functionality between Microsoft Excel and Word, each extracted observation was linked back to the original transcript, thereby retaining richness and avoiding "too thin cell entries" (Miles & Huberman 1994). The observations were coded at three levels, identifying the interviewee, the business process commented, and the theme (organisational attribute). The business process was recorded independently of the functional affiliation of the interviewee. For example, observations regarding shipment decisions were classified as pertaining to the "Deliver" process, and were commented upon by managers from Finance, Materials, Manufacturing, Distribution, and Sales. The themes began as a set of 13 seed categories, developed from the literature review, and complemented by themes which emerged from the data.

6.4 Findings of the case study

The empirical data was analysed to answer the three research questions mentioned in the research objective section of this paper. These questions form a vehicle to investigate the effect of ERP driven integration in today's multinational company.

Research question 1: Key organisational attributes

Research question 1 identifies the organisational attributes associated with ERP driven integration. These observations were coded based on whether the impact of the attribute was perceived to be related to organisational, decisional or integration themes, and categorised by process area. The field data is aggregated across both cases (n=2,818), and plotted according to three dimensions. Figure 6.1 summarises the results of this analysis of organisational attributes. Organisational themes (y-axis values) included Centralisation, Goals, Compliance and Skills. The 695 observations classified under the organisational themes related to the positive aspects of centralisation, goal clarity, compliance and the development of new skills. Integration themes (x-axis) included Correlation, Granularity, Accuracy / Consistency, Automation and Aggregation. Again, the 883 observations in this category emphasised the positive aspects of integration, particularly the analytical potential. The Decisional themes (denoted by size of bubble) were Manual, Flexibility, Gap Virtual vs. Physical, Uncertainty and Latency. The 1,060 observations under the decisional theme were largely negative feedback regarding the difficulties of exploiting ERP data.

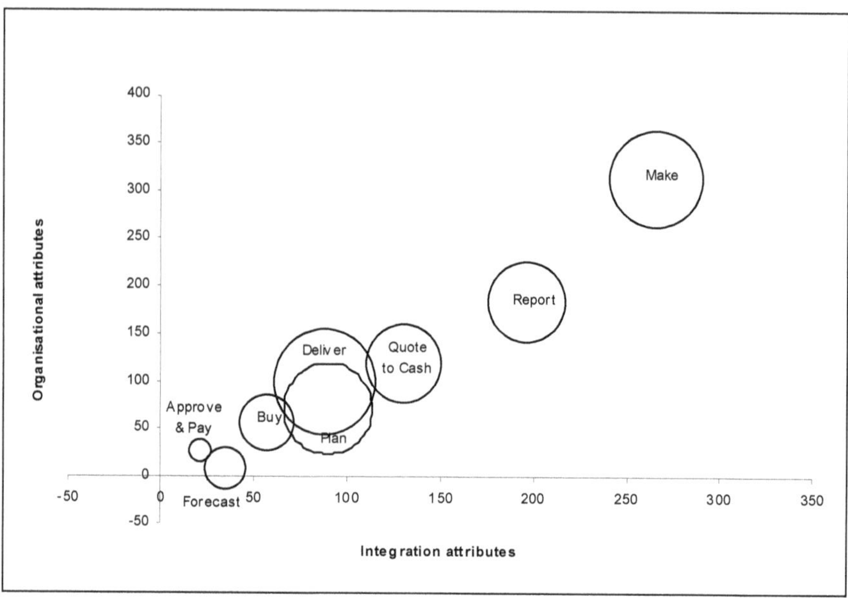

Figure 6.1: The organisational impact of ERP integration by business process area

These results reveal a strong linear relationship between centralisation and integration. That is, the stronger the consensus around the need for a centralising force in the organisation, the stronger the perceived need (among managers) for integration. This relationship holds across the different process areas. It could be deduced from this data that organisational goals are well understood and assimilated in the different functions, and that centralisation of the organisation is wholly accepted. There is a good understanding among managers of the impact of centralisation for data integrity, and a good understanding of the potential to use the associated wealth of highly granular information for different decision scenarios. This linear relationship would seem to suggest a broad acceptance among managers that centralisation is necessary from the point of view of goal focus, and that the more centralised the organisation, the more integration is required and accepted. The corollary of this finding, not tested in this sample, would be that more decentralised organisations would have difficulty accepting integration. On the other hand, what is equally striking from these results is the level of unanimity in the frustration felt throughout the business in exploiting corporate information for decision support. Because of performance and security issues with the technology, and its' fit with actual business activities, managers are obliged to resort to much manual manipulation of the information derived from the ERP system in order to get to the meaning they require.

It was of interest to note that the acceptance of centralisation varied between the two cases observed, with SIT showing more consensus on centralisation for Buying and Shipping, than KPC who were more forceful in their support for centralisation for Planning and Making. It is thought that the regulatory environment explains the KPC willingness to accept compliant manufacturing processes, whereas SIT had moved Purchasing to a global process, and were debating how to change the Deliver process from a site specific activity to a global basis. These nuances demonstrate that the acceptance of integration should be considered from a site and functional level.

Research question 2: Causality map between attributes

The analysis of Research question 1 served to establish the existence of a strong relationship between the centralisation attributes and the integration attributes. Integration is accepted by managers as it is understood that it is a pre-requisite for better control and visibility of organisational activity. The granularity of information available possibly encourages requirements for managers to correlate data in ways that were not envisaged by the integrated applications used, and with information from other sources. The increased accuracy of information benefits Manufacturing and Finance particularly. The downside of this integration is that ERP systems are inflexible and unforthcoming with meaningful information. Organisations seek to exercise control and reduce uncertainty by multiplying the number of data points, but the implementation of tools and procedures to collect the data in a changing reality becomes a cause of bureaucratic inflexibility. This inflexibility is a cause for users to resort to workarounds, which engender gaps between the physical reality and the virtual picture used to monitor its progress. These gaps or virtual blind-spots mean managers return to manual methods in manipulating information for decision making purposes. This additional manipulation introduces latency in reporting, which is compounded by response time issues deriving from the technical architecture. The net result is a requirement for skilled resources in the manipulation of corporate data to derive meaning. Thus, as integration increases with centralisation, there is a corresponding increase in the necessity for skills to manipulate and digest the ensuing glut of data. Finally, and perhaps most worryingly, users in the most sensitive execution areas (Manufacturing and Deliver processes) are handicapped by inflexibility in the transaction processing system, whereas their focus should be on material availability and customer satisfaction respectively.

These elements are depicted graphically in Figure 6.2.

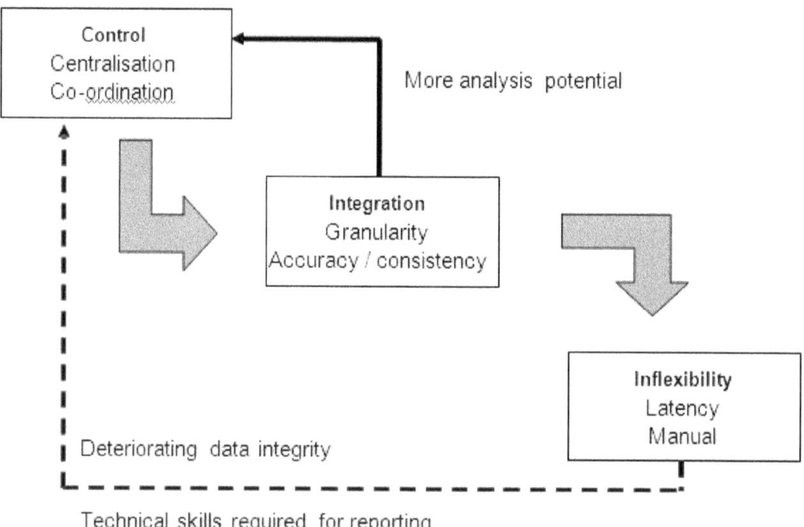

Figure 6.2: Understanding the causality between control, integration and its impact

Research question 3: Conceptual framework for ERP integration and functionality gaps

The first two research questions highlighted the themes related to the impact of ERP driven integration on the organisation, and the causality associated with these themes. The final research question draws on this output to suggest a framework for the conceptualisation of integration in the organisation, named here as "the Zipper effect" and shown in Figure 6.3. At go-live (t^0), a certain number of gaps will exist between the configured ERP processes and the way the company actually works. These will typically be dealt with by workarounds, but managers do not have visibility of the impact for data integrity of these workarounds, or their cost. The suggestion behind the Zipper effect is that these gaps between the physical and the virtual will inevitably emerge over time, but that acknowledging that they exist is the first step in addressing them. The second step is to establish processes for monitoring these gaps, analysing and explaining them. Once recognised, the third step for organisations is to have the resources and procedures in place to be able to resolve them.

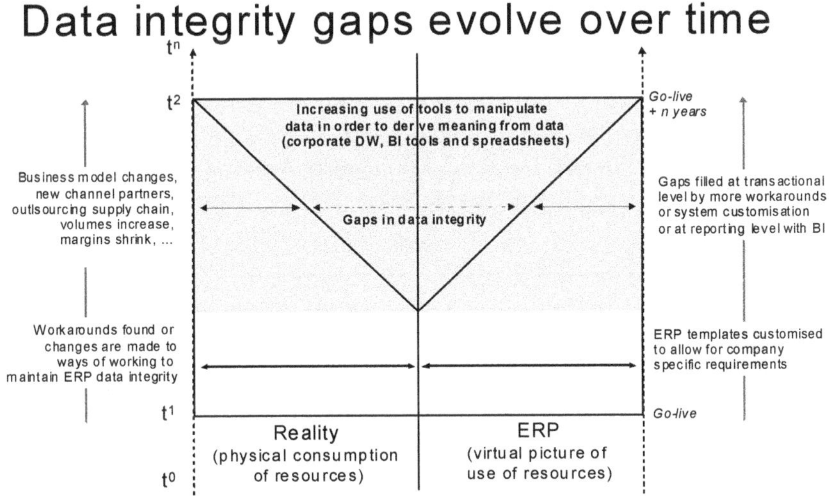

Figure 6.3: The Zipper effect: modelling the divergence of ERP from reality

6.5 Conclusions

This research highlights a fundamental difficulty for the use of ERP systems in large corporations. Integration involves "virtualising" the communication process through the use of information systems such as ERP. The accuracy of the information is a function of the closeness of the template parameters to the actual way of doing business. The two cases studied demonstrate that the virtualisation of business processes engenders constraints that negate the original purpose of improved control. These constraints arise from either the virtual or the physical context. The combination of a centralised technical architecture and large volumes of highly granular information creates latency issues (virtual context) which impacts at both an execution and a reporting level. The inflexibility of the standardised ways of working to the evolving business imperatives (physical context) obliges managers to resort to manual methods when analysing performance variances, defeating the original aim of an integrated approach to performance control, and incurring an additional cost.

Another key lesson from this study has been that an integrated model of how businesses function is theoretical and ill adapted to the reality of how businesses operate. Managers in both studies confessed to their inability to build conceptual models of the decision processes required in the demand and supply processes of the firm because of their sheer complexity. In such complex scenarios, the imposition of standardised procedures appears to inhibit rather than encourage an understanding of the key variables. Accordingly, the notion of integration should be treated as a normative force in organisational administration, along with other organisational attributes, but not as a once-off solution embodied in the ERP software. Raising the awareness of integration as a parameter of organisational design should be an objective for researchers and practitioners alike, rather than being left in the hands of vendors of "solutions".

6.6 References

Adam F. and Sammon D. (2004) The Enterprise Resource Planning Decade: Lessons Learned And Issues For The Future, IPG, Hershey, PA

Barua, A., Kriebel, C. H., and Mukhopadhyay, T. (1995) Information Technologies and Business Value: An Analytic and Empirical Investigation, Information Systems Research, Vol. 6, No.1, pp 3-23

Child, J. (1973) Strategies of Control and Organisational Behaviour, Administrative Science Quarterly

Davenport , T.H. (1998) Putting the Enterprise into the Enterprise System, Harvard Business Review, Jul-Aug

Dearden, J. (1972) MIS is a mirage, Harvard Business Review, Jan/Feb, Vol. 50, No. 1, pp 90-99

Gattiker, T.F. and Goodhue. D.L. (2005) What Happens After ERP Implementation: Understanding the Impact of Interdependence and Differentiation on Plant-Level Outcomes, MIS Quarterly, Vol. 29, No. 3, September, pp 559-585,

Galbraith J.R. (1974) Organisation design: an information processing view, Interfaces, Vol. 4, No. 3, pp 8-37.

Gorry, G. (1971) The Development of Managerial Models, Sloan Management Review, Winter, pp 1-16

Gorry G. & Scott Morton, M. (1971) A Framework for Management Information Systems, Sloan Management Review, Fall, Vol. 13 No. 1, p 49-61

Inkson, J., Hickson, D. & Pugh, D. (1968), Administrative reduction of variance in organization and behaviour, unpublished paper given to the British Psychological Society, Annual Conference, April

Knights, D. and Willmott, H. (1988), New technology and the labour process, Macmillian, London, pp 20-49

Leavitt, H. and Whisler, T. (1958) Management in the 1980's : New information flows cut new organisation channels, Harvard Business Review, Nov-Dec, pp 41-48

Lee, Z. and Lee J. (2000), An ERP implementation case study from a knowledge transfer perspective, Journal of Information Technology, Vol. 15, pp 281–288

Lucas et al. (1980) The Information Systems Environment, North-Holland Publishing Company, IFIP

Markus, M.L. and Robey, D. (1988) Information technology and organisational change causal structure in theory and research. Management Science, Vol. 34, No. 5, May, pp 583-598

Markus et al. (2000), Learning from adopters' experiences with ERP: Problems encountered and success achieved, Journal of Information Technology, Vol.15, 245–265

Miles, M., and Huberman, A. (1994) Qualitative Data Analysis: An Expanded Sourcebook, 2nd edition, Sage Publications, CA

Mintzberg, H. (1989) Mintzberg on Management, The Free Press, New York

Pennings (1983) Decision Making : an Organisational Behaviour Approach, Markus Wiener Publishing Inc., New York, pp 131-139

Pugh, D.S. (1997), Organization Theory: Selected Readings, 4th edition, Penguin Books, England

Simon, H. (1977) The new Science of Management Decision, 3rd edition, Prentice Hall, Englewood Cliffs, NJ

Thompson J. (1967) Organisations in Action, McGraw-Hill, New York

Yin, R.K. (2003) Case Study Research, Design and Methods, 3rd edition, Sage Publications, CA

6.7 Summary on a Page, using Toulmin's Argument structure:

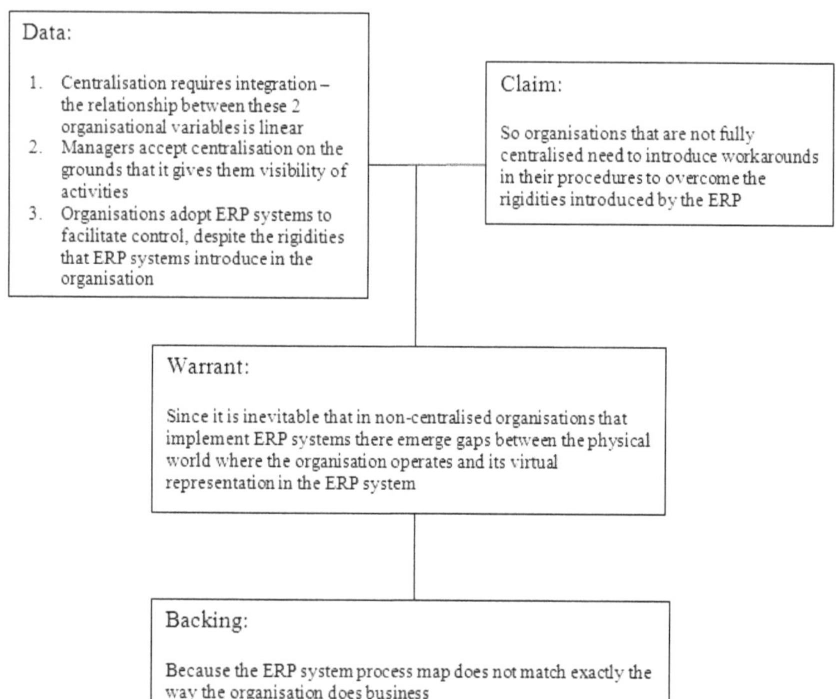

6.8 Case Study Review

Date of Review:	25JAN11
My Reference: ISBN: Other Reference:	IM.254.
Title/Document:	Towards a Model for Determining the Scope of ICT Integration in the enterprise: the Case of Enterprise Resource Planning (ERP) Systems, The Electronic Journal Information Systems Evaluation, Volume 13, Issue 1, pp.17-26
Author/Date:	Carton, F. & Adam, F. (2010)
Source:	EJISE
Theme:	The benefits and difficulties that emerge from implementing ERP systems in organisations.
Purpose of Paper:	To propose a framework that would allow the question of integration to be modelled alongside other related organisational attributes.
Classification/Philosophy:	Basic research/Interpretive
Research Question:	The research questions are stated as follows: • Concerned with discovering the key organisational attributes relating to the implementation of ERP • Concerned with developing a causality map between the prior attributes • Draw on the output from Q1 and Q2 to suggest a conceptual framework for the consideration of integration as a set of interdependent organisational attributes.

Methodology:	The authors use a case study approach. They state that the unit of analysis is at company level, and there are two cases. But is this so? Or is the unit of analysis the manufacturing plants in Cork? By the way the author treats the data, I am inclined to say that the unit of analysis is the ERP implementation project. The approach is mixed. Evidence collection denotes a qualitative approach, but in the analysis phase they are adept to quantifying key variables such as organisation attributes and integration attributes, in addition to secondary things such as the number of words in the interview transcripts (400,000 words.) Unfortunately no information on how this is done is revealed. Evidence collection was mainly done through interviews, for which there were 76 informants. Analysis of the evidence was done through what the authors call a robust coding procedure; curiously, this coding procedure departs from specifying a series of seed categories (centralisation of responsibility; standardisation of processes; gaps between template process and reality) from the literature, from where I infer that this is quite strongly a deductive approach. Emergent attributes were 'granularity of information', 'process flexibility' and 'manual manipulation' of data.
Results:	There is a strong linear relationship between the centralisation attributes and the integration ones. Centralisation is accepted by managers because they recognise it facilitates control and visibility of organisational workings. The increased accuracy of information that comes with integration through ERP systems

	benefits functions such as operations, logistics and finance. The introduction of the ERP facilitates more data points and availability of richer and more granular information. But the downside of this is that ERP systems incorporate rigidities and are unforthcoming with meaningful information. This inflexibility drives users to introduce workarounds, which engenders gaps between physical reality and the virtual picture used to monitor its progress. This, in turn leads to manual work to overcome the gaps between virtual and reality, which derives in latency in reporting. All this, additionally, requires incorporating high skilled workers to, with increasing effort, manage manual operations and overcome the gaps.
Managerial Implications:	**Claim**: The more centralised the organisation, the more integration is required and accepted. The corollary of this finding would be that more decentralised organisations would have difficulty accepting integration. *{Reflect on how this affects my model. A customer intimacy value discipline requires a more decentralised organisation, thus deriving value from an ERP system that leads to high integration would be less clear than in an operational excellence value discipline, where centralisation and standardisation is key. And what about in product leadership?* The Zipper Effect: The gaps between the physical and the virtual will inevitably emerge over time. Acknowledging that theses gaps exist is the first step in addressing them. The second step is establishing processes for monitoring theses gaps, analysing and explaining them. The third step is to put in place the resources and procedures to resolve them. The accuracy of the information or size of the gap depends on the closeness of the template parameters to the actual way of doing business. *{So, in order to close the zipper you need to configure the ERP system*

	to fit very closely with how the business works; or, conversely, apply a strong change management initiative so the real world processes are drawn close to those configured in the ERP system.}
Limitations / Future Research:	
Critique and Learning:	'Integration' is a key organisational attribute in this study, but it is not defined. The research questions are stated in a rather loose way – they should be more explicitly and formally articulated. And I am not sure that Q3 is a question at all. The graph in Figure 1 requires a lot more explaining (especially the abscissa and ordinates variables.) In the abscissa the authors seem to be quantifying Organisational Attributes, and in the Ordinates Integration attributes. How this is done deserves an explanation. In the analysis of evidence and presentation in the graph of figure 6.1 that reveals a linear relationship between Organisational and Integration attributes, the authors lump together the evidence from both cases. Is this valid? Are they not mixing apples and tomatoes? **Lessons Learned:** Longer lasting transformative benefits to the organisation are more likely to come from core value-adding activities of the company rather than administrative functions (citing Barua *et al.*, 1995). *{How does this relate to the 'efficiency driven' and 'revenue driven' ICT investments in my model?}* The authors introduce organisational attributes such as 'specialisation', 'standardisation', 'formalisation' and 'centralisation.' They also state that

	the challenge of studying such attributes is that there are underlying interdependencies between these attributes and contextual factors which are difficult to conceptualise. These attributes relate to each other: formalisation leads to standardisation that in turn leads to centralisation. 'Incorporating IT systems' is also an organisational attribute that interplays with the others. In figure 6.1 Organisation Themes (abscissa) include Centralisation, Goals, Compliance and Skills. Somehow the authors arrive at 695 observations which they classify under positive aspects of *centralisation, goal clarity, compliance* and the development of *new skills.* Integration themes in the ordinates include Correlation, Granularity, Accuracy/Consistency, Automation and Aggregation. There are 883 observations in this category that emphasise the positive aspects of integration, particularly the analytical potential. The third category is Decisional themes which are denoted by the size of the bubbles: Manual, Flexibility, Gap Virtual vs. Physical, Uncertainty and Latency. There are 1060 observations of the latter and largely refer to negative feedback regarding the difficulties of exploiting ERP data. Somehow all these observations are grouped under key processes: Make, Report, Quote to cash, Deliver, Plan, Buy, Forecast, Approve &Pay. Why would *quote to cash*, an absolutely fundamental process that runs through from end to end in nearly all organisations, have a smaller bubble than *deliver,* for example, is something that begs explaining. The acceptance of centralisation varies across the two organisations studied; that I do not find curious. What is more interesting is that acceptance of centralisation varies per business proc-

	ess from one organisation to the other. Logically, in a regulated industry such as pharma, acceptance for centralisation in a regulated process such as manufacturing is more readily accepted. The authors find almost unanimity in frustration throughout the business in exploiting corporate information for decision support. Because of performance and security issues with technology, managers are obliged to resort to much manual manipulation of the information derived from ERP system in order to get "meaning they require". Is meaning the right word in the previous phrase? This study arrives at that an integrated model of how an organisation works is theoretical and ill-adapted to how businesses work in reality. The imposition of standardised procedures appears to inhibit rather than encourage understanding of key variables. Accordingly, the notion of integration should be treated as a normative force in organisational administration.

Chapter 7

Consequences of Failing to Align Key Stakeholders in an ERP Implementation (UK, Manufacturing)

We seldom have the opportunity to study failure, despite that failure often offers more learning points than success. The paper analysed in this chapter is a single case study of a mid-sized company that manufactures hospital furniture. It complements its offering to clients with products from other vendors so as to give a broader solution to its clients.

This case study eloquently exposes the problems that businesses can confront when they fail to understand that ICT is only an enabler and not an end in its own right. It is a vehicle for change that needs to be governed by a robust change management proposition. The ICT project described in the case study failed and the root causes of this failure are clearly in human and organisational issues.

Another interesting observation that emerges from analysing this case study is that when failure becomes apparent the leadership team of the organisation tends to attempt at fixing the problem by throwing more resources at it – that is usually not effective and reveals avoidance of the real issues.

The Fundamental Challenge: Human and Organisational Factors in an ERP Implementation

Julie Dawson and Jonathan Owens
University of Lincoln, UK

Abstract: Organisations encounter obstacles when implementing ERP systems. This paper intends to explore some of the problems that occur throughout the implementation of an ERP system. Using a combination of the work of Markus et al (2001) and Kim et al (2005), a framework is constructed of Human and Organisational and Technical problems in ERP Implementations during the project phase. Drawing on empirical evidences from a UK furniture manufacturer, this study then discusses and analyses each problem identified in the framework and its affect on the implementation of their ERP system. The findings of this paper reveal that the fundamental challenge of ERP implementation is not technology but organisational and human problems, which, if not properly comprehended and addressed, can lead to ERP failure. Understanding that organisational and human issues are extremely important will encourage practitioners to address these problems and succeed in their ERP system implementations.

Keywords: ERP systems, implementation, human and organisational problems, technical problems

Originally published in the Proceedings of ECIME 2007, pp. 121-130.

7.1 Introduction

In the past two decades, companies around the world have implemented Enterprise Resource Planning (ERP) Systems (Nah *et al* 2006). An ERP system is a commercial software package (Davenport 1998, Markus *et al* 2000) that promotes seamless integration of all the information flowing through a company (Davenport 1998). Laudon *et al* (2006) explain that an ERP system collects data from various key business processes in manufacturing and production, finance and accounting, sales and marketing, and human resources. The system then stores the data in a single comprehensive data repository where it can be used by other parts of the business. Managers have precise and timely information for coordinating the daily operations of the business and a firm wide view of business processes and information flows.

ERP systems have near magical effects when they work as promised (Legare 2002), but unfortunately, a significant number of ERP implementation projects do not succeed (Sarker 2002). The fact that many ERP implementations fail or escalate out of control (Davenport 1998), has led academics to concentrate on what makes a successful ERP. Scholars have focused their research on critical success factors (CSF) (Parr *et al* 2000, Somers *et al* 2001, Nah *et al* 2001, Umble *et al* 2002), which focus on the factors that determine whether an ERP implementation will be successful (Umble *et al* 2002). Markus *et al* (2001) explains that most companies experience outcomes that fall some what short of what a "best in class" organisation might achieve. This directs their attention to the problems companies experience when they adopt, deploy, and use ERP systems. Markus' study in 2001 is unusual as it places considerable focus on the problems experienced in ERP implementations as opposed to simply defining CSFs. They explore the aspects of organisations ERP journeys. This study will focus is on the problems experienced in ERP implementations. The authors believe that focusing deeply on ERP problems will produce different findings opposed to focusing on CSFs. Research suggests that most companies experience problems with their ERP systems, particularly during the implementation phase (Parr 2000). Both technical problems and human and organisational problems can be attributed to ERP failure. '*ERP implementations are affected by both technical and social and organisational aspects*' (Elbanna 2003 p1). This is because the implementation of an ERP system is a socio-technical challenge (Kansel 2006). Laudon (2006) emphasise that information systems are sociotechnical systems. They are composed of machines, devices and 'hard' physical technology, yet they require substantial social, organisational, and intellectual investments to make them work properly.

This paper intends to differentiate between the human and organisational problems and the technical problems in an attempt to explore the presence of the opposing problems in an ERP implementation in a UK furniture manufacturer. According to Sarker (2002), there is a consensus among researchers that human factors, more than technical are critical to the success of ERP projects, this paper intends to explore this assumption. A combination of the work of Markus *et al* (2001) and Kim *et al* (2005) will be used to construct a framework of Human and Organisational and Technical problems in ERP Implementations during the project phase. Drawing on empirical evidences from a UK furniture manufacturer, this study then discusses and analyses each problem identified in the framework and its affect on the implementation of their ERP system.

7.2 ERP Phases

A phase can be described as a point in time (Markus *et al* 2000). Kim (2005) states that the identification of ERP problems, or impediments as they call them, for each phase provides greater detailed guidelines. Although there have been many definitions of phases across the ERP lifecycle (Esteves *et al* 1999, Parr *et al* 2000), this study will focus on the work of and Markus *et al's* (2000) ideal phases of ERP implementations. In particular the project phase of Markus *et al* (2000) shall be focused on. This is because, as will later become clear, the case study of the UK furniture manufacturer concentrates on this period. According to Markus *et al* (2000) the project phase comprises activities intended to get the system up and running in one or more organisational units. Key activities include software configuration, system integration, testing, data conversion, training and rollout.

7.3 ERP Problems

The ERP implementation problems identified by Markus *et al* (2001) and Kim *et al* (2005) will be detailed in this section. The rationale for using the work of these two authors is that both define the ERP phases using Markus *et al's* (2000) ideal phases and concentrate on the project phase in particular.

7.3.1 Markus et al (2001)

Markus *et al* (2001) conducted a study which reflects the experiences of approximately forty organisations that they have been involved in studying. Markus *et al* (2001) presents findings about adopters' problems with ERP. In the project phase of the ERP lifecycle, they reported that: software modifications, system integration, product and implementation consultants, and turnover of project personnel were the most challenging of problems to overcome. Table 7.1 details each of these challenging problems in the project phase.

Table 7.1: Markus et al's (2001) challenging problems with ERP adoption in the project phase

Challenging problems	**Project Phase**
Software Modifications	Difficulties in operating effectively with systems functionality Difficulty in getting modifications to work well and arrive in time Not understanding the ERP system before modifications were made, resulting in unnecessary modifications
System Integration	Difficulty integrating ERP system with a package of hardware, operating systems, database management systems and telecommunications systems suited to their organisations size, structure and geographic dispersion Difficulty finding experts to advise on operating requirements
Product and Implementation Consultants	Few IT products and service firms were willing to take end to end responsibility for project managing all parties (ERP vendor, vendors of supporting hardware, software and telecommunications capabilities and implementations consultants etc) ERP adopters reluctant to cede authority for project management to an outside party Conflict between parties Lack of continuity in personnel assigned to adopter projects Conflicts between adopting company and IT product or service vendors
Turnover and Project Personnel	Losing Key IT specialists and user representative

7.3.2 Kim et al (2005)

A later study conducted by Kim *et al* (2005), categorise ERP problems or impediments as they call them, into six different areas. These are: human resources and capabilities management, cross-functional co-ordination, ERP software and configuration, systems development and project management, change management and organisational leadership. Within these areas they compiled impediments identified from previous ERP implementation studies. Kim *et al* (2005) grouped together the impediments into phases. Kim *et al's* (2005) impediments within the project phase are demonstrated in table 7.2.

The authors have combined the ERP adoption problems defined by of Markus *et al* (2001) and Kim *et al* (2005) so a united framework of ERP problems in the project phase of the ERP lifecycle can be developed. This framework is then divided into human and organisational problems or technical problems.

Table 7.2: Kim *et al's* (2005) impediments with ERP adoption in the project phase

Critical Impediments	Project Phase
Human Resources and Capabilities Management	Difficulties in building team Lack of in house resources of project management skills Difficult to gain outside expertise Lack of adequate incentives Imbalanced team composition
Cross Functional Coordination	Lack of coordination mechanism to resolve cross-functional differences Lack of communication across cross-functional units Lack of communication across internal project teams Unwillingness to accept changes from other functional units
ERP Software Configuration	ERP systems that are too difficult to customise Complexity of ERP systems only a few people understand it beyond a single model which makes design difficult
Systems Development	Lack of Adequate resources to renew systems Frequent changes in requirements
Change Management	Lack of organisational change management expertise To much effort to redesign business processes, resulting in a heavy burden in reconfiguring the software Too much effort to align business process to the ERP process resulting in loss of competitive edge
Organisational Leadership	Perspective of ERP as just a technical system Inadequate management of stakeholder politics Lack of adequate monitoring and feedback

7.4 Human and organisational problems and technical problems in ERP adoptions

This is displayed in table 7.3. This paper defines technical problems as involving the machines, devices and 'hard' physical technology. Human and Organisational problems are categorised as attitudes, management and organisational politics and behaviour. It can be observed that six problems have been identified as human and organisational and three have been identified as technical. This combination of work will be used to analyse the case of a UK furniture manufacturer.

This research belongs to the qualitative school of research in information systems. An ethnographic approach is adopted.

Table 7.3: Human and organisational problems and technical problems in ERP adoptions

Human and Organisational Problems	Technical Problems
Product and Implementation Consultants	Software Modifications / Software Configuration
Turnover and Project Personnel	System Integration
Human Resources and Capabilities Management	Systems Development
Cross Functional Coordination	
Change Management	
Organisational Leadership	

7.5 Research setting and methodology

Ethnographies in there most characteristic form involves the ethnographer participating, overtly or covertly, in peoples lives for an extended period of time, watching what has happens, listening to what is said, asking questions, in fact, collecting all the data that is available to throw light on the issues that are the focus of the research (Hammersley *et al* 1995). Myers (1999) states that ethnographic research is well suited to providing information system researchers with rich insights into the human, social and organisational aspects of information systems.

The authors were employed by the UK furniture manufacturer to project manage the adoption of an ERP system. This gave the authors the opportunity to immerse themselves in the area of study. The ethnography data was collected between November 2005 and April 2006, a six month period. Data was collected via participant observation and social contact with the participants as well as referring to documentation such as project proposals, vendor contracts and company research. Note taking was carried out constantly throughout the ethnographical period. Not only observations were noted, the impressions and feelings which emerged were also recorded.

7.6 The UK furniture manufacturer

The UK furniture manufacturer specialise in manufacturing storage furniture for the healthcare industry. They offer a service to the industry in which they design, supply and install not only storage furniture but third party products to equip a hospital room for example with all the furniture it needs.

The notion of adopting an ERP system in the UK furniture manufacturer transpired after a systems review exercise in mid 2004. It became apparent that there was an immense need to improve their information systems. Business processes were very inefficient and frustrating to employees. One employee was quoted saying upon the authors arrival at the company 'System, what system?' The manufacturer was mainly controlled by Microsoft Excel. The specialised software that they did use was not used to its full potential; this was mainly due to inappropriate implementation as well as the ineffective software itself. At the time in 2004 there were opposing views of which direction to take the companies information systems. Some parties were confident that a best of breed software approach was the appropriate route, others were adamant that an ERP system would be the best solution, others simply didn't know enough (or care enough) about either option to make a choice. Research into ERP systems took place. In October 2004 IT exhibitions were attended and ERP vendors were asked to demonstrate their products at the company. After seeing a demonstration of Microsoft Dynamics GP the UK furniture manufacturer were suitably impressed. The company were able to compile a case for the ERP system and the best of breed option and convince those reluctant parties that an ERP system was the paramount option. In July 2005 a final version of the contract was compiled by the ERP vendor. The contract was later signed between both parties to implement Microsoft Dynamics GP. The UK furniture manufacturer decided to enlist an external consultant to put together an implementation plan for the ERP system, a plan was compiled before the authors recruitment. In November 2005, the authors were recruited to project manage the implementation of Microsoft Dynamics GP.

The authors joined the UK furniture manufacturer with theoretical experience of ERP implementations. They were confronted with an ERP system which had been selected and consequently had been contracted to be implemented. An implementation plan had been devised by a consultant and everything was set for the implementation to proceed. In April 2006, a decision was made to abandon the ERP adoption. Between November 2005 and April 2006 the ERP implementation encountered numerous problems. The following sections of this study will explore these problems and analyse them in relation to the human and organisational problems and technical problems framework identified in section four.

7.7 Human and organisational problems and technical problems with the UK furniture manufacturer's ERP adoption

In this section the human and organisational problems and the technical problems incurred by the UK furniture manufacturer will be analysed using the framework compiled in table 7.3.

7.7.1 Product and implementation consultants

Markus *et al* (2001) state that problems might occur because few IT products and service firms were willing to take end to end responsibility for project managing all parties. This problem did not affect the UK furniture manufacturer. The authors were employed to project manage the ERP implementation; they took end to end responsibility for project managing all of the product and service parties involved. Markus *et al* (2001), also state that conflict may occur between parties: the implementation consultant, the ERP vendors and the vendors of existing software. They also state that conflict may occur between the adopting organisation and parties. The UK furniture manufacturer also did not experience any disputes.

7.7.2 Turnover and project personnel

This problem was identified as such by Markus *et al* (2001). Markus *et al* (2001) recognised that internally adopters are unable to maintain continuity of personnel. Losing Key IT specialists and user representatives was identified as a problem. This was not a problem that the UK furniture manufacturer experienced. The personnel that were involved in the ERP implementation at the beginning of the project were involved in the project at the end.

7.7.3 Human resources and capabilities management

Kim *et al* (2005) firstly state that the problem they define as human and resources and capabilities management involves difficulties in building a team. The UK furniture manufacturer constructed a steering committee of user representatives, directors and project management personnel. The team was encouraged to join together in the first instance by the directors sponsoring the project. At the time of the recruitment of the authors it appeared that all of members of the steering committee were happy to be part of the team. The building of the team was not a problem for the furniture manufacturer. Kim *et al* (2005) suggest the balance of the team may also be a problem. The team at the UK furniture manufacturer was well balanced of user representatives, project management personnel and technical personnel. The balance of the team wasn't an issue. Kim *et al* (2005) also point out that lack of in house resources of project management skills can be a problem. According to Loh *et al* (2004), good project management is vital and that the scope of the ERP implementation project should be established and controlled. The authors were well experienced in managing projects, theoretically and practically. This problem was not an issue. Kim *et al* (2005) state that lack of adequate incentives may cause a problem. This wasn't particularly the case. The furniture manufacturer is a SME, the fact that improvements were going to be made which would improve the business seemed to be incentive enough. The frustration of existing systems motivated the steering committee to contribute to the implementation.

7.7.4 Cross functional coordination

Kim (2005) stated that cross functional coordination was a problem in the project phase of ERP implementations. An ERP system is cross functional. In the case of the UK furniture manufacturer the system was proposed to encompasses a large proportion of the business, covering many functions and departments. User representatives from each department were members of the steering committee. The coordination mechanism in place to resolve cross functional differences was the steering committee meetings. Communication was encouraged in these meetings. After deciding upon an incremental implementation oppose to a big bang approach, there was a lot of debate as to which departments would see the implementation of the ERP system first. This disagreement was resolved in the steering committee meeting. As the UK furniture manufacturer is a SME, the cross functional coordination problems were limited.

7.7.5 Change management

The authors were fully aware of change management theories and the steps they had to take to make the ERP implementation run smoothly. The project phase, as identified in section two involves: software configuration, system integration, testing, data conversion, training and rollout. The UK furniture manufacturer only really managed to get as far as software configuration stage before the project was abandoned. So although the project phase as a whole involves a lot of change, the stage the UK furniture manufacturer managed to get to, didn't involve a lot of change. Therefore, there was no real change for the users, so no problems occurred with the management of change.

7.7.6 Organisational leadership

Kim *et al* (2005) state that perceiving the ERP as just a technical system is a problem for organisational leaders. This point was profound in the UK furniture manufacturer. The user representatives and directors (the leaders) clearly referred to the ERP system as 'the system'. This led the authors to believe that the ERP system was seen by many as just computer software. The managing director saw the ERP implementation simply as an IT improvement, the ERP system wasn't viewed as a social system which would affect the structure, culture and politics of the organisation. The managing director didn't really understand the enormity of an ERP system and its affects on the organisation.

Kim *et al* (2005) suggests that the lack of inadequate management of stakeholder politics an organisational leadership problem for ERP implementations. The politics of information systems can be seen to have evolved from the long tradition of literature on the relationship between information and power (Bull 2003). The whole ERP implementation at the UK furniture manufacturer had a political dimension. The user representative who was the main leader for getting the ERP approved was a powerful influence. This representative was not necessarily the most informed party on IS, but taking control of vendor selection gave the user representative authority and control. The opposing user representative that was in favour of implementing a best of breed product in the UK furniture manufacturer was also a powerful influence. Although the ERP system was approved and was going ahead, the opposing user representative did not involve themselves in the planning stages (the chartering phase as Markus 2000 would call it). They did not involve themselves in vendor selection and they failed to state their requirements for the ERP system. This is called counter-resistance according to Bull (2003). Consequently the wrong modules were selected and possibly the wrong ERP system had been selected. The process began of trying to correct this. During this process it was established that the ERP system lacked functionality of a product configurator. The ERP vendors proposed a varying degree of options to overcome this problem, from building a bespoke configuration system, using an existing system or linking with another third party product. In making this decision, those opposing the ERP system evidently found an opportunity to discuss abandoning the project. They also began turning up late or make proceedings difficult in steering committee meetings. The management of stakeholder politics should have been focused upon throughout the project stage and prior to this stage. Because it wasn't, the problem of inadequate management of politics could be associated with the abandonment and consequently the failure of the ERP adoption. Lack of adequate monitoring and feedback was a problem identified by Kim (2005) under the heading of organisational leadership. The project was monitored and feedback was given by the directors attending the steering committees and offering there opinions and advice. There wasn't a problem of lack of adequate monitoring and feedback.

7.8 Technical problems

7.8.1 Software modifications / software configurations

The software modifications that were needed to implement Microsoft Dynamics GP were extensive at the UK furniture manufacturer. Holland (1999) states that an organisation should try to purchase the package that fits best into its business processes. They continue to explain that organisations should be willing to change the business to fit the software with minimal modification and work the existing functionality of the system. Working with the existing functionality in with the Microsoft Dynamics GP would have been impossible. The core capability of the UK furniture manufacturer is the fact that there are few limitations to the dimensions and specification of storage cabinets. Microsoft Dynamics was not specialised enough to manage this functionality, it did not have a product configurator. The UK furniture manufacturer realised the lack of capabilities of the ERP system very early on in the project, it was a very big problem for the company to overcome. Markus *et al* (2001) also state that a problem with ERP implementations in the difficulty in getting modifications to work well. The project didn't proceed at the furniture manufacturer up to the stage where modifications were commissioned. Modifications were discussed in detail, many options and degrees of modification were deliberated, but the ERP adoption was abandoned before any modifications were made.

7.8.2 System integration

According to Markus *et al* (2001), problems can occur when integrating an ERP system with a package of hardware, operating systems, database management systems and telecommunications systems which are suited to an organisations size, structure and geographic dispersion. These problems weren't approached with the UK furniture manufacturer as the implementation of the ERP system didn't reach the stage when these aspects were applicable. The UK furniture manufacturer did not experience difficulty finding experts to advise on operating requirements, which is also a problem defined by Markus *et al* (2001). This again was because they didn't reach that stage of implementation.

7.8.3 Systems development

Kim *et al* (2005) state that the problems that are affected in the project phase that they categorise as systems development are: lack of adequate resources to renew and maintain systems and frequent changes in requirements. The UK furniture manufacturer didn't progress along the project phase enough to experience problems with lack of adequate resources to renew and maintain systems. However, they did experience considerable problems with frequent changes in requirements. Shortly preceding the recruitment of the authors it was discovered that the modules of the ERP system that had been contracted to be implemented did not fit the business needs. The business needs initially were decided by a particular function, this function neglected the needs of other functions in the UK furniture manufacturer. Therefore there was a major change in requirements even before the implementation started to take place. The changes had severe impact on the cost of the ERP system, it increased. This change was certainly not welcomed by the Managing Director and the Financial Director.

7.9 Discussion

This paper is based on only a single exploratory case, so any conceptual insights will need to be verified through subsequent research. With this caution is mind, there do appear to be some interesting theoretical insights that can be derived from the case. The most challenging human and organisational problems encountered by the UK furniture manufacturer were labelled under the heading of Organisational Leadership. The challenging problems that were defined under the heading or Organisational Leadership were: having the perspective of ERP as just a technical system and inadequate management of stakeholder politics. The most challenging technical problems encountered by the UK furniture manufacturer were labelled under the headings of software modifications / software configurations and systems development. The challenging problem that was defined under the heading of software modifications / software configurations was: difficulties in operating effectively with systems functionality. The challenging problem that was defined under the heading of systems development was: frequent changes in requirements. The challenging problems of the UK furniture manufacturer can be observed in table 7.4.

Table 7.4: The challenging problems of the UK furniture manufacturer

Human and Organisation Problems		**Technical Problems**	
Organisational Leadership	Perspective of ERP as just a technical system	Software modifications / software configurations	Difficulties in operating effectively with systems functionality
	Inadequate management of stakeholder politics	Systems development	Frequent changes in requirements

It firstly needs to be mentioned that in total six human and organisational problems were identified in table 7.3 (the framework of organisational problems and technical problems in ERP adoptions) and only three technical problems were identified. This was because the framework was derived from the work of two authors (Markus *et al* 2001, Kim *et al* 2005), and that was what they stated. This point already states that scholar's believe that human and behavioural problems are more profound in ERP implementations. However, because two of the human and organisational problems were found to be relevant to the UK furniture manufacturer, and two technical problems were also found to be relevant, this upon first observation would suggest that the human and organisational problems and the technical problems carry equal importance in the ERP adoption by the UK furniture manufacturer.

However, the findings suggest that the problems experienced due to organisational politics in the planning phase of the UK furniture manufacturer led to the software modification / configuration problems in the project phase. Certain user representatives didn't involve themselves in the planning phase because they were resisting the power of the user representatives in favour of the ERP system, therefore an ERP system was selected which did not fit the business in all departments. Markus *et al* (2001) suggest that in practice, that it is the case that problems experienced in a prior phase which are not perceived as problems and rectified will impact on the subsequent phase. This has been the case in the UK furniture manufacturer. Consequently, if the problem of organisational politics had been resolved in the planning stage, a best fit ERP system could have been selected which would have meant that they would have been limited problems with software modifications. The problem of software modifications may be perceived as being the cause of the project being abandoned. However, the underlining root cause of the modifications was organisational politics. Because of this it can be argued that the human and organisational problems caused the technical problems and therefore were more profound in the case of the UK furniture manufacturer.

This study also found that the ERP system in the UK furniture manufacturer was viewed as just a technical system. Viewing the ERP system a technical system was defined by Kim *et al* (2005) as a problem, this study supports this assumption. The fact that the ERP system was viewed as simply a technical system may have led the adopting organisation to treat the project as unimportant. The organisational politics may not have been managed because the ERP adoption wasn't seen as important enough to provoke conflict. User representatives were left to there own devices in the planning stage, if one user representative didn't involve themselves, it wasn't seen as important to encourage their involvement.

The frequent changes in requirements can be seen to originate from the organisational politics too. If the differences between the user representatives were managed, the business requirements would have been accurate. As it was, the requirements were wrong, which led to frequent changes in requirements later on in the project. The changes in requirements led to the cost of the ERP system escalating. This resulted in the Managing Director and the Finance Director seriously questioning the project. There was a budget, and the ERP exceeded this budget. Money was one of the deciding factors that led to the ERP project being abandoned.

7.10 Conclusion

This paper has identified the problems that are experienced in ERP adoptions using the work of Markus *et al* (2001) and Kim *et al* (2005). A framework was devised from this work clearly stating which problems were human and organisational problems and which were technical problems. Using this framework the case of a UK furniture manufacturer's ERP adoption was analysed. The findings of this paper identify that in the case of a UK furniture manufacturer, the most profound problem was human and organisational. There was a human and organisational problem (inadequate management of organisational politics), which wasn't addressed because of another human and organisation problem (perspective of ERP as just a technical system) which instigated the technical problems (difficulties in operating effectively with systems functionality and frequent changes in requirements) which increased the costs of the system and led the ERP adoption to be abandoned.

Practitioners can learn from this case. It cannot be emphasised enough that human and organisational factors are extremely important in ERP implementations. Adapting organisations must make a conscious effort to management organisational politics. If they are not managed appropriately, practitioners ERP adoptions could end up as yet another failed implementation to add to the pile.

7.11 References

Bull C (2003), *'Politics in Packaged Software Implementations'*, Proceedings of the 11th European Conference on Information Systems, June.

Davenport TH (1998), *'Putting the Enterprise Back into the Enterprise System'*, Harvard Business Review, July-August, pp121-131.

Ehia I C and Madsen M (2005), *'Identifying Critical Issues in Enterprise Resource Planning (ERP) Implementation'*, Computers in Industry, Vol 56, Issue 6.

Elbanna AR (2003), *'Achieving Social Integration to Implement ERP Systems'*, Proceedings of the 11th European Conference on Information Systems, June.

Esteves J and Pastor J (1999), *'An ERP Lifecycle-based Research Agenda'*, Proceedings of the 1st International Workshop on Enterprise Management and Resource Planning Systems, November.

Esteves J and Pastor J (2004), *'Organisational and Technological Critical Success Factors Behaviour Along the ERP Implementation Phases'*, Proceedings of the 6th International Conference on Enterprise Information Systems, April.

Hammersley M (1991) 'What's Wrong With Ethnography?: Methodological Explorations' London, Routledge.

Hammersley M and Atkinson P (1995), *'Ethnography: Principles in Practice'*, Second Edition, London, Routledge.

Ho CF, Wu WH and Tai YM (2004), *'Strategies for the Adaptation of ERP Systems'*, Industrial Management and Data Systems, Vol 104, No 3, pp 234-251.

Holland CP and Light B (1999), *'A Critical Success Factors Model for ERP Implementation'*, IEEE Software, May-June, pp 30-36.

Kansel V (2006), *'Enterprise Resource Planning Implementation: A Case Study'*, The Journal of American Academy of Business, Cambridge, Vol 9, No 1, March, pp165-170.

Kim Y, Lee Z and Gosain S (2005), *'Impediments to Successful ERP Implementation Process'*, Business Process Management Journal, Vol 11, No 2, pp 158-170.

Laudon KC and Laudon JP (2006), *'Management Information Systems'*, Pearson Education, New Jersey.

Law CCH and Ngai (2007), *'ERP systems adoption: An exploratory study of the organizational factors and impacts of ERP success'*, Information and Management, Vol 44, Issue 4.

Legare TL (2002), *'The Role of Organisational Factors in Realising ERP Benefits'*, Information Systems Management, Vol 19, No 4, pp21-42.

Loh T C and Koh S C L (2004), 'Critical Elements for a Successful Enterprise Resource Planning Implementation in Small and Medium Sized Enterprises', International Journal of Production Research, Volume 4, September, pp 3433-3455.

Markus ML and Tanis C (2000), *'The Enterprise System Enterprise – From Adoption to Success'*, in R Zmund W, *'Framing the Domains of IT Research'*, Pinnaflex Educational Resources, pp173-207.

Markus ML, Axline S, Petrie D, Tanis C (2001), *'Learning From Adopters' Experiences With ERP: Problems Encountered and Success Achieved'*, Journal of Information Technology, Vol 15 pp245-265.

Myers M D (1999), *'Investigating Information Systems with Ethnographic Research', Communications of the Association for Information Systems'*, Volume 2, December, Article 23.

Nah FF and Lau JLS (2001), *'Critical Factors for Successful Implementation of Enterprise Systems'*, Business Process Management Journal, Vol 7, no 3, pp 285-296.

Nah FF and Delgado S (2006), *'Critical Success Factors For Enterprise Resource Planning Implementation and Upgrade'*, Journal of Computer Information Systems, Special Issue, pp99-113.

Parr A and Shanks G (2000), '*A Model ERP project Implementation*', Journal of Information Technology, Vol 15, pp289-303.

Ross JW (1999), '*Surprising Facts about implementing ERP*', IT Professional, Vol 1, No 4, pp 65-68.

Sarker S and Lee A (2002), '*Using a Case Study to Test the Role of Three Key Social Enablers in ERP Implementation*', Information Management, Volume 40, Issue 8, pp 813-829.

Somers TM and Nelson K (2001), '*The Impact of Critical Success Factors across the Stages of Enterprise Resource Planning Implementations*', Proceedings of the 34th Hawaii International Conference on System Sciences, January.

Umble EJ and Umble MM (2002), '*Avoiding ERP Implementation Failure*', Industrial Management, January / February, pp 25-33.

Umble EJ, Haft RR, Umble MM (2003), '*Enterprise Resource Planning: Implementation Procedures and Critical Success Factors*', European Journal of Operational Research, Volume 146, pp 241-257.

7.12 Summary on a Page, using Toulmin's Argument structure

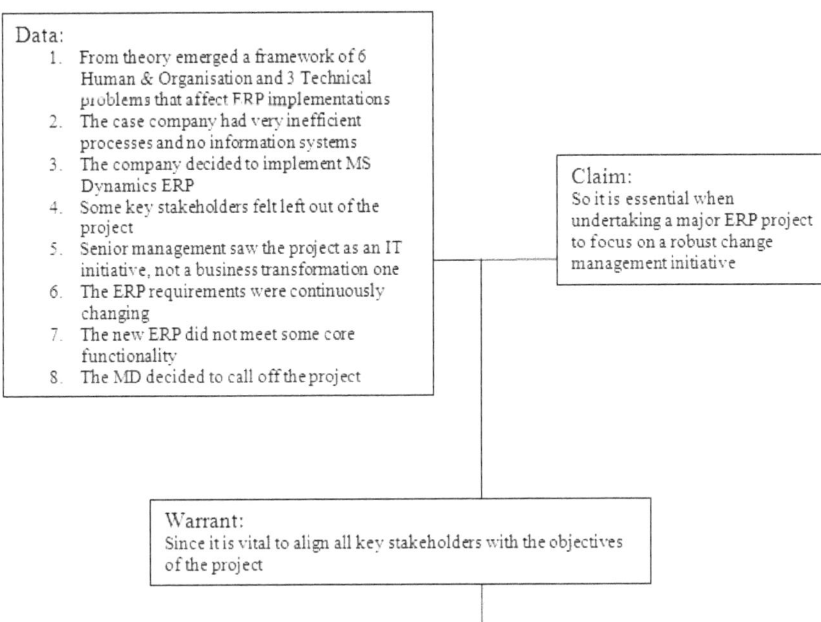

7.13 Case Review

Date of Review:	30JAN2011
My Reference: ISBN: Other Reference:	IM.258
Title/Document:	*The Fundamental Challenge: Human and Organisational Factors in an ERP Implementation,* Proceedings of the European Conference Information Management and Evaluation, University of Montpellier, France, 20-21 September 2007, Edited by Prof. Dan Remenyi, pp. 121-130
Author/Date:	Dawson, J. & Owens, J. (2007)
Source:	ECIME Proceedings
Theme:	The problems encountered in ERP implementations.
Purpose of Paper:	Attempt to differentiate between the human and organisational problems in ERP implementation on one hand, and the technical problems on the other.
Classification/Philosophy:	Basic research/Interpretative in that the researchers claim using and ethnographic approach, but I question this. The fact that they do a theoretic review and use a framework that comes out of it to analyse the case, is incorporating a deductive angle to the research. So on the Deductive-Inductive spectrum, their approach falls somewhere close to the middle.
Hypotheses/Research	Hypotheses or Research Questions are not explicitly specified. However, they do a review of the literature and arrive at a list of what they call

Question:	"Human and organisational problems and technical problems in ERP adoptions. They compile 6 "Human & Organisational Problems": Product and implementation consultants, Turnover & project personnel, Human resource and capabilities management, Cross functional co-ordination, Change management, and Organisational leadership. They also compile 3 Technical Problems: Software modifications/software configuration, System integration, System development.
Methodology:	The authors use the framework given in the hypothesis above, to analyse a case of ERP non-implementation at a UK furniture manufacturer. It is a single case study. Qualitative. The authors were engaged as project managers for the ERP project, and yet they say the method is ethnography (I believe it is really Action Research – see explanation in "Critique" below.) Evidence Collection: Was done mainly through observation and copious note-taking; this was complemented by documents. Evidence collection was done in the November 2005 to November 2006 period. **Evidence Analysis**: The evidence that emerged from the case was categorised along the 6 "Human & Organisational issues" and 3 "Technical Issues". **The Case**: A SME hospital furniture vendor; it manufactures its cabinets and complements its offering to hospitals by reselling other hospital furniture from third party vendors. The company had "very inefficient" business processes and virtually no information systems; what little information there was, was managed on Excel spreadsheets. There were two dominant positions with respect to what systems should be acquired and implemented: one position was to go for an ERP,

	and the other for 'best of breed' systems. This decision was being taken in 2004. Finally, the ERP position prevailed and it was decided to implement Microsoft's Dynamic GP. The project was kicked-off in H2 2005; the researchers were brought on as project managers in November when the project was already under way; by April 2006 the project was halted and scrapped. The case study is aimed at explaining why this happened.
Results:	This study concludes that the implementation of the ERP system at the UK furniture company failed for four reasons: 1. Senior management viewed the ERP implementation as simply a technical system (Human & Organisation) 2. The Project leadership did not do its homework in stakeholder management and thus never managed to bring on board those stakeholder that had initially favoured a best-of-breed solution, who had considerable power and in the end sunk the project (Human & Organisation) 3. Could not meet the requirements of what were core process for the organisation (Technical) 4. As the project progressed there were continuous changes in requirements that in the end led to significant budget overruns (Technical) In searching for the root cause of the problems, in this case it is clear that the two Human & Organisation problems are the root cause of the two Technical problems
Managerial Implications:	ERP Implementations need to be recognised by senior management as business transformation

	projects enabled by a technology, and not seen as simply Technological projects. This means that change management is of upmost importance and in particular the MD needs to take leadership and make sure she detects power disputes early on, and align the whole management team with the project's objectives.
Limitations / Future Research:	
Critique and Learning:	In section 2 (and in several later sections) the authors give the phases of an ERP implementation as: s/w configuration; systems integration; testing; data conversion; training and rollout. They leave out two critical phases: Design or business blueprint, and Cut-Over or Go-Live. The design stage is critical for defining the scope of the project and functionality of the solution, which in the end was the cited reason for scrapping the project. The authors say they take an ethnographic approach; I think they apply a perfectly valid approach, but I have doubts as to whether this is really ethnography, on two grounds. The first is that ethnography is by definition interpretative (Gabriel, 2008, pp.99-101) where the researchers come into the community they are studying with an open mind and, in most cases, to understand the world in the mindset of those being analysed. The fact that the authors do a literature review and use the framework that came out of it to analyse the case would be defeating this approach. The other reason for doubting this is ethnography is that the researchers have been appointed project managers and therefore have power over the community they are studying. Is having power over the community legitimate for ethnography? Clearly the researchers do not have control over all variables and external conditions of the 'experi-

	ment', but they certainly can make links between causes and effects. Would this not be more a case of quasi-experiment or Action Research? **Lessons Leaned:** **Definition of ERP**: A commercial software package that promotes seamless integration of all the information flowing through a company. It collects data from various business processes in manufacturing and production, finance and accounting, sales and marketing, and human resources, and stores it in a single comprehensive data repository where it can be used by other parts of the business. As a result, managers have precise and timely information for coordinating the daily operations of the business and a firm wide view of business and information flows. **Functional Misfit**: Clearly product configuration is a key functionality for this type of organisation – how did this gap not emerge in the software selection process? Clearly the company did not involve all the interested parties in the requirements definition and selection process. **Root Cause Analysis**: From personal experience going through these processes, it would have been the Production and Sales people who would have pushed for a best-of-breed solution, because that would give them the best solution for their core issues: designing products that perfectly met their clients' needs, and feeding those specification straight into the production line. These stakeholders lost out in the political battle as the decision was to go for an ERP. As a result they lost interest in the project and thus did not give their input for the ERP selection. They then just waited until the project got under way to torpedo it at the first opportunity. This must be a powerful group in

	the organisation, because the MD immediately took their side when they exposed the limitations of the solution. So the technical problems that emerged, as real as they were, were actually only symptoms; the root of the problem was poor change management; or more specifically, no stakeholder management. **Apply the Diamond Leadership Model**: It is interesting to consider the following: The problem emerged as functional limitations or in other words a process problem – at the Structure level of the organisation. The immediate reaction of the project leadership was to throw more money at the problem: develop the lacking functionality, or purchase a specific application that covered the functionality and integrate it with the ERP. In other words, given a Structure problem the leadership of the project went down one level to Resources to find an answer, when really they should have gone one level up, to Power. **Challenging Problems**: In their primary analysis of the case study (Section 8. Discussion) the authors conclude that 2 of the Human & Organisation problems and 2 of the Technical problems are relevant to the UK furniture company. However, they later advance this analysis and conclude that the Human & Organisational problems caused the Technical problems, and thus were the root cause of the problems. Could not the authors venture to propose that among these problems there is a hierarchy? That Human & Organisation problems are of a higher level than Technical problems?

PART III:
Market Power Driven ICT Investments

Chapter 8

Supporting Healthy Growth in a Building Contractor (UK)

This chapter will be centred on the experience of a UK building contractor that started up as a family business some four decades ago and is now a leading player in its market. This is a story of growth and the impact that it has on the internal workings of the organisation. This impact can be devastating to an organisation and if not taken care of frequently leads to failure shortly after succession from the founders.

Building contractors of a significant size have the organisational complexity of operating with staff at many different sites. It shares this with management consulting firms but with the added problem of operating in temporary, and often precarious, installations as are site offices.

Beale & Cole's leadership was determined to maintain growth in a sustainable manner, and thus decided it needed to strengthen its organisation by embarking on an ICT-enabled business transformation programme. The case illustrates some key issues to be considered in making decisions in this space.

The Effect of Information Systems on Firm Performance and Profitability Using a Case-Study Approach

Mojisola Olugbode[1], Ibrahim Elbeltagi[2], Matthew Simmons[3] and Tom Biss[1]
[1]University of Plymouth, UK
[2]Plymouth Business School, UK
[3]Beale and Cole Building Services Limited, UK

Abstract: Beale and Cole is a company that was experiencing significant levels of growth in its business. However, its existing operational practices and ICT infrastructure were incapable of efficiently sustaining their level of growth. A thorough analysis of the operational systems was carried out covering both the manual systems and those supported by its computerised accounting system. A number of beneficial changes were made, including the implementation of a major new business system replacing the old accounting system. In all these developments, the work of a teaching company associate, now known as knowledge transfer partnerships associate supported the analysis, but the full participation and support of all key personnel within the company was essential. Although there were problems during the implementation, these have being resolved and Beale and Cole now has a fully supported and integrated IT system which will maintain their competitive advantage and facilitate their continued growth and profitability.

Keywords: information, communication and technology (ICT), business systems integration, SMEs.

Originally published in the Electronic Journal of IS Evaluation Volume 11 Issue 1 pp. 11-16.

8.1 Introduction

A business information system is defined by Hooper and Page (1997) as "the sum of all the tools, techniques and procedures used by the business to process data". Fisher and Kenny (2000) suggested that organisations infuse information systems into their operations so as to enhance competitiveness and facilitate business growth and success. On the other hand, Laudon and Laudon (2001) believed that information systems are embedded in organisations and are the result of standard operating procedures, work flows, politics, organisational culture and structure. Although organisations have different information systems because they have varying information needs, they all strive for competitive advantage through continuous improvement; re-evaluation of the effectiveness and efficiency of their business information system (Chaffey and Wood 2005). The purpose of this paper is to investigate the Information System of Beale and Cole, to examine the course of action taken to implement changes to the existing IS practises, and to share experiences and lessons learnt from the change process and the effect on the organisation's performance.

Beale and Cole Building Services was established in 1967. The company started out in Exeter as a small family business but today, it is one of the leading firms of building services engineers in the South West of England with branches in Exeter, Yeovil and Plymouth. The company has witnessed a significant level of growth over the years. However, the existing operational practises, processes and supporting Information, Communication and Technology (ICT) infrastructure were inadequate to efficiently sustain this level of growth.

Subsequently in the summer of 2003, Beale and Cole in partnership with the University of Plymouth embarked on a Department of Trade and Industry (DTI) funded initiative known as the Teaching Company Scheme (TCS) now called Knowledge Transfer Partnerships (KTP). The main objective of this coalition was to implement new integrated business and supporting IT systems which would streamline operations, increase internal efficiency, facilitate sustained growth and increase profitability.

In order to achieve the objective of this investigation, a Knowledge Transfer Partnerships Associate with a background in business information management systems was recruited to conduct an in-depth analysis of the business information system and to propose and implement recommendations for improvement. Therefore, this paper will reflect on the experiences of this process by all parties involved in the project including management and staff of the organisation.

8.2 Initial review of Beale and Cole's information systems

This stage was conducted by the associate, Matthew Simmons. The first step was to review the internal processes and existing Information systems in the organisation so as to highlight the major problem areas. The main problems were found to be; duplication of effort, inefficiency in some processes including e-commerce strategy and problems with communication. We developed a simple model (see Figure 8.1) to explain all the main problems in detail and to highlight the impact of the improved information systems on operational performance and profitability in the organisation.

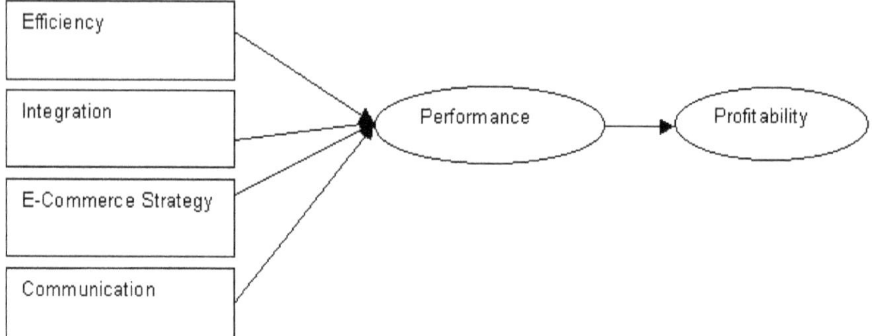

Figure 8.1: Proposed framework for the effect of information systems on performance and profitability

8.2.1 Efficiency

The unprecedented expansion and consequent physical and commercial growth of the organisation opened up crevices in the organisation's business processes.

Nicholls-Nixon (2005) found in his study that rapid growth in business generates dramatic changes in the scale and scope of a firm's activities. According to him, entrepreneurs in rapidly growing business enterprises experience more difficulties in comparison to small growth companies when deciding or establishing the type of changes or evolution required to support their level of growth. This is because they face greater managerial complexity than slow growth firms. One of the solutions she recommended to solve this complex issue was that high growth organisations should develop new skills and capabilities which will allow them to cope with the complexity. This can be attained by appointing new personnel or acquiring new resources such as new information systems targeted at improving organisational efficiency and effectiveness.

The main problem area highlighted by the associate was the organisation's accounting system. The company's business system had been purchased from a software company many years ago. Initially, the software was run on a leased line which was very expensive. This was later changed to a Virtual Private Network (VPN) by the associate thereby greatly reducing the operating cost.

The software was supposed to be an extensible accounting system capable of managing all financial aspects of the organisation and though it appeared to be a tool that can be fully integrated with MS excel or access so as to facilitate data analysis and report creation; it would have required a database translation to function effectively. However, as the structure of the database was weak, translating it would have been very difficult, time consuming and cumbersome. Moreover, the system was generic, had limited documentation which was very difficult to understand and as it was outdated, the system would have failed to meet legislative regulations by 2007.

Furthermore, the software company had since changed ownership. Presently, their have been no new developments but extensions and upgrades to their existing software. Although the supplier offered these more up to date upgrades (which was not free), it still appeared to use some of the features that proved unsatisfactory in the original system. Another drawback to using this system was the maintenance agreement. Although it had been properly structured, it was however inconvenient as the software company had a third party agreement with another company which managed the maintenance of the software. Invariably, turnaround time for maintenance could sometimes be very high, prolonged and time consuming.

Another operational concern was that the company had not altered its recording procedures despite its rapid growth. The method used for monitoring labour needed to be improved as it was not centralised and was deficient in forward planning. The job costing system that was used did not take into account the availability of labour while there was a lack of consistent structure in the recording of unstructured information about projects. Although a manual index of documents was stored online, it had become ineffective since the organisation had expanded to a second location.

A manual procedure of operation that needed much improvement was the time sheet recording. This involved engineers completing a complex time sheet which would then be faxed to the office for the contracts manager to check and calculate the necessary payment agreements. Once this stage had been completed, the time sheet would be passed on to the administration department where the time would be checked again before inputting it onto the system. Finally, the information would be printed out so that the details can be used to generate the engineers' wages. This procedure would normally take about 6 office hours and would involve about 60-70 engineers, all the contracts managers (7), 2 administrative assistants and a payroll officer.

8.2.2 Lack of uniformity and integration

The major concern was that there were many bespoke systems and undocumented manual system, and very little uniformity in operational procedures. This followed from the recent merging of a part of the company specialising in plumbing with the original business which specialised in electrical services. Crist (2002) observed a similar situation in his study suggesting that "traditional document control processes were usually a combination of manual and electronic systems which may result in duplication of effort and further expenditure of time". Winch and Carr (2001) recommended that an appropriate remedy was to use process mapping which focuses on actual flows of information within the organisation. They maintain that this method is less demanding with regards to resources and engenders a process whereby there are standardised protocols for business operations. Furthermore, Fisher and Kenny (2002) pointed out that there were two mandatory steps required to implement an organisation-wide information system and these are; well designed set of business processes or value chain and secondly, a cautious exercise in strategic thinking, operational planning and consultation with all end users of the system to facilitate user satisfaction and in turn better use of systems and improve performance.

Researchers like Weill and Baroudi, (1990) cited in Caldeira and Ward (2002) and Delone and Mclean (1992) established that user satisfaction was the most widely used variable for measuring IS success because there exists a strong correlation between this variable and firms' performance. However, other studies by Kim (1989) and Melone (1990) have disputed these findings as inconclusive because user satisfaction failed to consider the diverse roles, needs and interests of the users. In this study, a thorough analysis of the alternative systems was carried out by the associate and involving all the main users of the system to enhance user satisfaction. However, some users were initially opposed or averse to the change, while others had mixed feelings. The observation and interviews showed that with gradual induction of changes and good training, this might lead to improvement of performance.

8.2.3 e-Commerce strategy

Although Beale and Cole had a website, it did not give a clear and up to date picture of who they are and what they had achieved. The deficiencies apparent on the website meant it could not be effectively utilised as a strategic e-commerce tool for marketing the company's services. Taylor and Murphy (2004) highlighted that E-commerce strategies can be adopted by Small and Medium Enterprises (SMEs) for customer base expansion. Other researchers suggested that e-commerce strategy enhances performance in general and time-based delivery performance in particular (Jeffcoate, J., et al. 2002; Iyer, Karthik N.S., et al. 2004).

8.2.4 Communication

Information in the organisation was stored at a very high cost rather than being shared. The main modes of communication within branches were through phone and fax, face to face and limited use of e-mail, while for customer and suppliers, telephone and fax were used. There were also the lack of network capabilities for file sharing and organised postal system and no internal communications link for the offices. This translated to increased expenditure on telephones.

This existing communication arrangement promoted data duplication, loss of information, elongated processes and increased time frames for decision making. A lot of studies showed that clear communication channels within the organisation and between the organisation and its customers have a positive effect on firm performance, see for example (Carr, Amelia S. Kaynak, Hale, 2007).

8.3 Research methodology

This article describes qualitative research into the case study company through a series of in-depth interviews and observation. The evidence from the interviews and observation are compelling, and therefore the overall study is more robust. One of the limitation of case study is that it provides little basis for scientific generalization. To overcome this problem and for future research a multiple case studies approach is required. Multiple case studies are generalizable (though not necessarily to multiple populations or contexts).

8.4 Implementation of improved systems

To eradicate these deficiencies, a number of changes were made to the existing system. Where possible, the systems which differed on the two sites but served similar purposes were amalgamated and integrated. These changes were supported by a similarly configured file server with a permanent line between them.

The initial enhancements included:

- The introduction of electronic time sheets which has eliminated duplication reduced payment errors by 99.9% and saved 3 staff members half a day per week.
- Improvements to the telephony system and a change of supplier saved an estimated 312 person hours per year and reduced expenditure considerably.
- Standardisation of forms and procedures between sites, eliminating duplication of activity, reducing error and improving communication.
- Enhanced data security through integrating the IT and communications system, improving their reliability, robustness and increasing user confidence.
- Implementation of a suitable filing structure reduced time spent locating files and enabled improved archiving capabilities.
- Design and development of the website by an external developer. The site now has a professional image and highlights areas of specialisation of the company and past projects executed. Further developments will be made in the future to incorporate the website onto the business system.

After the successful implementation of a number of immediate improvements, it was further decided that the old accounting business system should be replaced. Numerous studies by (Delone and McLean, 1992; Yap et al 1992; Doukidis et al, 1994) have pointed out the importance of involving all key employees at this stage of the project in order to obtain commitment to the new system. In Beale and Cole, user participation and commitment was achieved through several brainstorming sessions, meetings and thorough analysis of the alternative systems with all the main users so as to agree on the selection criteria and which package best met those criteria.

There were clear differences of opinion about which was the best package for the company's needs. This was probably due to the superiority of one package for the estimating and costing side of the business and another for the financial reporting side. However, the full participation of all key members of the company ensured that there was a high level of commitment when the final choice of Estimation Plus, an industry specific software package, came to be implemented.

The Estimation Plus software was easier to use than its predecessor and allowed greater control. Some of the functionalities of the system were:

- It was segregated into sections and order list, which made it possible to determine materials required for a building and individual rooms within the building.
- Price enquiries could be sent to suppliers and purchasers.
- It made it possible for engineers to purchase materials through the system.
- Enquiries on job details and all contracts can be easily accessed.
- Outstanding debtor balances are effortlessly produced.
- The system allows users to create many of their own reports and also provides management reports which can analyse the business from 15 different perspectives.

8.5 Experiences gained from the implementation and impact of the systems change

The selection and implementation process took place during a period of rapid growth for the company. Consequently, all concerned were experiencing pressure on their time. The time taken to complete the selection process therefore exceeded the time planned. In an attempt to restrict the degree of consequent slippage in the implementation date, the time analysing the detailed requirements for implementation was restricted. Therefore all the areas of the business system were not completely configured before commencing the phased in implementation. They discovered after implementing some areas in the estimating and accounting software that some aspects of the system should have been done earlier. Consequently, some of the decisions taken such as cost code allocation were regretted and corrected. With hindsight, we feel that more time should have been spent getting used to the package under test conditions before its full scale implementation.

Although the new system is still in its early period of operation, there is wide agreement within the company that operational processes within the company are now running much more efficiently:

- The communications system has been streamlined. Consequently, there is improved integration and communication, particularly between the Exeter, Yeovil and Plymouth sites.
- Enhanced customer communications and improved opportunities for maintaining excellent customer relations.
- Improved management information for tactical and strategic planning and control.
- The documentation of systems and processes to ISO standards provided a framework for future developments in the organisation.
- The company has the potential and capacity for more rapid expansion and business growth.
- There has been increased turnover through business growth
- Implementation of improved business system has increased profitability and improved cost control in the organisation.
- The reports produced by the business system make information for decision making readily available to managers.

Presently, the company is considering the procurement of an electronic trade e-invoicing system which would be integrated into the business system. This e-invoicing would eliminate the need for manual input of invoices, greatly enhance cost control and reduce transaction and overhead costs.

8.6 Conclusion

This study describes the experiences and lessons learnt at Beale and Cole as they implemented changes to their existing IS practises in order to support the level of growth of the business. Initially, the change brought about mixed reactions, some doubt and some opposition amongst employees but these were gradually eliminated through their involvement in the search for alternatives and in the implementation stage of the change process. During the implementation stage, some teething problems were encountered. This was because the time frame allowed for implementing and studying the new system was restricted thereby leading to some errors but these were subsequently corrected.

These changes to the organisation's operational practises, business system and ICT infrastructure have improved operational processes and efficiency of the company. Consequently, this has reduced operating and transaction costs, increased turnover and enhanced profitability. The introduction of this fully supported and integrated IT system will serve as a strategic tool for Beale and Cole to sustain its continued growth and maintain its competitive advantage as one of the leading building services company in the South West region.

8.7 Acknowledgements

We wish to thank the Department of Trade and Industry who mainly sponsored the two year KTP initiative which made this study possible. Our sincere thanks and appreciation also goes to the Managing Director of Beale and Cole Building Services Limited, Mr Phillip Beale for allowing their experiences on this project to be documented and published.

8.8 References

Carr, A. and Kaynak, H. (2007) "Communication methods, information sharing, supplier development and performance: An empirical study of their relationships", International Journal of Operations & Production Management, Vol. 27, No. 4, pp 346 - 370

Caldeira, M. and Ward, J. (2002) "Understanding the successful adoption and use of IS/IT in SMEs: an explanation from Portuguese manufacturing industries", Journal of Information Systems, Vol. 12, pp 121-152.

Jeffcoate, J., Chappell, C. and Feindt, S. (2002) "Best practice in SME adoption of e-commerce, Benchmarking", An International Journal, Vol. 9, No. 2, pp 122-132.

Iyer, K., Germain, R. and Frankwick, G. (2004) "Supply chain B2B e-commerce and time-based delivery performance", International Journal of Physical Distribution & Logistics Management, Vol. 34, No. 8, pp 645-661.

Chaffey, D. and Wood, S. (2005) Business information management: Improving performance using information systems, Pearson Education Limited, Essex.

Delone, W. and Mclean, E. (1992) "Information systems success: the quest for the dependent variable", Information systems Research, Vol. 3, No. 1, pp 60-95.

Fisher, B. and Kenny, R. (2000) "Introducing a business information system into an engineering company", Journal of Information, Knowledge and Systems Management, Vol. 2, pp 207-221.

Doukidis, G., Smithson, S. and Lybereas,T. (1994) "Trends in information technology in small business", Journal of End User Computing, Vol. 6, No. 4, pp15-25.

Laudon, K. and Laudon, J. (2001) Essentials of information systems: Organization and technology in the networked enterprise (4th ed.), Prentice Hall, New Jersey.

Hooper, P. and Page, J. (1997) "Organising information and data flows in business systems", National Public Accountant, Vol. 42, Issue 9, pp 9-14.

Kim, K. (1989) "User satisfaction: a synthesis of three different perspectives", Journal of Information Systems, Vol. 4, pp. 1-13.

Melone, N. (1990) "A theoretical assessment of the user satisfaction construct in information systems research", Journal of Management Science, Vol.36, Issue. 1, pp 76-91.

Nicholls-Nixon, C. (2005) "Rapid growth and high performance: The entrepreneur's impossible dream", Academy of Management Executive, Vol.19, No. 1, pp77-89.

Taylor, M. and Murphy, A. (2004), "SMEs and e-business, Journal of Small Business and Enterprise Development", Vol.11, No. 3, pp 280-289.

Weill, P. and Baroudi, J. (1990) An empirical investigation of the relationship between firm performance and systems success, Working paper No.15, University of Melbourne, The Graduate School of Management.

Winch, G. and Carr, B. (2001) "Process, maps and protocols: Understanding the shape of the construction process", Journal of Construction Management and Economics, Vol.19, pp 519-531.

Yap, C., Soh, C. and Raman, K. (1992) "Information systems success factors in small business, Omega International", Journal of Management Science, Vol.20, No. 5/6, pp 597-609.

8.9 Summary on a Page, using Toulmin's Argument structure:

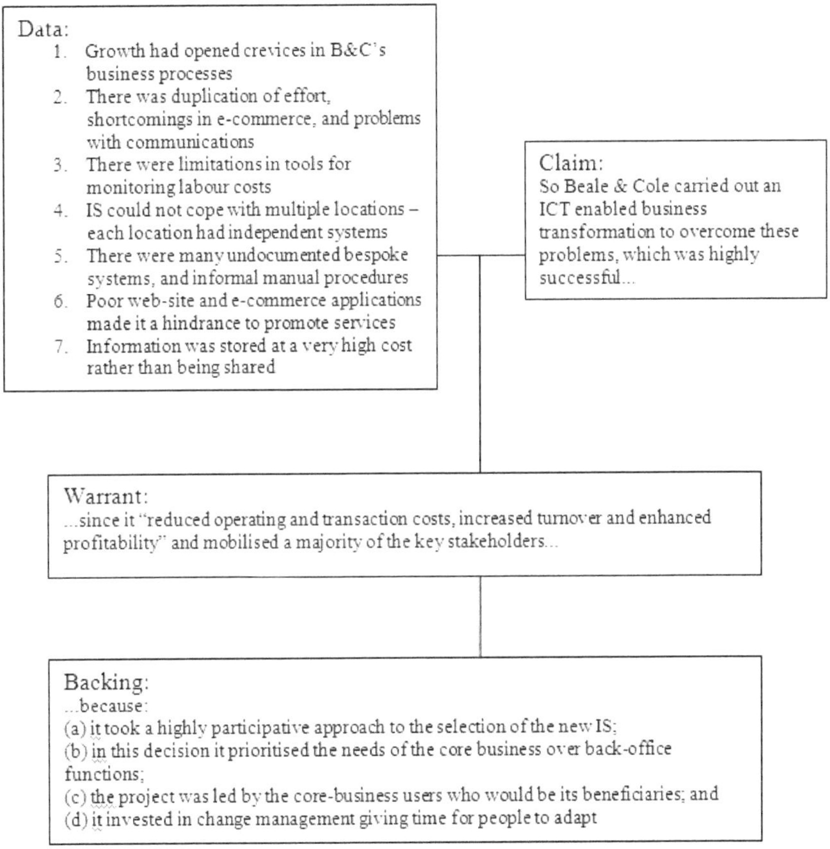

Data:

1. Growth had opened crevices in B&C's business processes
2. There was duplication of effort, shortcomings in e-commerce, and problems with communications
3. There were limitations in tools for monitoring labour costs
4. IS could not cope with multiple locations – each location had independent systems
5. There were many undocumented bespoke systems, and informal manual procedures
6. Poor web-site and e-commerce applications made it a hindrance to promote services
7. Information was stored at a very high cost rather than being shared

Claim:

So Beale & Cole carried out an ICT enabled business transformation to overcome these problems, which was highly successful...

Warrant:

...since it "reduced operating and transaction costs, increased turnover and enhanced profitability" and mobilised a majority of the key stakeholders...

Backing:

...because:

(a) it took a highly participative approach to the selection of the new IS;
(b) in this decision it prioritised the needs of the core business over back-office functions;
(c) the project was led by the core-business users who would be its beneficiaries; and
(d) it invested in change management giving time for people to adapt

8.10 Case Study Review

Date of Review:	12FEB2011
My Reference: ISBN: Other Reference:	IM.259
Title/Document:	The Effect of Information Systems on Firm Performance and Profitability Using a Case-Study Approach, The Electronic Journal Information Systems Evaluation, Vol. 11, Issue 1, pp.11-16
Author/Date:	Olugbode, M., Elbetagi, I., Simmons, M. & Biss, T. (2008)
Source:	EJISE
Theme:	Increasing the growth capacity of an organisation by implementing a new core business system.
Purpose of Paper:	To investigate the IS of Beale & Cole, to examine the course of action taken to implement the new IS, and to extract and share lessons from this process.
Classification/Philosophy:	Basic Research/ Interpretative
Hypotheses:	The authors do not explicit a research question. What lessons can be learnt from the implementation of a new IS at Beale & Cole?
Methodology:	The authors use single-case study, qualitative research. They give very little information on the methodology applied. They do not say how many people, and in what positions, they have interviewed. Neither do they place the evidence gathering in time. Because this research was de-

	veloped within a DTI sponsored programme to improve IT systems and streamline operations at Beale & Cole one of the authors was the DTI associate who worked on the project, interviews were obviously not the only source of evidence, as there must have been significant observation. But no information on this is given. The unit of analysis is the company, a building services engineering company (plumbing, and of late electric installation) that started up as a family business in 1967 and grew strongly in recent years to become one of the leading such firms in South West England. As a result its ICT infrastructure became inadequate to sustain more growth.
Results:	From the initial review of its IS, the main problems were found to be: • Intense growth caused opening up of crevices in the organisation's business processes. • Duplication of effort; inefficiency in some processes including e-commerce strategy; and problems with communications. • One of main problem areas was the accounting system, which was generic and lacked proper documentation; it was outdated and did not meet legislation requirements; poor quality service by s/w vendor. • Limitations in tools for monitoring labour costs • Could not cope with multi-locations: separate and independent systems. • There were many bespoke systems and undocumented manual systems. • Poor e-commerce application made it a hindrance to promote the organisation's services and show its success cases and experience. *{This is a clue that the organisation is thinking*

	in terms of revenue enhancement}. • Information was stored at a very high cost rather than being shared, and communications between offices and with customers was heavily phone and fax based. This created elongated processes and increased timeframes for decision-making. • Action: In response to these limitations it was decided to create a robust ICT platform to support the business and enable growth. **Outcome**: It is considered a success because it has "reduced operating and transaction costs, increased turnover and enhanced profitability." I qualify this as a revenue-enhancement driven ICT project because confronted with the alternatives of going for an accounting and finance centred project, or a core-business centred project, the organisation opted for the latter. Although not explicitly stated in the text, it can be inferred that the business managers got their way and most probably led the implementation project. Apart from this, when one reads the functionality of the new project in section 5, expressions such as "enhanced customer communications", "maintaining excellent customer relations", "business growth", "capacity for more rapid expansion", "information for decision making readily available" outweigh expressions such as "improved cost control". Finally, the business context of the project is also giving clues in this direction: the company had recently decided to expand its product/service offering by adding electrical engineering services to their traditional plumbing (offering more products to their present client base and market segment).
Managerial Implica-	Beale & Cole accomplished a successful ICT enabled business transformation. Their success can

tions:	be explained by the fact that, precisely, they viewed it as such and not as an IT initiative. The company's leadership brought in external help to give expertise and objectivity to the project, and involved all business units in the solution selection process. It also indicated that sustained growth was a priority, which derived in that a revenue enhancement business led solution was secured. The "losers" in the solution selection were enticed to join in the project by investing effort and taking their time to make the changes gradual.
Limitations / Future Research:	
Critique and Learning:	The authors have a rather restrictive view on the possibility of generalising from a single case study, and sound a bit confusing when they say this study should be followed by a multiple case study research. Generalising from a case to another case is perfectly valid in a single case-study. Clearly, we are not talking about generalising from a case to a population as in statistical generalisation, but it nevertheless can have a lot of value. The authors gather from the literature that the correlation between "user satisfaction" as a variable for measuring IS success, and company performance is inconclusive and explain this by saying that "user satisfaction" failed to consider the diverse roles, needs and interests of the users. *{This is really just a manifestation of the problems with thinking around a simple input-output model in IS evaluation, and ignoring the mechanism through which the input impacts the output. Another problem is that they are not taking into account the value discipline of the organisation.}*

	Lessons Learnt: **Definition**: Business information systems are defined by Hooper & Page (1997) as "the sum of all the tools, techniques and procedures used by the business to process data." The importance of Change Management: Initially some users were opposed to the changes, but this was contained through gradual induction of changes and good training. It was decided to replace the accounting and other systems by an ERP; they involved all areas in the decision-making process through workshops and other consultations. The organisation eventually decided for a solution that responded more to their core-business needs than financial and accounting. *{This is another clue that the project was focused on revenue enhancement}*. There were several groups with different interests, but through the participative selection process they eventually won over the losers. *{What a difference with the case where they had to scuttle the project because there were losers in the process who could never be pulled on board – I believe that the fact that in this case it was a business driven, rather than back-office driven system, also facilitates this. It requires less change management because the project is led by the business, and the majority of the users are the beneficiaries of the new system.}* There was time constraint that led to scarce user testing and eventual significant mistakes in such things as cost code allocation – but commitment had been built so they did step back and fix those problems.

Chapter 9

The importance of strategic alignment for CRM (China)

Client relationship management systems are typically market power driven ICT investments. In the case we shall see, Alfa Laval changed its value discipline from Product Leadership to Customer Intimacy. Its strategy after this switch was to grow through capturing and retaining Clients that, in order to be successful, required changes in its organisation.

Alfa Laval defied the prevailing trend by selecting a bespoke solution as opposed to one of the leading world class packages, which exposed the project to higher risks. However, this could have been compensated by the fact that senior management was highly committed to the project, and its ownership was transferred to local management that was responsible for its success. The commitment of senior management at a local level is decisive in this kind of project. Evidence of this is that there was no need for a large change management initiative (those who were getting the benefits from the project were actually leading it.)

Users found the CRM system cumbersome to use and with quality problems that would normally call for rejection of the system. However, users also found that access to Client information, actual and historical, was far easier than in the prior status – and this is a pivotal attribute for a system in an organisation that operates in a customer intimacy value discipline, where staff require far more information on their Clients than that required to complete transactions.

Let us get straight onto the case. It will highlight the importance of strategic alignment and business ownership for success in CRM implementation projects.

Evaluation of a CRM System Implementation in China

Sven Carlsson, Linda Frygell, Jonas Hedman[9]
Department of Informatics, School of Economics and Management, Lund University, Lund, Sweden

Abstract: This paper presents an evaluation of a multi-national company's Customer Relationship Management system in China. The implementation in China was part of the first wave of the global implementation of the system. The aim of the evaluation was to evaluate the first wave of implementation in order to improve the system and the implementation. Based on the evaluation a list of action items was generated, including improved resource planning, acceptance testing, training, timing, usability, new functionality, information and communication, and user forums.

Keywords: Implementation, evaluation, CRM system, China, culture, enterprise systems

Originally published in the Proceedings of the ECITE 2005, pp. 129-136

9.1 Introduction

This paper presents and discusses the evaluation of a Customer Relationship Management (CRM) system implementation in China. The case is a Swedish MNC, Alfa Laval, and its CRM-system ACE (A Commitment to Excellence). The purpose of the evaluation was to learn from one implementation to improve later waves of implementations.

The paper is organised in following way. The next section describes the evaluation approach. The third section presents the CRM system and how it was developed. The following section presents and discusses the results of the evaluation. Based on the evaluation we present a list of action items to be implemented to improve later implementation waves.

9.2 Evaluation Approach

The evaluation study was done during the fall of 2004 and the focus was on the CRM system implementation process and the CRM system in use.

---

[9] The authors contributed equally to this paper.

The data sources were interviews, internal documents, and observations. Documents were used to get an overall picture of previous actions and events. The internal reports, project specifications, and ppt-presentations consisted of more than 200 pages. The purpose of the observations was to get additional information that was hard to obtain through interviews. Events observed during observations included project manager workshop; super user training for Nordic Countries and the US; follow-up training in Beijing; telephone meeting with the ACE project manager for China; and office visits in Sweden. The main data source was interviews. The interviewees were chosen based on their roles in the project. In total 24 interviews with 23 employees were done. All the interviews have been individual interviews and have been recorded and have been recorded and transcribed.

The collected data was analysed continuously to enrich the following interviews. A continuous analysis meant that after each interview it was immediately transcribed and the content analysed in relationship to the objectives of this study. The very first interview, with the global Project Manager for the ACE implementation project, was an unstructured interview were the interviewee was asked to describe what had happened in the first implementation wave and what his reflections were. This interview led to a guideline for what to ask the Sales Company IS co-ordinators, and their input then further developed the local Project Mangers interview guides. Thereafter the interview guide for the ACE team members and the regular users were developed in relationship to Sales Company IS co-ordinators' answers.

After a first general analysis, themes, coding and pattern matching was performed. First, the interviews were divided into groups based on the interviewees' roles in the project. This meant, for instance, comparing the local project manager's answers in relation to one another, to find variances, similarities and differences in their answers. After that, all the question that had been asked to all people were analysed, this involved grouping the questions as being positive vs. negative or good vs. bad. All the questions were also separated into different themes which corresponded to the factors critical for system implementations as suggested in the research literature—a major literature review was done previous to the evaluation. The material was analyzed several times looking for different patterns in the total material and also in the material grouped by project roles, gender, previous IS implementation experience and other factors that could have affected the implementation process.

9.3 Alfa Laval's new CRM system: ACE

Alfa Laval was founded in 1883 by Gustav de Laval. The firm's initial success was based on his invention of the separator, used to separate milk from cream. Today Alfa Laval is organised around three business areas—see www.alfalaval.com. Traditionally Alfa Laval has been a decentralised firm organised around its areas of expertise with a strong product orientation. In the last years this has shifted toward a market orientation, with a strong focus on the customers' needs instead of the products.

Prior to 2001, different types of CRM systems were used by Alfa Laval's market and sales companies and the corporate support staff. In 2001 the IT board of Alfa Laval decided to standardise the CRM systems around the world. In the process following the decision standard applications and the in-house systems were evaluated. In 2002 it was decided that Alfa Laval should use one of the in-house developed systems as the platform for building a new global CRM system.

The next step was a pilot installation and in May 2002 the IT board decided to approve a pilot project in the Nordic Sales Company. In March 2003 the Nordic Pilot case was finalised and the main conclusion was that the pilot project clearly demonstrated that the system could add significant value to Alfa Laval's business units. In April-May 2003 preparation for continued development (CRM phase 2) and a global roll-out (CRM phase 3) was undertaken and in June 2003 the IT board was presented with the proposals for continuation. The final version of ACE was estimated to be ready at the end of April 2004. CRM phase 3 is the global roll-out that will take place in four main waves, each wave will be treated as an individual project and include approximately 400 users. The original time schedule for the CRM phase 3 wave 1 was specified to start first of July 2003 and end 31st of April 2004.

The countries/regions participating in the first have been: China, Malaysia (incl. Vietnam), Mid Europe (Denmark, Germany, Austria and Switzerland) and France. Within each wave a specific sub-project will be set up for each sales company. The project team will be staffed with people from the local organisation with a local project manager. For each sub-project there will also be a dedicated ACE team, with a project coordinator, from the Sales Tools Group (Corporate IT) supporting the local project. The local project leader reports to the steering committee for the local sub-project. The project manager for the implementation wave in question will report to the local sub-projects in each wave as one consolidated project to the Central Steering Committee.

9.4 Findings

This section presents the evaluation findings. It is organized around themes that emerged from the analysis described in Section 9.2.

9.4.1 Organisational culture and Chinese culture

System implementations are affected by and can affect the organisational culture. One of the reasons for looking at the organisational culture during the evaluation is to see if there is a strong organisational culture that is the same and apparent throughout the whole organisation. We also wanted to see if there are any differences in how the employees that develop and implement ACE perceives the organisational culture compared to how the sales company where ACE is being implemented view their organisational culture since this can affect the implementation.

Surprisingly, we found an unwillingness to share the customer information amongst sales people. This can be related to the fact that personal relationships are considered important in China, but it could also depend on the way sales people traditionally worked in China, i.e. before ACE. That relationship building is important in the sales company is not possible to verify in the evaluation. Cheng et al. (2003) argue that in a Chinese context supervisory commitment plays an important role in employees' job-satisfaction, turn over intention and job performance as well as in their individual and organisational outcome. This is probably true in the sales company in China and for hierarchical organisational cultures in general. Although we assume that supervisory commitment not only plays an important role for the employee's job performance in China but in all the countries in the first wave, since it is an important factor for successful system implementations as well.

9.4.2 Top Management and Project Management

In the case there are two different top management levels to consider: the top management centrally and the top management locally. How the central top management commitment has been will not be examined in this post-implementation evaluation. The commitment from the local top management in China was according to themselves obvious and clear to the employees/users. For the ACE team it was clear even though some of the members thought that they (the management team) said more than they actually did. Even if it is not visible to the end users the local top management has been committed in that they have supplied the users with quite a lot of training occasions and assigned key employees to the project.

An important factor for a best practice project management framework is to have project schedule and plan to reach the projects goals (Umble et al. 2003). There has been a plan and specifications for the different tasks involved in the implementation process for all the countries participating in the first wave. Also monitoring and feedback about the projects progress was done by having both regular meetings and reports in three of the countries. In general the opinion on how the IS SC (Sales Company) co-ordinators have worked and how committed they have been was rated as quite high during the beginning of the implementation, but a bit lower towards the launching of the system. The lower commitment at the end is probably due to the fact the IS SC co-ordinators also are involved in the development of ACE which is an on going process.

Management must be aware of the different social, technical and political sub-systems that co-exist in the organisations and also be aware of their goals, attitudes and objectives otherwise they might work against the CRM implementation (Ocker and Mudambi, 2003). One example in China is that there has been awareness of one small group of older sales employees having difficulties with the English language. The problem being that ACE is in English even if there are possibilities to enter customer information with local language characters. Extra help has been supplied to this group in order to make it possible for them to accept and use ACE in their daily work.

9.4.3 Change management

Employees must understand the vision, purpose and changes that the CRM will lead to (Chen and Popovich, 2003). In the sales companies the vision and the purpose of ACE seems to have been communicated quite well, in some countries better than others. The impact that the system will have on the sales peoples' work seems to have been underestimated to some extent. If this depends on the system not meeting the expectations, the inflexibility to actually align ACE with the countries business processes (BP) or something else is not clear. The work procedures might not have change dramatically, but they have changed for all the end-users. The sales people in China found that they had to spend more time in front of their computers, which for a sales person can be an unwanted change that is great enough to create a negative system view and resistance.

9.4.4 Business Process Reengineering

Chen and Popovich (2003) and Kotrov (2003) argue that IS can be an enabler to change and redesign of BP in order to achieve improvements in organisational performance. We got comments that ACE was inflexible and that it was therefore unnecessary to map BP. But, if a system is inflexible it is very important to map the BP "to be" so that they will support the way the system works and so that users through, for instance, training can understand and be aware of the adjustments needed.

Light (2003) found that some companies had trouble aligning their CRM applications with their business processes. This limitation to the CRM packaged software depends on the tendency to have standardised views of relationship management processes. ACE is not a standard software package from a software vendor. But because ACE is a global system that needs to accommodate all the sales companies within the organisation it is possible that it is quite standardised in its procedures and therefore harder to align with the BP.

Business Process Reengineering (BPR) can be done as a part of a system implementation (Robey et al. 2002). In China some respondents thought that this should not be part of the ACE implementation but a project on its own since a complex CRM system affects so many different BP. In the

ACE case the GAP analysis was supposed to be the BPR and since this was not performed in neither of the countries no formal BPR was done.

9.4.5 CRM system and data quality

The system quality is at the moment not perceived to be very high by the respondents. ACE is said not to be user friendly and the user interface is confusing which could be adding to the local supporting costs and in the end also the central support costs. There are too many bugs, the system is cumbersome to work in and the natural way to do business is not supported by ACE according to the users. The users thought that the information quality in ACE was not good enough and the information was not always reliable and some user worried about old information being in the system. Another thing was that there were not enough customer information in the system depending on restrictions to the level of detailed information possible to type in and display in the system. Users also complained about for instance the format of things like the quotation number, which was to long and not very user friendly.

At the time of this post implementation evaluation ACE users found it quite frustrating to use the system and they did not understand the logics of ACE. Some users work was partly facilitated by ACE. The searching for customer data and finding historical records was for instance easier now when they could use the searching and history functionality in ACE. The data quality has an impact on the user's productivity. One respondent said that they had to phone the customers to confirm and check the customer information quite often and then update with the correct information in ACE. This procedure was thought to be quite time consuming.

Collecting and reviewing existing customer data records is vital for the CRM implementation and all people interviewed agrees with this. The data cleaning process started fairly early in the ACE implementation process, but for China it took more time and resources than expected even though it as been rather thorough some of the common problems pointed out by Ryals and Payne (2001) like missing customer data and out of date information about the customer is still a problem affecting the respondents' daily work.

9.4.6 User acceptance

Nelson et al. (1991) argue that if an organisation wants the employees to accept an IS they must make sure that the employees have the ability to use it. One way to make sure the employees have the ability to use the system is to offer enough and satisfactory training. All the countries in the first wave appear to have been very aware of the need for training and have also supplied their users with quite a lot of end-user training.

User involvement is according to Hartwick and Barki (1995) important in explaining system use. End user involvement in the ACE implementation project has not included the end users very much. They have, in China, been asked to supply the ACE team with their business cards for the data cleaning but that activity does not mean that they have been involved in the implementation. The usage behaviour can be reasonably predicted between two to four months after roll-out according to Rawstorne et al. (2000) which means that the usage behaviour is to early to control just a couple of weeks after go live, but for the end users in China that started to use the system at the first go live date more than two months had passed at the time of the interviews.

9.4.7 Training

Krumbholz et al. (2000) points out that one of the main reasons for failure of large and complex systems is the lack of adequate training. The cost of training and support is often under-estimated and is usually a lot higher than originally anticipated and this is probably the case for the ACE implementation as well, due to the fact that there has been more training occasion than what was predicted in the plans from the beginning. Making the training content as similar as possible to the user's actual job enhances user's learning, motivation and actual usage according to Gallivan (2000). The training was modified with cases that had local customer names etc. but no real local adjustments were made when central IT had their training sessions. To be able to get the full benefits of a complex system like a CRM application it is necessary to show the users how the application enables different strategies and different approaches to the user's job and this can be done through behavioural training that focuses on developing new job practices. To be able to do this during central training more involvement from the local ACE team would have been necessary. The central training is more or less the same in all the different countries and is not adjusted according to the country specific guidelines.

Should the users be able to play around with the system before the first end-user training or not? It depends on if it is better for the users to have seen the application before training and perhaps be able to ask questions, or if the philosophy is that it is better to be able to direct the users so they will not make mistakes and learn things that they later on have to unlearn and relearn. Kleintrop et al. (1994) proposes that letting users use, play around with and practice skills necessary in the system before implementation is an important condition for achieving successful use of the system. In the ACE case users are able to use and practice the system before launching at the training session. If users should be able to see and play around in the system on their own before the first end user training is up to the local ACE teams to decide as there are both advantages and disadvantages to consider. Co-discovery learning where users are interacting with a co-worker while engaging in discovery learning, can be used on the job or at traditional class room training and some respondents would have like more discussions and interaction at the training sessions. Another finding is that employee's usage is influenced by co-workers more than formal training (Gallivan, 2000) and this is probably true and also somewhat confirmed by statements where the respondents say that training is one thing and actually using the system is something else. When the users get stuck and do not know what to do them usually prefer to ask a super user and most probably in the future their co-workers as they with time will be more knowledgeable in how ACE works.

Apart from enhancing employee's skills and knowledge, education can boost motivation and commitment as well as reduce employee's resistance to the CRM application (Xia and Lee, 2000) and the accompanying change. The first central training session did not precisely affect the motivation and commitment positively or reduce the resistance to the application. What it might have done is lower the expectations of the system so that the end users got a more realistic picture of what they would be able to expect from ACE. Unfortunately negative impressions last longer and has a greater impact than positive ones and from the comments about the central training and what people remembered negative impact seems to last for quite some time. Goodhue (1995) suggests that the users that had support closer to them found the software to be easier to use and felt they got more of the assistance they needed and this is probably a correct observation and possibly one of the reasons for using super users for close and direct support. When using super users it is important that they can help the regular user and in China they have had extra super user training to secure good support.

It is common that training is focused on while a system is being implemented and especially just before go live dates. But later on when the user is familiar with the system and comfortable using it no training opportunities are offered. For complex systems like a CRM system there might be a need for even more follow up training, not immediately after the go live date but later on in order to use the system to its full potential and not let it become a global customer data base. But obviously the local top management in co-operation with the maintenance team is supposed to assess what needs to be done in the future to secure good usage of ACE.

9.5 Action items

The result of the evaluation were summarised and presented as action items to the project management in Lund. These action items are presented below and some of them have been implemented and thereby have had an impact on further implementations.

Better Resource Planning and Allocation: Lack of especially central resources was something that the sales companies were worrying about, especially since their maintenance teams still needed a lot of central back up and many bugs were still in the system.

Time and timing: Timing – the IS SC co-ordinator need to push the local ACE teams to finish activities on time and with "high quality". "High quality" implies in this case for instance that the customer data is classified according to predefined categories. Something else that needs to be considered is that having long (more than one year) implementation processes might lead to loss of focus from all levels (local steering committees, local ACE teams, end users and central IT) in the organisation.

Acceptance testing: The time allocated for acceptance testing was not enough, the local project teams did not realise the importance of the testing and consequences from not having a proper acceptance test. Furthermore was there no clearly stated testing procedures specified from local or central project teams. For the next wave this must not be forgotten or overlooked since the impact of not having the system ready in time for end user training has very negative impact on the general user acceptance and in the end the users' willingness to use the system according to set procedures and guidelines.

Training and super users: Central IS SC co-ordinators need to find a way to involve and use the super users more during training sessions in the sales companies. This is good both from a super user's learning perspective and can also be a way to better assess the language problem that might exist in some countries. Something else that could be considered more is what other training possibilities are there, except classroom based end user training? Examples of other training scenarios could be; self training programs, web based learning programs or virtual classrooms or on the job training. This is not just something for central IT to think about but also for the local maintenance teams since they might be the ones that should supply training during the ACE system's lifetime and perhaps not only when there are system updates.

Information and communication: How to communicate and inform employees was discussed during the first project manager workshop and communication plans were established for the different sales companies. But something that was overlooked and forgotten was general information to other countries not involved in the current wave. More information is also needed to the sales companies that have already implemented the system and for sale companies that are going to implement so that they can keep themselves updated on what is going on with the ACE project from a global perspective.

Usability: In the development phase the developers used scenarios and cases to make specifications for user requirements. A usability expert has also been consulted but still a lot of users in China did not feel that the procedures in ACE support the natural way of working with business. Perhaps this is a cultural thing and the users that were asked to participate in development have other preferences and procedures than the Chinese users. To make sure that ACE is user friendly it might be a good idea to validate and test the usability again. Not just with an expert but with actual users from different sales companies.

Integration or missing functionality: Integration with other systems was something that the users mentioned were less than optimal at the moment. There were for instance a lot of bugs related to opening a calculating system from the ACE application and end users would also like more integration with already existing systems. Another functionality related future requirement was for external sales people to be able to access and use ACE.

User forum, bugs and request handling: The user forum as it was when the interviews were conducted was not good enough for the local maintenance leaders. It was hard to find information due to unclear structure and the response times were slow from central IT.

9.6 Concluding remarks

Alfa Laval's CRM concept which is stated to be customer centric, based on getting more new customers, keeping customers and growing. Is in general well aligned with what is stated in the research literature to be important for an organisation to consider before implementing a CRM system. Sales people, who are said to be important for a good CRM implementation, have been very involved in the local ACE projects. Although one problem with involving and relying on sales people is that they need to share their time between selling and working with ACE. This competition for time was something that was obvious, but not impossible to overcome, to many of the ACE team members in China.

Finally, even if the first wave of implementing countries has closed their local ACE projects there is still a lot of work to be done in regards to maintenance and user acceptance of the system. At Alfa Laval the majority of the users seems to be willing to give ACE more time and understands and accepts that the system is not perfect from the start. This means that there still is a chance to make this implementation a success and beat the odds.

9.7 References

Ashurst, C. and Doherty, N. (2003) "Towards the Formulation of a 'Best Practice' Framework for Benefits Realisation in IT Projects", *Electronic Journal of Information Systems Evaluation,* Vol. 6, No. 2, pp1-10

Chen, I. and Popovich, K. (2003) "Understanding customer relationship management (CRM) – People, process and technology", *Business Process Management,* Vol. 9, No. 5, pp672-688

Cheng, B., Jiang, D. and Riley, J. (2003) "Organizational commitment, supervisory commitment, and employees outcomes in the Chinese context: Proximal hypothesis or global hypothesis?", *Journal of Organizational Behavior,* Vol. 24, No. 3, pp313-334

Gallivan, M. (2000) "Examining Workgroup Influence on Technology Usage: A Community of Practice Perspective", *Proceedings of the 2000 ACM SIGCPR conference on Computer Personnel research*

Goodhue, D. (1995) "Understanding user evaluations of information systems", *Management Science,* Vol. 41, No. 12, pp1827-1845

Hartwick, J. and Barki, H. (1994) "Explaining the Role of User Participation in Information System Use", *Management Science,* Vol. 40, No. 4, pp440-465

Kleintrop, W., Blau, G. and Currall, S (1994) "Practice makes use: using information technologies before implementation and the effect on acceptance by end users" *Proceedings of the 1994 computer personnel research conference on Reinventing IS: managing information technology in changing organizations.*

Kotrov, R. (2003) "Customer Relationship Management: strategic lessons and future directions" *Business Process Management Journal,* Vol. 9, No. 5, pp566-571

Krumbholz, M., Galliers, J., Coulianos, N. and Maiden, N. (2000) "Implementing enterprise resource planning packages in different corporate and national cultures", *Journal of Information Technology,* Vol. 15, No. 4, pp267-279

Light, B. (2003) "CRM packaged software: a study of organisational experiences", *Business Process Management Journal,* Vol. 9, No. 5, pp603-616

Nelson, R., Kattan, M., and Cheney, P. (1991) "An empirical re-examination of the relationship among training, ability, and the acceptance of information technology", *Proceedings of the 1991 conference on SIGCPR* pp. 177-186

Ocker, R. and Mudambi, S. (2003) "Assessing the Readiness of Firms for CRM: A Literature Review and Research Model", *Proceedings of the 36th Hawaii International Conference on System Science 2003* pp. 181-190

Rawstorne, P., Jayasuriya, R. and Caputi, P. (2000) "Issues in predicting and explaining usage behaviours with the technology theory of planned behavior when usage is mandatory", *Proceedings of the twenty first international conference on Information Systems*

Robey, D., Ross, Jeanne, W. and Boudreau, M-C. (2002) "Learning to Implement Enterprise Systems: An Exploratory Study of the Dialects of Change", *Journal of Management Information Systems,* Vol. 19, No. 1, pp17-46

Ryals, L. and Payne, A. (2001) "Customer relationship management in financial services: towards information enabled relationship marketing", *Journal of Strategic Marketing,* Vol. 9, No. 1, pp3-27

Umble, E. Haft, R. and Umble, M. (2003) "Enterprise Resource planning: Implementation procedures and critical success factors", *European Journal of Operational Research*, Vol. 146, No. 2, pp241-57

Xia, W. and Lee, G. (2000) "The influence of persuasion, training and experience on user perceptions and acceptance of IT innovation", *Proceedings of the twenty first international conference on Information Systems*

9.8 Summary on a Page, using Toulmin's Argument structure:

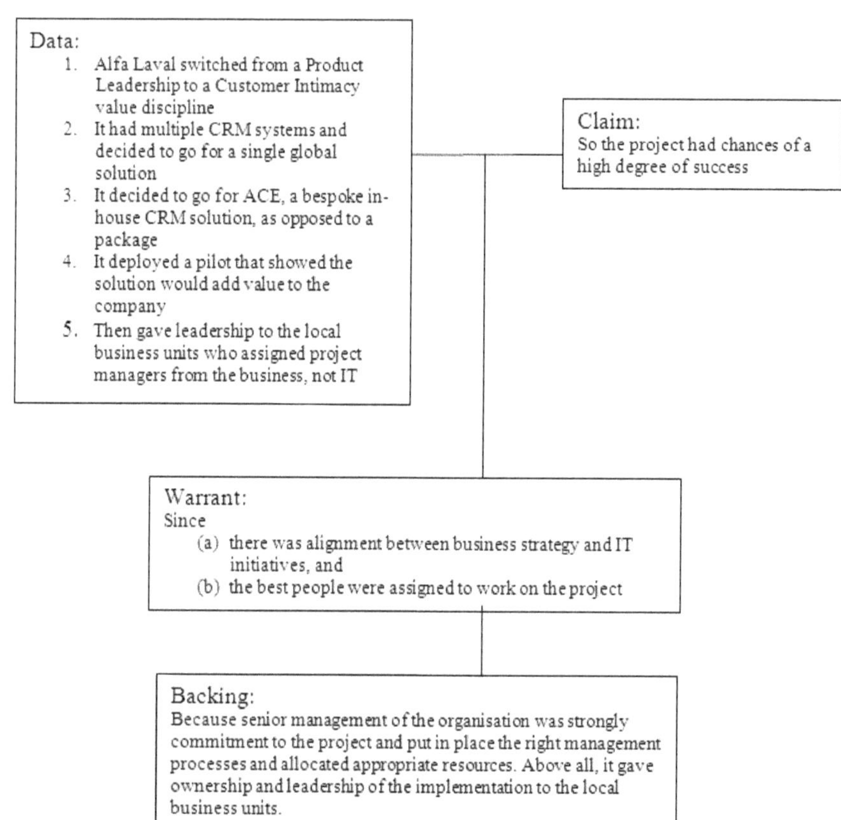

9.9 Case Study Review

Date of Review:	28JAN11
My Reference: ISBN: Other Reference:	IM.256
Title/Document:	Evaluation of a CRM System Implementation in China, ECITE 2005 Proceedings, pp.129-136
Author/Date:	Carlsson, S., Frygell, L. & Hedman, J. (2005)
Source:	ECITE Proceedings
Theme:	Success and failure factors in CRM implementation projects; a post-implementation evaluation.
Purpose of Paper:	To evaluate the first wave of implementation roll-out of a CRM solution for Alfa Laval, with an aim at incorporating lessons learned into the following waves. The study is done on the basis of one country implementation (i.e., China) of a group of countries that this wave comprised.
Classification/Philosophy:	Basic research/Interpretive
Hypotheses/Research Question:	The authors do not specify a research question, but it can be inferred that the question is: What lessons can be learned from the China implementation that would increase the chances of success in other Alfa Laval markets?
Methodology:	Single case study (lost opportunity to carry out an Action Research project). Qualitative. Evidence collection was mainly based on interviews, but supported by other methods such as observation and analysis of documents. There were also visits

	and telephone meeting with members of the Laval offices in Nordic Countries and USA. There were a total of twenty four interviews with 23 informants. The first interview was completely open with the Global ACE Project Manager; the output of that interview served as input for designing a semi-structured interview guide for interviews with the Sales Companies' IS co-ordinators, which in turn served to refine guides for interviewing the 'regular' users. From the description of the design of the interview guides, it can be inferred that on the Deductive-Inductive spectrum, this research is skewed towards the Inductive end. However, when the authors describe their analysis method they appear to have categorised the evidence into "themes which corresponded to the factors critical for systems implementations as suggested in the research literature," which moves them straight back into the deductive camp. As is common in this approach, the evidence collection and evidence analysis phases are intertwined. Analysis was done through a theme, coding and pattern matching process. The categories that emerged from the analysis appear to be: "Organsational culture and Chinese culture", "Senior Management and Project Management", "Change Management", "Business Process reengineering", "CRM system and data quality", "User acceptance", "Training". Or did they emerge from the literature and were then input for the analysis? Finally, the authors say the "material was analysed several times looking for different patterns in the total material and also in the material grouped by project roles, gender, previous IS implementation experience..." so it appears they combined holistic

	and reductionist treatments of the evidence.
Results:	See Managerial Implications and Lessons Learned
Managerial Implications:	Quality is essential for system acceptance, but also time and timing are important: focus at all levels is lost if a project of this kind lasts over a year. Alfa Laval's strategy of becoming customer centric, based on capturing and retaining customers, and growing, is a highly favourable environment for a CRM implementation. Alfa Laval heavily involved its sales staff in the deployment of this CRM solution. Despite the short term cost of this approach in terms of sales force distraction from sales, the company is confident of getting a payback on the project in the longer term. Despite that at the time of this research, shortly after going live with the system, there was still a lot of work to do to obtain the benefits from the project, the majority of the users were willing to give the initiative more time to get it right. That is an indication that this implementation has good chances of becoming a success.
Limitations / Future Research:	
Critique and Learning:	It would be interesting to have described why Alfa Laval challenged the trend and decided to go for a bespoke, in-house, CRM solution (which they call ACE) as opposed to a world class standard package, of which there were several well established alternatives at the time of the decision. On the basis of the pilot implementation, Alfa Laval decided that "the system could add significant value" to its business units. One would think that

	making explicit the criteria on which this decision was based is key to understanding the case. The authors find it "surprising" that the sales people in China were unwilling to share customer information with other people. They attributed this to that "personal relationships are considered important in China". Would it not be more straight forward to assign this to the fact that salespeople lose power when they lose their grip on customer information? **Lessons Learned:** Alfa Laval appeared to shift its value discipline from "Product Leadership" to "Customer Intimacy"; it supported this shift with the implementation of a global CRM solution rather than a multitude of different solutions per country and process that it had before. Alfa Laval assigned leadership for the CRM implementation in the different markets, to the local business unit. The local business provided the Project Manager and staffed the project team. The Global ACE project gave support from the centre and support with local IS staff. Alfa Laval's senior management support was made evident not only in words, but also tough acts: (a) Freeing-up end-users for extensive training; and (b) Assigning key people (with potential) to the project team. Senior managements' commitment seemed to drop-off towards the end of the project, close to the go-live date, but even then was still quite high. This is probably aligned with the authors' conclusion that these projects need to be kept short in duration, and certainly below one year. With reference to Change Management, despite

	some inconveniences for end users in terms of having to spend more time in front of a screen, it appears to have worked quite well. It should be kept in mind that IS-SC is a sales company were the majority of staff are focused on sales and thus a CRM application directly benefits their work. *{This seems to corroborate that change manage ment is not such a big issue when dealing with a customer facing solution whose project is being led by the business - as opposed to IT}.* CRM System and Data Quality: Quality is not perceived to be very high because of the 'bugs' (this problem would have been less severe with a world class package) and, which is more surprising, "the system is cumbersome to work in and the natural way to do business" is not supported by it. One would have thought that this would have been the main criteria for adopting a custom-made system as opposed to a CRM package. On the other hand "searching for customer data and finding historical records" was significantly facilitated *{this is well aligned with the Alfa Laval having switched to a Customer Intimacy value discipline.}* Training: An interesting insight from this research is that co-worker's influence on the adoption of a new system is more important than training, so that is why super-users are so important.

Chapter 10

Valuing Tacit Knowledge in Engineering Services (Netherlands)

This case study narrates the experience of a Dutch engineering consultancy in the Transport Planning space that engages in a programme to improve the quality of its services by improving its knowledge management. It does so by incorporating a social networking tool such as *wiki* to promote knowledge sharing in a horizontal fashion across the whole organisation.

The case study will highlight that implementing a wiki tool for this purpose will encounter challenging cultural and behavioural issues. In the cultural domain it is worth mentioning that a project like this requires the organisation to start valuing "soft" knowledge components contained in people's minds in the form of tacit knowledge in additional to the "hard" explicit knowledge that can be shared through technical and scientific white papers. Or the fact that using these tools is far more natural to the younger people in the organisation than to the elder ones. On the behavioural front, there is resistance by the most experienced people in the organisation to adopt the tool because, until it achieves a certain maturity, they will find they are contributing to the tool far more than they are getting from it.

A review of by now classic knowledge management theory, the adoption of a Web 2.0 tool, and the struggle of a company to excel in a *product leadership* value discipline, make this case study highly useful to attempt to extend our theory of converting ICT investments into value.

Wiki-Based Knowledge Management in a Transport Consultancy, a Case Study

Robbert in 't Hout, Jos Vrancken, Pieter Schrijnen
Delft University of Technology, The Netherlands

Abstract: Developing a Municipal Traffic and Transport Plan (MTTP) is a long lasting and complex process. Many different disciplines are involved, as well as many stakeholders. The process may take more than two years. The larger municipalities in the Netherlands mostly develop their own plans. But for the medium sized and smaller municipalities private consultancies play a major role in the development of the MTTPs. This article describes a case study concerning improving the MTTP development process in such a consultancy. The company did reasonably well in the field, but could do better: a part of the knowledge present in the company wasn't shared well enough, especially the exchange of knowledge and experience between senior and junior consultants which needed improvement. To improve the sharing, a wiki was developed. In interaction with the consultants a structure was proposed, allowing them to add the information they valued relevant for the development of the MTTPs. The wiki appeared to reveal not only explicit knowledge, but also tacit knowledge. On top of that, the tacit knowledge often was personal, subjective, and even divergent. The juniors were more eager to work with the wiki than the seniors. There still exists a difference between the generations in their ability and readiness to use ICT tools. Sharing the tacit knowledge, revealing the subjective perspectives of the consultants was confronting the company with its implicit learning styles. The staff of the company believed they worked with objective knowledge, and that only such knowledge was relevant in planning and decision making. The wiki revealed that the subjective aspects actually played a role within the company. After some interactions with the manager of the department, the structure of the wiki was adapted. One part of the wiki was meant for explicit, objective knowledge; the other part for tacit, subjective knowledge. Arrangements were made to create the role of moderator for the themes in the wiki - seniors that could decide how to deal with the subjective information. The conclusion of this case can be that wikis aren't just neutral tools. They need to be tuned to the learning styles that are available within the community that will use the tool. Pilots can help in revealing the way organisations deal with knowledge management. The article follows the chronology of the project. It starts with a short picture of the process of developing an MTTP and with a summary of the learning theories used to assess the challenges of the company. The article proceeds with the design of the wiki and the introduction of the first layout. It then describes the reactions from the consultants and the manager, and the adaptation of the wiki. The article ends with some conclusions on the way wikis can be designed.

Keywords: municipal traffic and transport planning, wiki, social software, knowledge management

Originally published in the Electronic Journal of IS Evaluation Volume 13, Issue 2, pp. 133-142.

10.1 Introduction

Traffic and transport are indispensable aspects of a town, related to virtually every other aspect, such as employment, environment, spatial planning, safety and social equity. Careful planning of traffic and transport and its infrastructure is therefore a major concern for every municipality. In the Netherlands every municipality is required by law to organise traffic and transport by a policy plan. This policy plan is known as the Municipal Traffic and Transport Plan (MTTP). After the final decision making an MTTP is valid for a period of about fifteen years.

Developing an MTTP is a highly complex process, usually taking about two to three years. It involves many different disciplines (economy, environment, public transport, traffic safety, etc.) and many stakeholders (such as citizens, drivers, bicyclists, pedestrians, Chamber of Commerce, companies, NGOs). Due to the complexity of the development of an MTTP and due to the fact that a municipality develops these plans only once every fifteen years, the development of an MTTP is usually done in close cooperation with consultant companies specialised in traffic and transport planning.

These companies also need to deal with the complexity and diversity of the process. Within the companies, various specialists are involved in the development of MTTPs. Their involvement is often temporary and often applies only to a single topic within an MTTP. A project manager will be responsible for the whole process. She has to integrate the generated knowledge, and has to keep the overview of the process within the company and within the municipality.

One of these companies asked for help in improving customer satisfaction. It turned out that the knowledge management practices within the company offered a good opportunity for improvement in order to achieve this goal. The article describes how a wiki, a kind of social software, was applied to enhance the knowledge management practices. The introduction of the wiki generated some resistance: it confronted the company with the lack of diversity in learning styles. The wiki was adapted to meet that challenge as well.

The article is organised as follows. Section 10.2 explains the research objective and research approach followed. Section 3 is about key notions and theoretical foundations. Section 10.4, 10.5 and 10.6 describe the company characteristics and the tooling built to support its knowledge management. Section 10.7 contains the evaluation of both the tool and the process of its introduction. The final section summarizes conclusions and recommendation that follow from the evaluation.

10.2 Challenge and approach

The challenge as expressed by the consultancy wasn't specific enough to create a well defined project plan. Improving customer satisfaction can be done in many ways. To support the company we chose to execute an in-company case study, in accordance with the recommendations from (Yin, 2003, pp. 13-14). The research plan had a flexible character, tuning its activities in accordance with the findings during the project. The true nature of the challenge indeed became clear during the course of the research. The approach described below is the approach actually followed. It comprised the following three phases.

10.2.1 Problem analysis and determining the research objective

The problem analysis was done in three steps:

- Discovering how the company perceived its own problem, by means of interviews (section 10.4).
- A theoretical analysis of knowledge management and learning processes, by means of a literature study (section 10.3).
- An investigation into current knowledge management practices and the support for learning processes in the company (section 4).

The theoretical analysis showed the importance of the distinction between explicit and implicit knowledge, as explained in the next section. It also revealed the variety of the learning styles actually in use in different organisations. This made it necessary to find out what knowledge-related practices in the company were available. The literature also indicated that sharing implicit knowledge might create a challenge for the organisation and would require a learning process itself.

The first set of interviews pointed out that the internal exchange of knowledge and experiences could be improved. The level of exchange of knowledge and experiences between senior and junior consultants, and between consultants with different expertise, was low. In consultation with the company the project moved towards creating a tool for this exchange.

10.2.2 Selection, building, filling and deployment of a prototype of the tool

In this phase, a particular kind of social software, the wiki, was selected as a promising device for the exchange. The prototype was built as a tool to store and exchange explicit knowledge. It also offered a number of functions to support the externalisation of tacit knowledge, such as commenting on the value and applicability of the explicit knowledge in the wiki, and storing experiences, recommendations and opinions. The prototype was filled with a fair amount of explicit knowledge on two specific topics of MTTP development. It was also filled with personal views and experiences, perceived as relevant to the authors. This device was deployed and advertised in the company (sections 10.5 and 10.6).

10.2.3 Evaluation and adaptation

An evaluation of the prototype by means of interviews with users and staff led to some practical adaptations. But the evaluation also revealed a number of constraints in the way the company could handle different forms of knowledge. The staff had trouble with the sharing of personal views and intuitions. The wiki had to be restructured into a double system: one part for explicit knowledge, one part for the tacit knowledge. Moderators were appointed that could discriminate the quality of the contributions.

After the adaptations, a final evaluation of both the tool and the process of development and introduction was done. It resulted in a number of recommendations on how the consultancy can support their knowledge management practices with a tool such as a wiki and how company culture can be changed by such a tool and has to be changed for the viability of such a tool (section 10.7).

10.3 Knowledge and learning

This section gives the theoretical framework for the project. *Knowledge* and *learning* are complex notions for which various definitions can be found in literature. The section starts with an overview of definitions of knowledge. It then focuses on mental models and ends with theories on learning, for individuals and organisations.

Literature on knowledge and knowledge creation often distinguishes two types of knowledge. The terms depend on the specific field of the researchers, but the analogy is remarkable. The main distinction is knowledge as stock versus or knowledge as flow, Mode 1 knowledge and Mode 2 knowledge, or explicit knowledge versus tacit knowledge.

The stock-approach uses the perspective that knowledge is an objective entity. It can exist outside individuals. Knowledge can be stored in knowledge systems. The flow-approach links knowledge with experiences, perceptions, and attitudes. In this view knowledge is a competency (Kessels 2001).

The distinction between Mode 1 knowledge and Mode 2 knowledge (Mode 1 K and Mode 2 K) addresses the difference between scientific knowledge and knowledge generated in actual decision making. Mode 1 K refers to traditional scientific knowledge, structured in disciplines, each with their own rules for the generation of new knowledge. Universities are the birthplace of such knowledge. Mode 2 K is application-oriented; it relates its relevance to the context in which it is generated and applied. Policy processes often need Mode 2 K more than Mode 1 K (Gibbons et al. 1994, Gray 1999, Robertson 1999).

An analogous distinction often made is the distinction between *implicit* and *explicit* knowledge (Nonaka 2000, Brömmelstroet & Schrijnen 2009). Explicit knowledge is knowledge that can be stored in data systems, libraries, on paper or on any other information carrier. Implicit knowledge, also known as *tacit knowledge*, is the knowledge possessed by human beings which is stored in their thoughts, behaviour and even in their identity. Examples of implicit knowledge are experience, skills and intuition (Nonaka 2000).

Some implicit knowledge can be made explicit almost effortless, and therefore is easy to share with others. This is for example factual knowledge like the organisation of a municipality: who can be addressed as responsible for each element of the planning process. Other tacit knowledge is harder to share, for example when a senior consultant shows his sophisticated technique to deal with a group of stakeholders to his junior, who is not able to copy his technique directly (or even in years).

People may not be aware of the implicit knowledge they hold. Large difficulties can be encountered before such knowledge is made explicit. A good example for this kind of knowledge is intuition. The difference between tacit and explicit knowledge becomes obvious in the difference between a professional with years of experience and a junior consultant, who just graduated and who may have a good command of explicit knowledge in the field, but lacks the tacit knowledge that can only be acquired by years of experience. Facts and figures are often quite obvious, with the right modelling program they can be achieved easily. The interpretation of such data is done through years of experience, processed into tacit knowledge. This is where the quality of consultancy companies can be found.

A second important notion is that of the *mental models* that each individual holds (Senge 2006, Rudrauf et al. 2003, Forrester 1975). Research in the field of cognitive psychology and the recent brain sciences reveal the same type of insight into the way people perceive the world. Each individual perceives the world through a "filter". This filter selects the input of the outside world on the basis of earlier experiences. The mental models that people hold create these filters. The mental models store the perceptions people have created of all the information and experiences that they acquired during their lives. Information that is new and that cannot be placed in an existing mental model is often discharged, or it is interpreted as the-same-as earlier interpretations.

Through these filters, learning is confined to those fields that the person can handle, whether she is aware of that or not.

These mental models are essentially different for different people. This explains for example why people react differently to the exact same situation. That has nothing to do with the situation, but everything with the person's experiences in the past. This notion is especially important in group processes, for example in consultancy companies. The differences in perception between people become apparent and have to be taken into account.

According to Kolb, learning is a process whereby knowledge is created through the transformation of experience (Kolb 1984). Kolb observed that individual people have different learning styles. People can favour their own feelings or their own actions as the source for learning. They can also favour abstract reflection, or observing others. Most people combine two of these preferences. Kolb observed that people that can handle all four styles are the most competent in learning. He translated this notion into the learning cycle – the process whereby people learn through 1. Concrete experience, 2. Reflective observation, 3. Abstract conceptualisation, and 4. Active experimentation.

Individual people learn best through experiencing, evaluating results, generalising the experience into more generally applicable abstract concepts and lessons, applying the formed abstract concepts in a new activity. Persons that do well in just one or two of these steps fall short when they need to innovate.

This also goes for groups and organisations. Teams that are able to acknowledge variety as a source for learning, and that can apply different learning styles have greater chance to generate more knowledge and become more innovative than individuals. Yet, group learning is more complex than individual learning. Every team has to deal with a variety of learning styles and a variety of mental models. Every team needs to create a common language about the challenges, the roles, and the available experiences. Every team needs to create common scaffold for learning to achieve (Senge 2006, Van den Bossche 2006, Schrijnen 2005).

Nonaka (2000) describes learning in teams and organisations as forms of interaction between implicit and explicit knowledge. People often work together and directly share their experiences and insights. Knowledge is shared or created here through Socialisation. When people make their experience explicit, when they formalise their insights, then one can speak of Externalisation. When people connect different sources of explicit knowledge they actually make a new Combination. And, when people learn to work with the new knowledge, they will Internalise it. Together these four elements create the SECI-model. Nonaka stresses that organisations that can apply this variety of learning strategies do better than organisations that stick to one strategy.

As with individuals, organisations actually appear to have different learning styles. De Caluwé (2006) characterises five types of organisations. The three most relevant types for this paper are: the engineering organisation, the political organisation and the learning organisation.

According to de Caluwé engineering organisations consider themselves to be rational organisations. They prefer to apply and generate explicit knowledge. They work with numerical data, think in terms of measuring, controlling, and engineering. These are often engineering companies, using scientific knowledge to address problems. De Caluwé gives this type of organisation the colour blue.

Municipalities or other public authorities often work as political organisations. Such organisations think in terms of power, interests, conflicts, coalitions, consensus and public support. In the scheme of De Caluwé, their colour is yellow.

The focus of learning organisations is on processes, on motivating people to learn and improve themselves. According to learning organisations, learning and organisational change are strongly connected. Learning organisations are consultancy agencies and organisations that work with processes. Their colour is green.

No organisation fits for one hundred percent in one of these profiles. An organisation characterised as one of the above has always some elements of a different colour, especially when organisations become larger. Yet, most organisations show some preference for one of these cultures, with the analogous learning styles.

It is obvious that in complex working processes a limited set of approaches to perceiving and to learning can be a serious impediment to productivity. The awareness of its own tacit approaches towards knowledge sharing and knowledge creation can be seen as an important asset for any organisation. Being able to switch between styles (or colours) allows organisations to develop themselves to higher levels of performance (De Caluwé 2006).

In conclusion, the project had to reveal the content of the challenge (what kinds of knowledge were needed to improve the MTTP development) as well as to reveal the way the organisation dealt with the process of knowledge management.

10.4 The case study

The case concerns a Dutch traffic and transport consultancy. This company has a dominant position on the MTTP market in the country. This market is dynamic, so the company wants to ensure its future role in this market. The company invited us to work on improving the MTTP development process. Their presumption was that more knowledge about the needs of the clients could help them to create better MTTPs.

The first activities in the company consisted of a series of interviews with junior and senior consultants working in the firm. The interviews addressed the actual activities of the consultants in the MTTP development process, the challenges they met, the internal and external communication, and their intuitions with respect to chances for improvement.

Through these conversations a picture was created shared by most of the interviewed persons. This company is better equipped for vertical communication, the communication in project groups and management, than for horizontal communication, which is the communication between peers and different project groups. The low level of horizontal communication is due to the geographical distribution of various departments of the company. Consultants also often work in the offices of the municipalities.

This constellation gives little room for critical reflection on each others' results among peers. The consultants of the firm also tend to put little effort in sharing their experiences, other than through the sharing of the outcomes of their work – the final plans.

Another outcome is that the level of exchange between the different disciplines within the company appears to be very low. Most communication is between professionals with the same vocational background (for instance modellers, traffic experts, public transport experts).

Besides the low level of reflection the current approach to knowledge management is limited and traditional. It consists of an archive, partly on paper, which is accessible only via the staff managing the archive. It contains exclusively factual knowledge, with little or no reflection on it and no opinions.

These characteristics are in line with the characteristics of a typical blue engineering organisation, with a content focused mentality. Knowledge management is traditionally focused on sharing explicit knowledge, with little interest for the implicit knowledge.

Obviously the implicit knowledge is present within the company. It is being created continuously, by many professionals, and with good quality. Unfortunately those professionals create the same type of knowledge again and again. That asset is not available for the whole organisation, only for those employees who happen to be near the source.

Before this case study the company was not aware of the limitations of the current approach to knowledge storing, sharing and creation and knowledge management as a whole.

The interviews revealed that the collective and the individual's learning processes both need improvement. Furthermore the different professional disciplines in the organisation need to enhance their understanding of the difference between each other's present mental models.

When applying the concepts of Kolb and Nonaka, it is obvious that the company can improve its performance most likely by enhancing the process of observing each other work, by making implicit knowledge explicit. Especially the phase of externalisation needs improvement. That is the phase where the created implicit knowledge is made explicit, where it is made accessible for other members of the company.

10.5 Creating a support system

This analysis was shared with the staff of the consultancy. In close consultation we chose to move the project towards the creation of a support system for the exchange of the knowledge available within the company. This support system should encourage organisation wide knowledge sharing and group learning.

Theoretical considerations and the specific requirements of the company generated these requirements for the support system. The system should:

- Help in finding and accessing explicit knowledge;
- Give information on the current affairs of the colleagues;
- Help to find people with specific expertise, experience and knowledge;
- Support externalise implicit knowledge and thus making it accessible to others;
- Allow people to mirror their own mental models to those of their colleagues;
- Support group-wise reflection, teamwork;
- Support the exchange of tacit knowledge;
- Make interaction place and time independent.

A comparison of various types of social software tools showed the wiki tool as an appropriate answer to these requirements (Wikipedia 2010). A wiki is a form of social software. Social software supports social interaction and collaborative processes. It a web site, but the essential difference with a normal web site is that any reader can add pages and change existing pages. It is a dynamic tool. Wikis can be easily accessible and effortless in use, as well as safe from non-invited intruders.

Wiki software includes or is compatible with most other forms of social software. Other examples are blogging, social tagging, networking sites such as Face book, Twitter, Ning and LinkedIn, and media exchange sites such as YouTube.

The power of a wiki lies within its basic editing principles: it is easy to create, remove, edit a page or link it to another page. The history of the changes (and its authors) is recorded. The editing of a page of a wiki is as simple as working with MS Word.

10.6 The MTTP wiki prototype

The MTTP Wiki has been designed and built according to the requirements listed above and on the basis of several interviews with senior employees. The application was built with Google Sites, which works just fine for a prototype (http://sites.google.com/?pli=1). When the MTTP wiki will extend, a platform within the company will be better for security reasons, and for the integration with other applications.

The experiment started with an empty frame. With the help of a number of employees of the company it has been filled with content. The main structure of the MTTP wiki is:

- Organisational
- Stages of the MTTP Development Process
- Themes

The Organisational part contains an overview of the employees involved in MTTP development, the policy making process of municipalities, the instruments used in MTTP development and a number of practical pages, such as a starting page, help function, user manual, MTTP templates, etc.

The Stages part gives a description per step of the development process of MTTPs. In the case of this company these are: acquisition, proposal, policy development, measures, plan development, use, maintenance and support. Each stage is provided with explicit knowledge, such as checklists, pertinent instruments, models and templates; and implicit knowledge, for instance tips, best practices and personal experiences.

The Themes part gives lots of factual information about a number of relevant subjects or *themes*. Currently included are: transport infrastructure, spatial planning, traffic (car, cycle, pedestrian, and truck), public transport, parking, traffic safety, environment, law enforcement, hazardous goods and speed limits.

The wiki has various search options and a site navigation facility. It also has a blog function per user, to stimulate to share the personal note on the generated knowledge.

Access to the wiki is limited to employees involved in MTTP development. Apart from the fact that the wiki contains confidential information, this is also necessary in order to create the perception of safety, necessary when people are supposed to (constructively) comment on and criticise each others' contributions.

At the time of writing, the content is not yet on the desired level for all parts. But the wiki is already at such a level of quality that it serves as a starting point for the development of an operational wiki on the servers of the company.

10.7 Evaluation of the prototype

The prototype is evaluated in a second round of interviews with the users and intended users of the wiki. Also the manager responsible for the pilot was interviewed. The interviews were taken during the pilot phase. Most of the feedback from the interviews was immediately translated in adapting the wiki.

Some comments could be dealt with easily. Other comments concerned the way the consultants in the company viewed the process of knowledge management. Some of these comments were:

About the practicality of the tool:

- Logging in for the first time was cumbersome; this deterred some potential users.

About the content of the tool:

- A lot of information that one might expect on the wiki was not yet present.

About the process of knowledge sharing:

- For most users the time they invested in the wiki was not yet worth the effort, because they had to add more information than they could retrieve from it;
- Some discussion took already place, concerning content and personal experience, this has been experienced as a useful functionality;
- Positive experiences were mentioned in the acquisition stage; here the wiki was already helpful.

In these comments, there appeared to be a noticeable difference between junior and senior consultants. The senior consultants spent less time on getting to know the wiki. They considered themselves less in need for the information from the wiki. Furthermore they are also less acquainted to the use of computers and social software. The senior consultants were therefore less positive about the concept of a wiki to support the MTTP development process than the junior participants in the experiment. The junior consultants also were less afraid to share uncertainties than the seniors.

The comment of the manager was rather severe. It revealed some of his mental models about learning, and it revealed again the core culture of the company. He said that he expected to receive a full overview of all explicit knowledge available in the organisation, whereas the juniors could live with a wiki as work in progress. Furthermore, he didn't like the fact that people expressed their intuitions, private perspectives, personal reflections. That type of information wasn't relevant for the MTTP development process. He considered it a threat to the quality of the work of the company. He clearly preferred a wiki solely based on objective, explicit knowledge.

In a collaborative reflection on the relevance of sharing tacit knowledge, the manager became aware of the existence of different approaches towards knowledge management and learning. After a while he could acknowledge that his expectation fitted a blue – engineering – organisation, whereas the wiki adhered to a green – learning – organisation. He himself had to reframe his perspective on knowledge management, in order to allow the professionals in his department to communicate and learn in different ways. With this awareness, he could give his support to the new approach.

A further requirement was added to the list:

- Allow people to express opinions while keeping a clear distinction between factual knowledge and opinions.

This requirement gave rise to a redesign of the structure of the wiki. It now has a space for explicit knowledge, and it has a clear space for implicit knowledge, for subjective stories, for blogs, for hunches and questions. The dual structure enables the sharing of both types of knowledge. In this way, the wiki really enables the consultants to work on the externalisation of their implicit knowledge.

In the design of this wiki, it is the responsibility of the contributor to assure the quality of her contribution, for instance by actively inviting others to review it. Simultaneously, for every theme a moderator is appointed to check on a regular base the quality of the content on the wiki.

The quality of knowledge and information added to a wiki is always an important point of attention. Factual information needs to be reliable. The participants that add personal, implicit knowledge and intuition need to do so with integrity. Applying the rule of reliability and integrity allows the professionals of the company to not only share crystallised knowledge, but also to learn form each others hunches, intuitions, questions, personal opinions.

To emphasise this aspect, the texts of the interviews were added to this part of the wiki.

The content of this wiki is in a continuous process of improvement, representing the state of art of the MTTP development within the company. It represents the concept of knowledge as flow, as well as the concept of knowledge as stock. This approach mirrors the way blue cultures learn.

So, the experiment did have several important second order effects:

- The organisation became aware of the opportunities that tools such as a wiki can have;
- The organisation became aware of its lack of horizontal communication among peers.

- The organisation also became aware of the effort that it takes to introduce and fill a wiki and to keep it alive. It realised how radical and comprehensive the change would be when seriously introducing a wiki and adapting work procedures to it. This would be little short of a change in company culture.

Overall, given the fact that there already was a clear need for change, the experiment ended with the company becoming genuinely interested in the new concepts, the new way of working and the tools supporting it. It was going to seriously consider the strategic decisions needed to develop and introduce an operational wiki, for MTTP development as well as for its other activities.

10.8 Conclusions and recommendations

This case study was about improving the process of developing municipal traffic and transport plans in a medium sized consultancy, by means of enhanced knowledge management. The core idea was to support this knowledge management using a social software tool, the wiki. This choice was based on theories on knowledge, learning and knowledge management. The implementation of the wiki created another level of learning within the company – not just on the content of the MTTPs, but also on the way the company dealt with knowledge management. The case study leads to two main conclusions.

A wiki can be very useful for the purposes of knowledge sharing and group wise learning in complex development processes. It has a number of practical functions:

- It serves as a database for implicit and explicit knowledge;
- It helps in sharing knowledge and experiences acquired during development processes;
- It helps to find experts and their knowledge in specific areas;
- It helps in organising the reliability of the resources it offers;

It also has a number of functions that have to do with the learning culture in an organisation:

- It helps people to make their mental models explicit and become aware of their subjectivity;

- It helps in creating knowledge collectively, in a group process, in which contributions from one participant are reviewed and adapted by others; it stimulates exchanging tacit knowledge;
- It stimulates peer-to-peer, horizontal communication; among other things, it is not hampered by place and time dependency, such as in voice communication, or ordinary meetings.

The introduction of a wiki in a large organisation will meet lots of difficulties. This has to do with the fact that the development, filling and introduction of a wiki are short term cost factors, whereas the benefits are long term. When in use, contributing to it remains a short term cost factor with no immediate benefit. In situations under time pressure, more common that not in consultancy companies, there will be a tendency to only consume from the wiki and not to contribute to it. Without extra measures to deal with this problem, there is a serious risk that the endeavour may fail.

This brings us to the following recommendation for consultancy companies that consider the introduction of a wiki as a tool for knowledge management. Such a step can require a fundamental change in the company culture. A change like this can only be successful when based on a strategic decision with comprehensive commitment from all levels of the company.

A wiki requires a minimal size and a minimal level of regular contributions in order to become viable and fruitful to its participants. First of all, it should be made easily accessible independent of the user's location, safe and attractive to use, and adequately supported by the necessary training and maintenance. Until it reaches the critical mass, most people will consider it a cost factor. that it will remain a cost factor as long as it has not yet reached critical mass. Support by management is necessary to overcome the short-term-cost-versus-long-term-benefit problem. One may think of measures such as the following:

- Measure the contributions to the wiki per employee and reward those that contribute to it more than average. Refer to these data in the regular performance interviews with employees.
- Integrate the wiki into standard working procedures. If project management data and project repositories become part of the

wiki, it will become nearly impossible to write proposals or project deliverables according to company standards without the wiki. Even though this is not the primary goal of the wiki, it helps in achieving regular use of it and thereby helps to achieve its primary goals in knowledge creating and knowledge sharing.

- Stimulate especially the junior employees to work with the wiki. Stimulate them to help senior employees to get involved with the wiki too.

However difficult it may be to introduce social software tools such as wiki's, one should be well aware that the productivity gains of an effective knowledge sharing and group collaboration tool are likely to be considerable and may become a decisive competitive factor in the near future.

10.9 References

Van den Bossche, N. (2006) Minds in teams. The influence of social and cognitive factors on team learning. Thesis, Delft University of Technology, Delft.

Brömmelstroet, M. te, P.M. Schrijnen (2009) From Planning Support Systems to Mediated Planning Support, Environment and Planning B: Planning and Design, Vol 37 no. 1, pp. 3-20.

De Caluwé, L. de, H. Vermaak (2006) Learning to Change: A guide for Organizational Change Agents, Sage, Thousand Oaks, Cal.

Forrester, J.W. (1975) Collected Papers of Jay Forrester, Productivity Press, New York.

Gibbons, M., Limoges, C., Nowotny, H., Schwartzman, S., Scott, P. & Trow. M. (1994) The new production of knowledge, Sage, London.

Gray, H. (1999). Re-scoping the university, in: H. Gray (Ed.) Universities and the creation of wealth. Buckingham: The Society for Research into Higher Education & Open University Press.

Kessels, J.W.M. (2001). Verleiden tot kennisproductiviteit (Seducing towards knowledge generation). Inaugural speech as Professor Human Resource Development. University of Twente, Enschede.

Kolb, D. A. (1984). Experiential learning: Experience as the Source of Learning and development. Prentice Hall, New Jersey

Nonaka, I., R. Toyama, N. Konno (2000). SECI, Ba and leadership: a Unified Model of Dynamic Knowledge Creation. In: Longe Range Planning, 33 (1) pp 5-34.

Robertson, D. (1999). Knowledge societies, intellectual capital and economic growth. In: H. Gray (Ed.) Universities and the creation of wealth. Buckingham: The Society for Research into Higher Education & Open University Press.

Rudrauf, D., A. Lutz, D. Cosmelli, J.-P. Lachaux and M. Le Van Quyen (2003): From autopoiesis to neurophenomenology: Francisco Varela's exploration of the biophysics of being. In: Biological Research 36 (1), pp. 27-65.

Schrijnen, P.M. (2005) Training professionals for Cross-Boundary Planning, Transportation research record, 1931, pp 1-7.

Senge, P. M. (2006). The fifth discipline, the art & practice of the learning organisation, Random House, London.

Senge, P.M., R. Ross, B. Smith, C. Roberts, A. Kleiner (2000) The fifth discipline fieldbook, Doubleday, New York.

Weggeman, M. (1997). Kennismanagement (Knowledge Management), Scriptum, Schiedam.

Wikipedia (2010). http://en.wikipedia.org/wiki/Wikipedia. Website, accessed July 8, 2010.

Yin, R.K. (2003). Case study research. Design and Methods, Sage Publications Inc., Thousand Oaks, Cal.

10.10 Summary on a Page, using Toulmin's Argument structure:

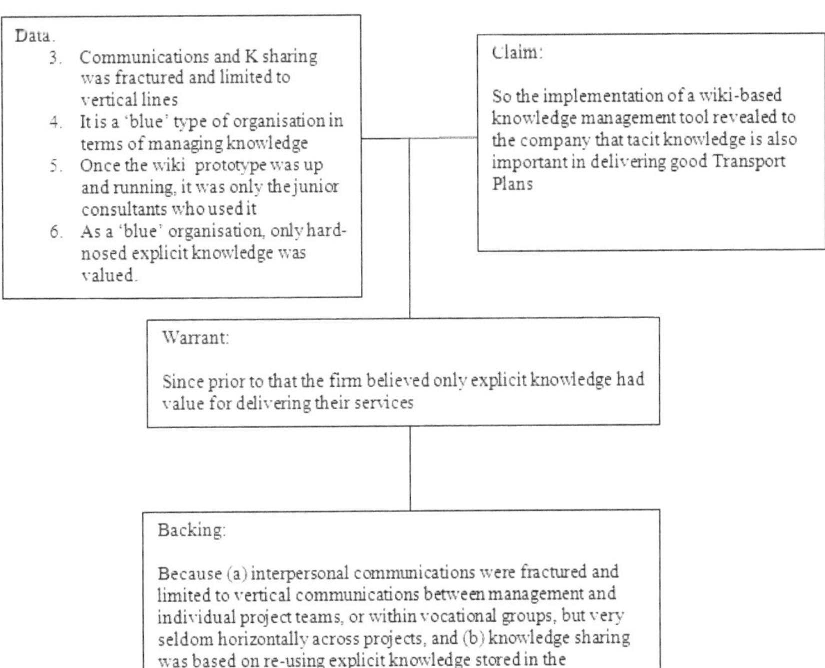

10.11 Case Study Review

Date of Review:	26JAN11
My Reference: ISBN: Other Reference:	IM.255.
Title/Document:	*Wiki-Based Knowledge Management in a Transport Consultancy, a Case Study,* The Electronic Journal Information Systems Evaluation, Volume 13, Issue 2, pp.133 – 142.
Author/Date:	in 't Hout, R., Vrancken, J. & Schrijnen, P. (2010)
Source:	EJISE
Theme:	The paper describes how a wiki, a kind of social software, was applied to enhance knowledge management practices.
Purpose of Paper:	
Classification/Philosophy:	Basic research/ Interpretive.
Hypotheses:	The research question was not explicitly stated. This can be explained by the fact that the objectives of the consultancy that gave place to this project was not specific – it was something generic such as improving customer satisfaction. After starting the scope was focused on improving knowledge management in the organisation.
Methodology:	There is no specific section describing the methodology, as one would expect in an academic paper. It is a single case study, with some clear components of action research. Qualitative. The

	unit of analysis is at company level, in this case a Transport Consultancy. Because the objectives of the intervention were not clear at the outset, and emerged as the project progressed, one would infer that on the Deductive-Inductive scale this research is skewed towards the latter. However, it is not fully Inductive because a literature review on KM was done at the beginning of the project, which helped depart with some concepts in mind. Evidence collection was initially done through interviews to senior and junior consultants, but there was also observation and second interviews at the time the pilot was being implemented. The research can be broken down into three stages: **Stage 1**: A series of interviews to define the problem, which resulted in needing to improve knowledge management. **Stage 2**: Develop a wiki prototype and put it to use. **Stage 3**: Observe the prototype, interview users, evaluate it, make improvements, and re-deploy it.
Results:	The unit of analysis is a 'blue' type organisation. People shared factual, explicit knowledge. However, it emerged that their knowledge sharing is fractured. Communications within the firm tended to be vertical, between management and project groups, or at most between professionals with the same vocational background; but there was very scarce communications horizontally between peers or across project groups. This was made worse by the fact that people worked in different geographies and tend to work at the Clients' offices. The culture is also such that people were not prone to reflecting on projects and

	share those reflections with peers; knowledge sharing was generally limited to the products of their projects. Most transfers were done via the archive, which was still quite paper-based and information obtained through archive clerks. It was decided to set up a support system to encourage organisation-wide knowledge sharing and group learning. This support tool should take the form of a wiki. Once the wiki knowledge management tool was set up, it was found that for most users the time they invested was not yet worth the effort, as they had to add more info than they could retrieve from it. The other issue that emerged is that the most experienced people would not use it. This was in part due to natural affinity with tools such as wiki, but mostly because they are the ones who less needs it. Finally, junior consultants were less afraid of sharing uncertainties. There are many disincentives for the most experienced. So, as a result, those who could most contribute do not get involved because they get little from it! *{This is an interesting insight that will affect the incorporation of most other technologies. It is vital input to be able to define the change management treatment for each project. Reflect on this and relate to the change management approach of each kind of value building project in my model}* When the prototype was presented to the MD of the firm, he did not like the fact that 'soft', opinionated 'knowledge' was getting mixed up in the communications channels with factual, explicit knowledge. The prototype had to be altered to manage both types of knowledge separately and distinctively. The MD had a 'blue' type style, and

	was confronted with a 'green' style tool, which, as theory would anticipate, does not make him receptive. *{Lesson: Knowledge management tools depend heavily on the approach to knowledge management of the organisation's leader.}* The final outcome of this experiment appeared to be that the company became genuinely interested in the new concept, the new way of working, and the tools that support it. However, the researchers do not explain how they overcame the cultural barriers in what appeared to be a short period of time. *{Through these knowledge management changes and tools it appears that the organisation got prepared for delivering a Product Leadership value discipline. Knowledge management at the firm shifted from heavily "technology-based networks" to a "people-based network" model. These are typical strategies of customer intimate and product leadership value disciplines.}*
Managerial Implications:	There is a period after implementation and until it is over a critical size, that the short term costs of contributing to the KM tool exceeds the immediate term benefits. So how are these projects made sustainable? Senior management dogged commitment until the project gets over the hurdle; give incentives for contribution until the tool gets populated; incorporate the wiki into standard working procedures. There is always a tendency to consume more than contribute from one of these systems. How can we overcome this? Through what kind of incentives?
Limitations / Future Research:	

Critique and Learning:	A specific section describing the methodology would considerably improve this paper. Description of the methodology is dispersed throughout several sections of the paper, and some important explanations such as how was the evidence analysed are not explicitly included. **Lessons Learned:** KM Literature: The authors review the by now more or less classic literature, with Nonaka's SECI model for group learning taking a central role. There is an interesting discussion on the role of mental models on learning, and the differences between individual learning and group learning, and highlighting the fact that the latter is more complex than the former because it requires to deal with as many different mental models as participants in the group. The authors also describe Kolb's learning cycle by which people learn through 1. Concrete experience, 2. Reflective observation, 3. Abstract conceptualisation, and 4. Active experimentation. Classification of Knowledge: The authors present 3 different classifications of knowledge, and they all seem to have two categories. The first classification is knowledge as stock (objective entity that can exist outside individuals), or as knowledge as flow which links it with experience, perceptions and attitudes. The second refers to Mode1 (scientific, originated mainly in universities) and Mode 2 (application oriented, where the context in which knowledge is generated is highly relevant). The third is the well known Explicit (can be stored in data systems, in libraries, on paper) and Implicit or tacit, which is possessed by humans and stored in their thought, behaviours and even identities. For the sake of completion, I would also add Popper's classifica-

	tion into Objective knowledge (any knowledge that can be criticised) and Subjective (cannot be criticised). **Classification of organisations from a KM perspective**: The authors cite De Caluwe's (2006) classification, taking the three main categories: (a) Engineering organisations, or 'blue', consider themselves rational; they prefer to generate and apply explicit knowledge; they work with numerical data, think in terms of measuring, controlling, and engineering; they are usually engineering companies using scientific knowledge to tackle problems. (b) Political organisations, or 'yellow', think in terms of power, interests, conflicts, coalitions, consensus and public support; typical of these are municipalities and public authorities. (c) Learning organisations, or 'green', tend to focus on processes, motivating people to learn and improve themselves; for them learning and organisational change are strongly connected; typical of consultancy agencies and organisations that work with processes. *{There could be a connection between these knowledge management styles and the value discipline of the organisation. If that is so, I could find a connection between this and the IT value building model.}* **Definition**: Social software is software that supports social interaction and collaborative processes. Relating this to our model, in the design of a wiki it is essential to build in the contributors' responsibility for the quality of the input, and that they should request reviews of their contributions by peers and experts.

PART IV:
Extending the Theory

Chapter 11

Discussing the Cases *vis-a-vis* the Theory

We now discuss each of the case studies presented in Parts II and III in the light of the theoretical conjecture constructed in Chapter 2. We take each case study in turn and identify the value discipline of the organisation being studied. We then analyse the ICT project involved and classify it into *efficiency driven* or *market power driven.*

Once we have defined the value discipline of the organisation and categorised the ICT projects we discuss the success or failure of the project in terms of value creation and map it on to the *Theory of Market Power ICT Investments for Value Creation* and thus arrive at whether the case corroborates or falsifies the theory.

11.1 Corroborating the need for well planned change management in an *efficiency-driven* ICT project

The case of Company X (Chapter 4) presents a situation where two large competitors in a mature market decide to merge their manufacturing operations so as to overcome a problem of long overdue plant obsolescence and at the same time avoid building overcapacity in the market, by pooling investments. Although not explicitly stated it can be inferred that Company X, the result of the merger, operates in an *operational excellence* value discipline where its value proposition is based on *best total cost.*

ICT integration was planned through the implementation of a large Enterprise System (ES). This project clearly fits into the characterisation of an efficiency driven ICT project, as depicted in Table 3.1. It is aimed at supporting the coordination of plant capacity and thus avoiding overcapacity in the market. As indicated in the text of the case study, the project was led and carried forward mostly by the IT department which, again, is typical of an efficiency driven ICT project. As such it requires significant effort in change management.

On the one hand it appears that user training was reasonably effective as the users did not complain about their knowledge of the system; actually it emerges from the user satisfaction survey that they perceive themselves as knowledgeable of its functioning. On the other hand, it is obvious from the survey that the users expectations of the system were let down. This is surprising because the ES appeared to meet its functionality ("...there has not been any order that we would not have been able to deliver.") and yes, there were system quality problems (bugs) due to opting for a tailor-made ES (and to doing insufficient tests) as opposed to a packaged one, but users can be persuaded to be patient in the early stages of deployment of the system. So where does this dissatisfaction emerge from?

The impression one gets from reading the case study is that the organisation invested enough on one aspect of change management (i.e., training) but overlooked other key dimensions such as stakeholder management and expectations management. After an organisation's 3-year effort in developing and implementing an efficiency-driven ES solution, user expectations can become unrealistically high, making change management critical for integration success.

With respect to our theory, this case seems to be telling us that as in financial services, in a manufacturing environment an operation excellence company can possibly convert an efficiency-driven ICT project into value, but it will require a well planned and resourced change management programme.

A final reflection from this case study is that determining IS success is problematic, as is finding reliable measures for it. The problem is that ICT is not an end in itself, but only an enabler; so it is not ICT that succeeds or does not succeed, it is whatever it enables. If there is a measure of ICT success, it is an indirect one, in terms of metrics of the enabled phenomenon. Both executives and academics usually evaluate acquisition performance and acquisition strategies in terms of monetary criteria such as cost savings (economies of scale) and synergies (reducing or exploiting redundant capacity) as benefits obtainable from post-merger IS integration. That is why it is so important to use a three construct model to understand how an ICT input contributes to an output such as organisational performance.

11.2 Customer-driven innovation in ICT-use leads to value-building

The narrative in chapter 5 describes not a single organisation but a multitude of small and medium sized hotels. Although the text does not explicitly reveal this, it can be inferred that the value disciplines adopted by these organisations may have variations, but these should not be too wide as all the hotels belong to the same network. They appear to be small hotels that give a limited breadth of services, but do so in a personalised way. This leads us to believe that these hotels tend to operate in a *customer intimacy* value discipline.

The concept of 'collective use' as opposed to simple individual use introduced by the author in this paper is particularly interesting in the context of the theory being analysed. By a collective the author refers to an interdependent group of individuals with a common direction or goal. So collective use is more than just social or task oriented interaction; it requires collaboration, communication, and coordination. The author goes on to explain that collective use can take two forms: *shared* and *configural*. The latter construct occurs when members of the collective use a system more or less frequently and for different purposes, "but there is a stable pattern in their use." *Shared* constructs occur when the collective uses the system in a homogeneous way. In practitioner terms, configural use happens when an individual user signs on to the system to perform several roles, as is characteristic in small and medium enterprises (SMEs); shared use, on the other hand, takes place when each individual in the organisation signs on to the system to perform a specific role and always the same role.

So this leads to *Collective, Innovative, Configural* (CIC) use of ICT, of which the two "C"s are now defined, but not yet the "I". The author defines *innovation* not as creative work-arounds to use the system by those who do not know its functionality well (practitioners will have no trouble in relating to this, as it is common in organisations that under-invest in change management and user training), but rather innovative use that has been "hierarchically institutionalised as an acceptable/required way to handle a circumstance of system use."

It emerges from the text of the case study that the driver for the hotels to implement this application was the pursuit of efficiency. However, the case study denotes a significant variation in the use of a common transaction system across quite similar organisations that operate in the same hotel networks. The application is an efficiency-driven system, but when the organisation adopts a CIC use of the system, it can also be revenue enhancing. This is a powerful insight: The same application can be one or the other depending on the degree of *innovative* and *configural* use. In cases where the system proved to have poor or inexistent functionality, *collective* understanding and agreement were essential in managing this lack of functionality so that the customer was not affected. In the cases where there were consistent patterns of innovative use, these were triggered by front-desk staff to manage customer transactions quickly and efficiently, and/or to maximise customer satisfaction with the booking process. This is innovation triggered by the pressure of customer facing transactions. It emerges from the text of the case that those organisations that engage in this dynamic are the ones that derive more value from their investment in this application, through customer satisfaction that translates into revenue enhancement. This case therefore extends the application of our theory to SME hotels which, when operating in a customer intimacy value discipline, maximise value from this application when they use it to solve customer facing issues.

The concept of collective deserves further attention. A collective restrains each member's sense of the outside world, beyond the collective. It is only a small number of fish in a school that know where food is or that a predator is approaching (as few as 5 percent according to Iain Couzin at the 2011 AAAS[10] meeting). The rest use that small group as leaders and guides – they move collectively but are quite absent of what is happening in their outside world, that beyond their school. Similarly, it is just a few voters in a democracy that have direct knowledge of what, why and who they are voting for – the rest takes them as referents (Ford, 2011; The Economist, 2011). This can be extended to an organisation and how it uses its systems. A few have direct knowledge of the system (known as super-users) while the rest tend to refer to them when in difficulty. It appears that those employees in SME hotels who are in con-

[10] American Association for the Advancement of Science

tact with Clients are the ones who get direct input from the outside, which would explain why they are the triggers of innovation in system use.

Collective use requires group learning, which puts additional demands on the implementation of an ICT project. The in't Hout (2010) paper on implementing a wiki-based knowledge management tool introduces an interesting discussion on the role of mental models on learning, and the differences between individual learning and group learning, and highlighting the fact that the latter is more complex than the former because it requires to deal with as many different mental models as participants in the group. This stresses the importance of the training dimension of change management in efficiency-driven ICT implementations.

In summary, when there is CIC use of an efficiency-driven ICT application it is possible to achieve market power as well. This will happen in SMEs where CIC use is more feasible. So in SMEs it is important to reach CIC use, and change management is led by the 'owner' of the business who leads the implementation. In large organisations where specialisation is compulsory for competitiveness, the *configural* aspect of CIC use is not achievable, but this should not stop *innovative* and *collective* use. In market power driven ICT projects the 'owner' of the application is on top of things and thus the dynamics of the project is more alike SMEs. But in back-office, efficiency-driven initiatives there are no such direct ownership by the leadership of the project. In this kind of organisation and ICT project a specific change management initiative is far more necessary to realise the benefits pursued by the project. This case study also highlights the importance of the human factor in 'landing the ICT aeroplane' and reinforces the concept that there is no such thing as an ICT implementation project, but rather an organisational change project enabled by ICT.

11.3 For ICT investments to produce long lasting transformative value they need to be applied to the core functions of the organisation

The study on ERP implementations in a pharmaceutical and in an information technology companies presented in chapter 6 makes some interesting contributions. From the evidence presented in the case study by Carton & Adam (2010) it appears that the pharmaceutical company is a global leader, quite possibly in a *best-product* value proposition. On the other hand, the *IT* company is morphing from a product-based company to a customer intimate one that is determined to improve quality of service to clients.

Neither of the companies analysed in the case study appear to operate in an *operational excellence* value discipline. As a consequence, the fact that they are both implementing an *efficiency-driven* ICT enabled transformation while pursuing *customer intimacy* or *product leadership* value disciplines should make them illuminating cases for analysing our theory, which predicts that it is highly unlikely that these projects will convert into value.

A finding from the analysis of the case study is that there is a strong linear relationship between the centralisation attributes in an organisation, and the integration ones. It also emerges from the case that centralisation is accepted by managers because they recognise it facilitates control and visibility of organisational workings. The more centralised the organisation, the more integration is required and accepted. A corollary of this finding would be that more decentralised organisations would have difficulty accepting integration. The explanation for this is that problems arise when implementing ERP systems (or other standardisation and efficiency-driven solutions) in organisations whose business model is based precisely on offering innovative products or customised services and thus require decentralisation to make sure the best brains are put to develop new products or to working with the customer to tailor services, respectively.

Having stated that centralisation is incompatible with the value disciplines of both companies, it is not surprising that there is general coincidence in rejection of centralisation across the two organisations studied by Carton & Adam (2010). What is more interesting is that the degree of rejection varies per business process from one organisation to the other. Logically, in a regulated industry such as the pharmaceutical, centralisation in a closely monitored process such as manufacturing is more readily accepted than in an unregulated one such as IT. It emerges from here that a normative force such as *regulation* impacts the degree to which centralisation is accepted by an organisation's leadership even in organisations that pursue *product leadership* or *customer intimacy* value disciplines.

The increased accuracy of information that comes with integration through ERP systems benefits functions such as operations, logistics and finance as the introduction of the ERP facilitates more data points and availability of richer and more granular information. But longer lasting transformative benefits to the organisation are more likely to come from core value-adding activities of the company rather than administrative functions (the authors cite Barua *et al.,* 1995) and in *product leadership* or *customer intimate* organisations these activities centre on developing innovative products or in designing best total solutions for clients. So this helps explain why it is hard to convert efficiency driven projects into value in organisations that pursue other than an *operational excellence* value discipline.

The Carton & Adam (2010) paper reinforces that the downside of efficiency-driven systems such as ERP is that they incorporate rigidities and are unforthcoming with meaningful information. This inflexibility drives users to introduce workarounds, which engenders gaps between the physical reality and the virtual picture used to monitor its progress in an ERP system. The authors call this gap that will inevitably emerge over time between the physical world and its virtual representation in an ERP system as the Zipper Effect. The Zipper Effect leads to manual work to overcome the gaps between virtual and reality, which derives in latency in reporting. All this, in turn, requires incorporating high skilled workers to, with increasing effort, manage manual operations and overcome the gaps. The accuracy of the information or size of the gap depends on the closeness of the template parameters in the ERP system to the actual way of doing business. So in order to close the zipper you need to configure the ERP system to fit very closely with how the business works; or, conversely, apply a strong change management initiative so the real world processes are drawn close to those configured in the ERP system.

As seen in previous sections, creativity channelled towards introducing workarounds to an information system does not only engender gaps between reality and the virtual model of the organisation, but it also drains opportunities for real innovation. Change management has to be oriented to closing the gaps and get people to work according to the system through training or change the system to adapt to how the company wants to do business. Simply avoiding the issue and letting users decide how to adopt it is not an option for organisations that intend to convert ICT investments into value.

In line with what our theory would have predicted, the authors find almost unanimity in frustration throughout the business in exploiting corporate information for decision support. They establish that managers are obliged to resort to much manual manipulation of the information derived from the ERP system in order to get "meaning they require." Our theory anticipates this in that an efficiency-driven ICT project such as those undertaken by both companies are aimed at streamlining and automating back-office processes and not geared at generating the information that managers need in a *product leadership* or *customer intimate* oriented company.

A final lesson that can be drawn from this case study is that an integrated model of how an organisation works is theoretical and ill-adapted to how businesses work in reality. The notion of integration can be treated as a normative force that acts upon the organisation and there is real danger that the imposition of standardised procedures that comes with it will inhibit rather than encourage understanding of the key variables.

11.4 A power struggle that leads to scuttling an ERP implementation (and thus destroying value) illustrates the need for change management

The Dawson & Owens (2007) paper presented in Chapter 7 deals with a medium sized (SME) hospital furniture manufacturing company based in the UK. From the text of the case study it can be inferred that the company operates in a *customer intimacy* value discipline. This emerges from the fact that it makes tailor-made furniture for its clients' needs, and complements this with third party products to offer a *best total solution.* This approach discards a *product leadership* value discipline, and the inference is reinforced by the information that the company was very inefficient in its internal processes, which also discards *operational excellence.*

Senior management at the company arrived at the conclusion that it needed to streamline its processes and implement an information system to support the new processes. Confronted with the decision to go with an *ERP* or a *best-of-breed* system, the company opts for the former, prioritising the pursuit of efficiency. So again we are confronted with a *customer intimate* company that embarks on an efficiency-driven project and there is little doubt that it destroyed value, as the project had to be scuttled before even going live. It consumed cash, management attention and intense effort from staff but made no contribution to solving the organisation's problems.

Where are the causes of this failure? In the first place the project failed to cover core functionality for this type of company as is *product configuration*. How did this gap not emerge in the software selection process? Clearly the company did not involve all the interested parties in the requirements definition and selection process.

From personal experience going through these processes, it would have been the *Production* and *Sales* people who would have pushed for a best-of-breed solution, because that would give them the best solution for their core issues: designing products that perfectly met their clients' needs, and feeding those specification straight into the production line. These stakeholders lost out in the political battle as the decision was to go for an ERP and as a result they lost interest in the project and thus did not give their input for the ERP design. They then just waited until the project got under way to torpedo it at the first opportunity. This must be a powerful stakeholder group in the organisation, because the MD took their side when they exposed the limitations of the solution. So the technical problems that emerged and are described in the text of the case, as real as they were, were actually only symptoms; the root cause of the problem was poor change management; or more specifically, no effective stakeholder management.

It is interesting to reflect on how the leadership of the project reacted to the problem. The problem emerged as a functional limitation or in other words as a process problem – this is at the *Structure* level of the organisation. The immediate reaction of the project leadership was to throw more money at the problem: develop the lacking functionality, or purchase a specific application that covered the functionality and integrate it with the ERP. In other words, given a *Structure* problem the leadership of the project went down one level to *Resources* to find an answer, when the solution was really one level up, at the *Power* level in the form of stakeholder management (Terry, 1987).

The authors of the case study arrive at the by now quite uncontroversial claim that it is essential when undertaking a major ERP project to focus on a robust change management initiative since it is vital to align all key stakeholders with the objectives of the project. This is because these are not merely ICT projects, but major business transformation ones in which human and organisational problems will derive in technical problems. This case is an indication that the *Theory of Market Power ICT Investments for Value Creation* we presented in Chapter 2, is clearly extensible to organisations other than banks in Chile as it corroborates our conjecture that:

> *Organisations that operate in a customer intimacy or product leadership value discipline, will only convert into value those ICT investments which enable them to increase their Market Power.*

11.5 Prioritising customer-facing-staff requirements leads to value creation in an ICT implementation for customer intimacy

From the evidence given in the text of the Beale & Cole case study (Chapter 8) it is not evident what the value discipline of the organisation is. However, by the way the organisation has grown and the fact that it has managed to survive for many years despite highly fragmented processes, disconnected operations, manual procedures and a low level of automation, clearly its value proposition is not based on *operational excellence.* There must be some other way it is offering value to clients: either *best total solution* or *leading products.* There are no indications that it is the latter, and the fact that it has recently incorporated a new product line through acquisition (i.e. electrical services) is a clue that it is betting on *best total solution* and thus a *customer intimacy* value discipline. This is corroborated by the *modus operandi* of the organisation where its talents work in a de-centralised manner as they perform their work on client sites in direct contact with their clients' staff.

Having determined the value discipline of the organisation, we turn to categorising the ICT enabled transformation project described in the case study. It has characteristics of a revenue-enhancement driven ICT project because confronted with the alternatives of going for an accounting and finance centred project, or a core-business centred project, the organisation opted for the latter. Although not explicitly stated in the text, it can be inferred that the business managers (as opposed to the back-office support managers) got their way and most probably led the implementation project. Apart from this, when one reads the functionality of the new project in section 8.5, expressions such as "enhanced customer communications", "maintaining excellent customer relations", "business growth", "capacity for more rapid expansion", "information for decision making readily available" outweigh expressions such as "improved cost control". Finally, the business context of the project is also giving clues in this direction: the company had recently decided to expand its product/service offering by adding electrical engineering services to their traditional plumbing (offering more products to their present client base and market segment). So it can be established that this initiative aims at increasing the company's market power through differentiation (i.e. better service quality and reliability) and ease of search (i.e. a more robust e-commerce infrastructure.)

The authors of the case study claim that the outcome of the project is highly successful since it "reduced operating and transaction costs, increased turnover and enhanced profitability."

The conclusion of this analysis of the Beale & Cole case study is that it is a company that operates in a customer intimacy value discipline and has carried out a revenue-enhancement project that has increased its market power and converted that into improved performance measured by market share and profitability. It can be interpreted from here that our theoretical conjecture that "Banks that operate in a *customer intimacy* or *product leadership* value discipline, will only convert into value those ICT investments which enable them to increase their Market Power" could possibly be extended to the engineering contractors sector. This claim is made conditional because the case demonstrated that a customer intimate contractor can also convert market-power projects into value; but it does not establish that the contractor cannot convert efficiency-driven projects into value, which if proven that it can it would not make our theory extensible to this industry.

11.6 Despite transactional limitations, achieving good access to customer information defines success in a customer intimate environment

The Alfa Laval's case (Chapter 9) describing the implementation of a CRM solution in its sales subsidiary in China denotes a company that has decided to switch its value proposition to clients from *best product* to *best total solution*. Changing value discipline is a complex process that cannot rely merely on leadership intentions and communications. It requires a major business transformation process. This company has enabled this transformation by using the implementation of a global CRM solution as a vehicle for business change.

The business transformation process described in the text of the case is clearly a *market–power building* project; it responds to most of the characterisations given in table 3.1. The objective is to assist Client facing staff do their job better. It is true that the quality is not perceived very high because of the 'bugs' (this problem would have been less severe with a world class package) and, which is more surprising, "the system is cumbersome to work in and the natural way to do business" is not supported by it. One would have thought that this would have been the main criteria for adopting a custom-made system as opposed to a CRM package. But, more important than all of this, "searching for customer data and finding historical records" was significantly facilitated, which is in the essence of a customer intimacy value discipline: having much more information on customers than that required to merely complete transactions.

The project is not led by the IT function or from another back office function at the Centre, but by the actual Chinese business unit whose leadership will benefit from its use and is responsible for its delivery. The text does not mention a specific change management stream, but this seems to corroborate our theoretical conjecture of Chapter 2 in that it is not really needed because the project affects a relatively small group of people in China who are the direct beneficiaries of the system.

Again, because this project is not *efficiency-driven,* it does not help us to determine whether the conjecture that *customer-intimate* organisations will *only* turn into value initiatives aimed at building market power. However, it does corroborate that customer intimate organisations are successful at delivering *market-power* building projects. A CRM project like this will act in increasing both *differentiation* and *ease of search.*

11.7 When implementing knowledge solutions, change management should focus on committing the most knowledgeable

The case of the Dutch consultancy described in Chapter 10 is interesting in that it is the only case amongst all those analysed where the unit of analysis is an organisation that commits to a *product leadership* value discipline. As part of its effort to emphasise its *best product* value proposition to clients, it bets on maximising the application of the knowledge of the organisation to solving client problems. The means for doing this is to implement a wiki-based tool that will break down communications barriers between its professionals, and incorporate tacit knowledge into transport plans development as part of its quest for differentiation.

Clearly the implementation of a wiki-based knowledge management tool is not an efficiency driven project; it is not aimed at standardising procedures or automating processes but at getting more brains involved in solving client problems. The result of this project will probably be more man-hours in developing transport plans, but the final outcome will be better plans. So this is clearly a Market-power driven project.

This project was not without problems. Once the wiki knowledge management tool was set up, it was found that for most users the time they invested was not yet worth the effort, as they had to add more info than they could retrieve from the system. Another issue that emerged is that the most experienced people would not use it. This was in part due to generational issues as the most experienced are in an age group that did not have a natural affinity with tools such as wiki, but mostly because they are the ones who less needs it. The most experienced people would tend to rely precisely on their experience to tackle a new project, while the younger ones would be more open to seeking for help through the knowledge management system. Finally, junior consultants were also less afraid of sharing uncertainties. In short, there are many disincentives for the most experienced to use the system so, as a result, those who could most contribute do not get involved because they get little from it!

This is an interesting insight that will shed helpful light on the problems concerning the introduction of most networking technologies, especially social networking ones that appear to be an emerging trend in *product leadership* organisations. Similarly to the case of *efficiency-driven* ICT projects, change management becomes an important issue, but the focus of change management seems to be different. While in efficiency-driven projects the focus of change management is essentially in training and getting the users to be able to use the system properly for their transactions, in the case of knowledge networking projects the need for change management seems to be more focused on stakeholder management. It is about enticing the most experienced to assume the short-term cost of contributing to the system even when they understand that their payback will not come until the system is mature.

It is worth noting that when the prototype was presented to the MD of the firm, he did not like the fact that 'soft', opinionated 'knowledge' was getting mixed up in the communications channels with factual, explicit knowledge. The prototype had to be altered to manage both types of knowledge separately and distinctively. The MD had a 'blue' type style, and was confronted with a 'green' style tool, which, as theory would anticipate, does not make him receptive. So another success factor in these projects appears to be to accommodate the knowledge management tools to the knowledge sharing style of the organisation's leader.

The final outcome of this case study appears to be that the company became genuinely interested in the new concept, in the new way of working, and the tools that support it. Through these knowledge management changes and tools it appears that the organisation got prepared for delivering a Product Leadership value discipline. Knowledge management at the firm shifted from a heavily "technology-based network" to a "people-based network" model. These are typical approaches for customer intimate and product leadership value disciplines (Griffiths & Remenyi, 2007).

The discussions carried out in this chapter support (or at least do not challenge) the fact that our theory on deriving value from ICT investments in Chilean banks is extensible to other industries in multiple geographic markets. This conversion of ICT projects into value is dependent on the strategic value of ICT investments and how they connect to the value discipline of the organisation. The following chapter will thus dwell on the strategic value of ICT and attempt to develop a model to help understand the connection between these constructs.

Chapter 12

Pursuing Value through Strategy-Technology Alignment

In this chapter we go back to the literature to understand the meaning of the *strategic value* of ICT. This will enable us to move from the two categories of ICT projects given in Chapter 3 (i.e., *efficiency driven* and *market-power* driven) to a classification framework of four dimensions that achieves more granularity.

Linking the strategic value of ICT to the different value disciplines that an organisation can adopt, and including *Tailored Change Management* as a construct, we propose a model of ICT valuation. Finally, we propose what we have called the *Catapult Theory for Deriving Value from ICT Investments.*

12.1 The Strategic Value of ICT

The discussions of the previous chapter motivate us to propose a model that connects the strategic value of ICT to the value discipline of the organisation. Doing this requires us to explain what we mean by strategic value of ICT.

An article published by Carr (2003) in Harvard Business Review that drew a parallel between ICT and some mature technologies provoked deep reflections and discussions amongst practitioners and academics on the strategic value of ICT. One of the papers in this global exchange (Bannister & Remenyi, 2005) classifies the strategic value of ICT into seven categories, as follows:

Strategic value as fundamental to the organisation's business/industry. The authors say that many industries exist in the form they do today only because of IT. It is quite possible for those of us who remember seeing Neil Armstrong take his first step on the moon to imagine a world without computers or modern communications technology – the Apollo spacecraft that landed Armstrong there had less IT processing power than our cars today. We have moved a long way since then and many industries today are totally dependent on IT to function at all, or are moving in that direction. Examples include financial services, retail, the music industry and the airline industry.

Strategic value as long-term value. These are applications of IT that introduce changes in the cost structure of the organisation that adopts them. They are those IT investments that lead to a lower variable cost at the expense of a higher fixed cost. There are two types of IT applications that render strategic value of this form. First, there are those whose benefits are tangible[11], but in order to realise them the organisation needs to increase its output or scale of activity. Typical examples are transactional systems that automate processes, such as *ERP* systems in any organisation, or *billing & customer care* applications in utilities. Second, there are applications that improve cost structure but whose benefits are not tangible in the sense given above. They are enablers, and in order to reap the benefits the organisation will have to give new uses to the application. An example of this is a portal application. An organisation may implement a portal for HR self-service knowing that the portal technology will not pay-back on that sole use. But having the portal in place will allow for additional uses in future, such as an *internet sales* application or a *corporate responsibility* (CR) information diffusion tool.

Strategic value as a driver of or platform for change of direction. Information technology can provide a basis for change of direction. This sort of technology gives companies the attribute of systemic flexibility, which can be classified into four types (Slack, 1991, cited by Albertin & Albertin, 2005, p.32):

- Speed of developing and launching new products
- Product portfolio flexibility: ability to change product mix
- Production scale flexibility
- Delivery flexibility: ability to alter dates and quantities of orders

---

[11] By tangible we refer to those investments whose benefits can be traced right down to the bottom line of the P&L statement.

The IT applications that develop this form of strategic value tend to be more about information management (i.e., information on Clients, demand forecasting, order tracking) than about process automation as was mentioned for long-term value.

Strategic value as necessary for survival. There are many examples of where IT is necessary to even operate in an industry. No bank could hope to compete today with just paper systems or, even, without an ATM network. If it is not already so, it will not be long before airlines and hotels, which do not have Internet booking services, will not survive. If you want to provide services to the government, you will need to use electronic procurement and so on.

Strategic value as platform for innovation. As Curley (2004) says, the problem with IT is that people's ability to imagine what can be done with it lags the technology's capabilities. Innovation can be defined as the ability to generate great ideas, plus the ability to execute them, and clearly IT can play a role in enabling both of these dimensions. Although this requires both process automation and information management applications, more important than either of those are applications that bring people together to share knowledge (e.g. groupware, social networks).

Strategic value as discontinuity/first mover. The decline of opportunities to gain breakthrough competitive advantage is the basis for Carr's 'follow, don't lead', recommendation. The evidence, as well as the argument, would appear to be on Carr's side in this case. It is even embedded in the industry's own hyperbole where, for example, companies such as SAP promote their products as embedding best business practices by industry. If this is so, then anybody with a chequebook and enough cash in the bank can have access to best business practices.

Strategic value as incremental improvement. A leading proponent of this school of thought is Ciborra (2004) who argued that long term, sustainable competitive advance does not come from technological breakthroughs, but from a myriad of ways of doing things better and a process of continual improvement. Ciborra used paradoxes to illustrate his thinking, such as 'plan for small breakthroughs'. This is, if not the antithesis of Carr's follow rather than lead approach, at least an alternative that is not defeatist. Ciborra does not recommend that companies wait for the next information technology gizmo to launch a great leap forward, but suggests that successful companies are always on the lookout for small ways to use IT to make themselves that little bit better.

12.2 A Strategic Value of ICT Model

The previous sections presented a framework for understanding the different forms of strategic value that a technology, in particular IT, can contribute to the organisation. The intention now is to develop that framework into a model that will help practitioners convert ICT investments into value for the firm. It will do so by explaining the relationship that exists between the relative importance of each of these forms of strategic value, and the value discipline of the organisation.

As ICT penetrates society industries become more *information intensive,* meaning that players in those industries tend to have only two resources with which to differentiate from their competition: talent and information. Many services already fall into this category (e.g., freight forwarding, banking, brokerage, news services, universities, VoIP-based-telecommunications) as do some product based industries (e.g., film industry, news papers, music, software). For this kind of industry it can be said that "Strategic value as fundamental to the organisation's business/industry" and "Strategic value as necessary for survival" can be consolidated into a single category that will be called "Strategic value as infrastructure".

Companies that offer a *best total solution* value proposition do not necessarily offer the lowest price or the latest product features, but they still provide a better overall result for their Clients than the competition. A *customer intimate* firm knows that its Clients have a hierarchy of needs beyond their requirements for a product, and uses its superior expertise in the Client's underlying problem to change the way the customer does business. It takes responsibility for results and customises services to meet the specific needs of their Clients. They are Client and field driven, and are organised around entrepreneurial Client teams. Their information systems prioritise customer databases linking internal and external information, and knowledge bases built around expertise (Treacy & Wiersema, 1995, pp.125-142).

Lowest total cost, which does not mean lowest price, is the value proposition of *operational excellence* companies. They, like Henry Ford, know that variety kills efficiency, so they deploy an operating model that is highly regimented, procedure- and rule-driven. They reject variety because it burdens the organisation with costs, and produce no-frills products for the middle of the market where demand is large and customers are more interested in cost than in choice. Information systems are mostly aimed at standardising and automating processes; they do not just track the process, but they contain and perform it. The systems produce detailed data for measuring and monitoring and so enable rigorous quality and cost control (Treacy & Wiersema, 1995, pp. 50-58).

The *product leadership* value discipline underpins companies that aim at delivering a *best product* value proposition to their Clients. Invention is critically important, but it goes hand-in-hand with commercialisation and market exploitation. The operational model is based on highly talented people working in loose-knit structures. Product leaders create flexible organisational structures with processes that provide efficient co-ordination, while accommodating inventiveness and discipline. This requires having person-to-person communications systems that prioritise technology enabled co-operation and knowledge management (Treacy & Wiersema, 1995, pp 87-100).

As these brief descriptions of the three value disciplines imply, no organisation can be at the same time customer intimate, operational excellent and product leader. What makes them strong on one dimension will, almost by definition, make them less-than-excellent on the other two. Market leaders need to decide on which of these dimensions they will excel, and limit themselves to meeting minimum performance thresholds on the remainder.

With these concepts in place, we shall now relate the relative importance of the different forms of strategic value of IT mentioned in section 12.1 with the value disciplines. Five key concepts emerge from analysing these definitions. The first is that strategic value as a "driver of or platform for change of direction" is clearly linked to the ICT requirements described for an organisation following a *customer intimacy* value discipline. Similarly, the strategic value as "Long term value" and as "Platform for innovation" fit in with the ICT requirements specified for *operational excellence* and for *product leadership,* respectively.

The second is that if, as supported by Treacy & Wiersema (1995), competitive advantage comes from decisively developing an organisations value discipline, and ICT plays a role in developing it, the "strategic value of IT as a Competitive Advantage" is a second order form of strategic value, that derives from the first order forms described before (i.e., "long term value", "platform for change" and "platform for innovation").

Drawing from the findings in Chapter 2 that information intensive organisations only convert into value[12] those ICT investments that are aligned with its value discipline, the third idea that emerges is that the value discipline plays a moderator role in the relationship between the first order forms of ICT strategic value (i.e. "long term value", "platform for change" and "platform for innovation") and the second order form (i.e., "competitive advantage")

The fourth concept is that, as depicted by Carr and dealt with in the previous sections of this paper, once a technology becomes an infrastructure, its absence will have a negative impact on performance (i.e., it will literally drive the organisation out of business during the absence of the technology) but its presence will not give a competitive advantage. So strategic value "as competitive advantage" is not a second order form of strategic value "as infrastructure".

The final idea that emerged is that this concept of ICT strategic value can be used as a reference theory to understand the impact of ICT investments on enterprise performance (Crowston & Treacy, 1986; Ginzberg, 1979; Griffiths, 2005). This can be represented graphically, as shown in figure 12.1.

---

[12] An economics approach to value is taken here (as opposed to meanings used in other fields such as strategy, organisational behaviour, marketing, labour economics, etc). Read *et al.* (2001, p.97) propose the following definition, which we adopt: *At its simplest level, value is created by generating revenues from the delivery of products and services to customers that exceed the cost of the delivery process.*

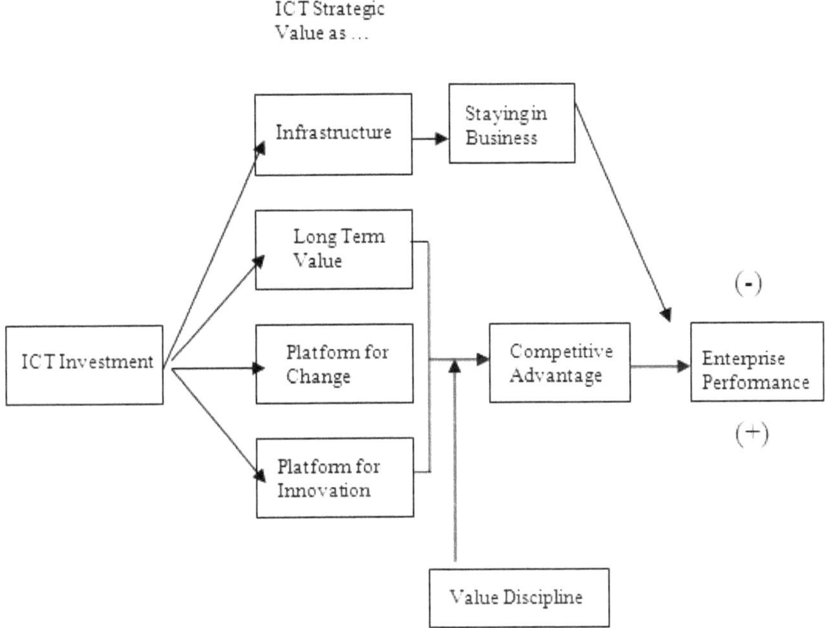

Figure 12.1 A Strategic Value based model for ICT investment decisions.

Two things may need explaining in figure 12.1. The first is the negative sign on the arrow from "Staying in Business" to "Enterprise Performance", which indicates that an ICT investment which takes the form of Strategic Value as Infrastructure will not have a positive impact on performance, but its absence will have a negative one.

The second is the role of the "Value Discipline" construct as a mediator. The conjecture that is being made here is that an ICT investment will only develop competitive advantage if it is aligned with the value discipline of the organisation. For example, an ICT investment aimed at developing strategic value in the form of "Long Term Value" will only produce competitive advantage in an Operational Excellence organisation. Conversely, an Operational Excellence organisation that makes an ICT investment aimed at developing value in the form of "Platform for Innovation" or "Platform for Change" will not develop competitive advantage. Likewise, an ICT investment aimed at developing strategic value in the form of "Platform for Change" will only produce competitive advantage in a Customer Intimacy organisation and, conversely, if such an organisation makes ICT investments aimed at building strategic value in the form of "Long Term Value" or "Platform for Innovation" it will actually destroy value. The same reasoning can be made for "Product Leadership" value discipline organisations.

The other issue that came up systematically in the seven case studies is the need for *change management.* Clearly, because ICT is an enabler and not an end in its own right, an ICT investment that is not used will not lead to competitive advantage. It will, thus, be a futile investment and therefore one that consumes resources and destroys value. So deriving value from ICT investments requires applying a *change management* initiative that helps the members of the organisation alter their work habits to maximise the use of the new tool and adopt the new way of doing things. Furthermore, it also emerged from the seven case studies that the *change management* initiative is not a "one size fits all" type solution. Far from it, the *change management* approach needs to be adapted to each type of ICT strategic value investment.

On the one hand, the case of the Dutch engineering firm analysed in Chapter 10 appears to indicate that "Platform for Innovation" type investment requires the change management programme to focus on stakeholder management, with the purpose of getting the experienced and knowledgeable members of the organisation to invest time and effort in the build-up phase, during which the effort they put into working with the system is significantly higher than the benefits they get out of it. On the other hand, the IS integration project in the Finnish manufacturing company (Chapter 5), the hotel core application in the Australian hotel chains (Chapter 5), the ERP implementations in a pharmaceutical and an computer companies in Ireland (Chapter 6), or the ERP implementation in a UK furniture manufacturing company (Chapter 7) indicate that change management in "Long Term Value" application implementation must be focused mainly on *user training,* on *stakeholder management* to neutralise powerful stakeholders that do not benefit from the new investment, and on *risk management* as these projects are long and draw on resources across most areas of the organisation.

Finally, the cases of the "Platform for Change" solution implementation in the UK contractor (Chapter 8) and the Chinese sales operation (Chapter 9) would indicate that in this type of ICT investment *change man-*

agement should be oriented at motivating the business units to take ownership of the project (rather than relying on the IT Department) and allocating their best people to the implementation.

This leads me to believe we should add an extra construct that we shall call "Tailored Change Management" that is a predecessor of "Competitive Advantage" and whose "Tailored" component will depend on the type of ICT investment (figure 12.2).

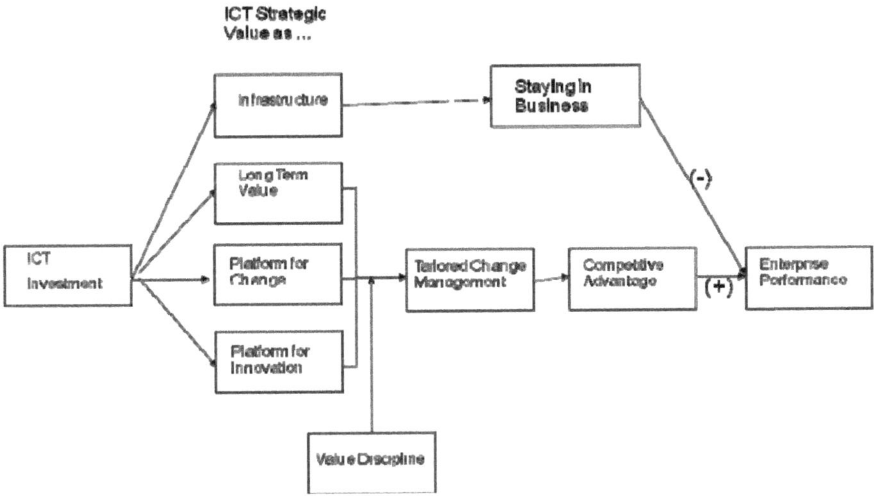

Figure 12.2: Value Catapult Model for ICT Investment.

From my experience working with practitioners as a consultant, the introduction of a *change management* construct into the model is of vital importance. The ICT profession decidedly underrates the importance of change management. When a CIO is confronted with a cost estimate for his new ICT implementation project that exceeds his budget, the first thing he will axe is the change management programme. He will not even consider the possibility of reducing the scope of the project to fit his budget or the possibility of breaking down the project into phases that meet his budget for the first year or two. For some reason he believes that he will get more value for his organisation if he maximises functionality at the cost of not ensuring that the users of the organisations actually use it properly. He will tend to believe that time will fix this problem; that with time people will learn to use the system at its full potential. This is nonsense. Witness of this is the number of projects that are abandoned, information systems that are by-passed, systems that do not have trustworthy data on real time, organisations that operate on the basis of spreadsheets, and IT managers that fall into oblivion after large projects. The key to delivering value from an ICT investment is that the functionality that is put in place is mastered by the users very quickly. From my experience successful systems are those with which the users are fully committed from the day of 'go-live,' that do not have any sort of parallel application or manual procedure, and whose data is trustworthy. This will only happen if a robust change management programme is put in place.

12.3 Catapult Theory for Deriving Value from ICT Investments

We can now use the model to articulate what we will call the *Catapult Theory for Deriving Value from ICT Investments.* It is named ´Catapult' partly in allusion to the shape of the model but more so to the fact that it is designed to penetrate the fortress of confusion that surrounds success in terms of value-creation in ICT investments (implementation and adoption.) The theoretical conjecture can be states as follows:

- ICT investment in *Infrastructure* will not add value to the organisation but it is required to stay in business.
- Organisations that adopt a value discipline of *operational excellence* need to focus their ICT investments on *Long Term Value* initiatives. They will convert these investments into value provided they apply a *change management* programme that emphasises *user training* to make sure the organisation changes its work procedures in line with the new system; it must also emphasis *stakeholder management* to neutralise powerful stakeholders that do not benefit from the new investment; and it must emphasise *risk management* as these projects are long and draw on resources across most areas of the organisation. These investments will strengthen the organisation's *competitive advantage* that will translate into value through improved performance. These organisations will not convert into value ICT investments in the form of *Platform for Change* or *Platform for Innovation.*

- Organisations that adopt a value discipline of *customer intimacy* need to focus their ICT investments on *Platform for Change* initiatives. They will convert these initiatives into value provided they apply a *change management* programme that emphasises motivating the business units that will benefit from the initiative and be its *key users* to take ownership of the project (rather than relying on the IT Department to lead it) and to allocate their best people to the implementation. These investments will strengthen the organisation's *competitive advantage* that will translate into value through improved performance. These organisations will not convert into value ICT investments in the form of *Long Term Value* or *Platform for Innovation.*
- Organisations that adopt a value discipline of *product leadership* need to focus their ICT investments on *Platform for Innovation* initiatives. They will convert these initiatives into value provided they apply a *change management* programme that emphasises *stakeholder management* with the purpose of getting the experienced and knowledgeable members of the organisation to invest time and effort in the build-up phase during which the effort they put into working with the system is significantly higher than the benefits they get out of it. These investments will strengthen the organisation's *competitive advantage* that will translate into value through improved performance. These organisations will not convert into value ICT investments in the form of *Long Term Value* or *Platform for Change.*

Chapter 13

Reflections, Conclusions and Managerial Implications

This book highlights the fact that although we have gone a long way in the last fifty or sixty years to incorporating information and communications technology into the workings of business and organisations in general, there remains a remarkable lack of theory to assist practitioners in deriving value from the resources they put into this technology. I have tried to countervail this problem by proposing a method to developing empirically based theory, and used it to develop the *Market Power as a Driver for ICT Investment Decisions* theory applicable to information intensive industries such as financial services. A key concept underlying this theory is the classification of ICT projects into *efficiency driven* and *market-power driven*.

A series of case studies published in EJISE and in the proceedings of ECITE and ECIME were then used to extend the theory to businesses in other industries. Through the use of these published case studies the theory was not only extended to other industries, but it was also made "rounder" – while the prior theory focused only on organisations with a *customer intimacy* or *product leadership* value discipline, the present one predicts outcomes for organisations in all value disciplines. It also improved the classification of ICT projects from merely *efficiency driven* and *market-power driven* (which is clear but rather coarse) to four categories (i.e., "Infrastructure", "Long term Value", "Platform for Change" and "Platform for Innovation") which has the merit of significantly greater granularity.

The great debate initiated by Carr (2003) mentioned in Chapter 12 came, took life at a roaring speed, lasted for a few months and then simply went away. The discussion was sanguine and highly opinionated but there was no real conclusion at the end of it – all sides simply walked away with apparently unchanged points of view and went back to their routine activities. In my view no structural constructions came out of the debate. The model presented here can be used to overcome the controversy. It captures Carr's acceptable idea that investments aimed at the infrastructural use of ICT will not have an impact on performance, but not making the required infrastructural investments will have a negative impact (i.e., similar to other infrastructure technologies such as electricity and railway transport). However, it rectifies Carr's unacceptable position that there are no opportunities for creating value through the application of ICT. We have shown that ICT investments aligned with the value discipline of the organisation and accompanied by the required changes in the way people work will help build competitive advantage that in turn creates value through improved enterprise performance.

I hope this book will helps CEOs and business managers understand how ICT can fit and strengthen their organisation's strategy and close the gap between corporate strategy and ICT strategy. It stresses that ICT should be fully incorporated into the strategic planning processes, and not merely used to articulate ICT plans to enable the execution of corporate strategy. The ICT dimension of the strategic plan of the organisation needs to include what ICT investments it will prioritise for the current and following years, and the model and theoretical conjecture presented in Chapter 12 is a robust basis on which to define those priorities.

This book should be highly useful to CIOs and IT managers as well. It should enable them to contribute positively to their organisation's performance enhancement through promoting those ICT investments that are aligned with the organisation´s value discipline. The theory presented in this book should be valuable in helping the CIO and IT managers decide what components of ICT will be outsourced and which will be kept in-house. Most CIOs are clear in stating that they will keep in-house all ICT components that are strategic but the problem is in the following step, in actually defining criteria for the insourcing-outsourcing dilemma. This model and theoretical conjecture is the key to defining that criteria to draw the border between what will be outsourced and what will stay in-house. Last but not least, I hope this book will also help CIOs and IT managers internalise the importance of having a competent change management programme tailored specially to the needs of the project in hand, using the criteria proposed in section 12.3.

I hope this book also challenges young academics to pursuing theory building in this field, and to question the theory I am proposing. The "Catapult" theory fits in snugly with the evidence and theory presented in Chapter 2, and it clearly extends its validity to a considerably broader domain. It also fits closely with the evidence contained in the seven published case studies analysed in Parts II and III of this book. However, no theory ever agrees with all the evidence in its domain, and I am sure that academics testing it against new evidence will find discrepancies. Citing Feyerabend (2002 [1975])[13] this is both because evidence is always contaminated by old ideologies and because knowledge permanently evolves. Thus the disagreement between theory and evidence is a sign of progress and its absence would mean the end of science.

In summary, if this catapult makes at least a small crack in the stoned walls of ICT value obscurity, it will have achieved its goal.

---

[13] "A straight forward and unqualified judgement of theories by 'facts' is bound to eliminate ideas simply because they do not fit into the framework of some older cosmology," p.52.

References

Alvesson, M. & Sköldberg, K. (2000) Reflexive Methodology: New Vistas for Qualitative Research, Sage Publications Ltd

Backhouse, R.E (2002) The Ordinary Business of Life: A History of Economics, Princeton University Press, New Jersey 08540

Bannister, F.E., (2001) Value Evolution: Changing Perceptions of the Role and Value of Information Technology in Irish Public Administration: Historic Development and Future Directions, PhD Thesis, University College, Dublin.

Bannister, F. and Remenyi, D. (1999) In Defense of Instinct: Value and IT Investment Decisions, Henley Working Paper 9914.

Bannister, F. & Remenyi, D. (2005) In Answer to Carr: Reflections on the Strategic Value of IT, Proceedings of the 12th European Conference on Information Technology Evaluation, Turku, pp.77-87

Barua, A., Kriebel, H.C., and Mukhopadhyay, T. (1995) Information Technology and Business Value: An Analytic and Empirical Investigation, Information Systems Research (6:1), March, pp. 3-25

Benaroch, M. & Kauffman, R. (1999) A Case for Using Options Pricing Analysis To Evaluate Information Technology Project Investment, Information Systems Research 10 (March): pp.70-86

Benbasat, I. & Zmud, R.W. (1999) Empirical Research in Information Systems: The Practice of Relevance, MIS Quarterly (23:1), pp.3-16

Bharadwaj, A. (2000) A Resource-Based Perspective on Information Technology Capability and Firm Performance: An Empirical Investigation, MIS Quarterly, 24(1) March: 169-196

Bharadwaj, A., Bharadwaj, S., and Konsynski, B. (1999) Information Technology Effects on Firm Performance as Measured by Tobin´s q, Management Science, (45:7), pp. 1008-1024

Bickman, L.B. & Rog, D.J. (1998) Handbook of Applied Social Research Methods, Sage Publications: London

Borges, J.L. (2000) Nueva Antologia Personal, Siglo XXI Editors: Mexico City

Bryman, A. (1989) Research Methods and Organisation Studies, Unwin Hyman, UK

Brynjolfsson, E. (1993) The Productivity Paradox of Information Technology, Communications of the ACM (35), pp.66-67

Carr, N.G. (2003) IT Doesn't Matter, Harvard Business Review, May, pp. 41-49.

Chamberlain, E.H. (1932) The Theory of Monopolistic Competition: A Reorientation of the Theory of Value, Harvard University Press, Cambridge, M.A.

Christensen, C.M. & Raynor, M.E. (2003) Why Hard-Nosed Executives Should Care About Management Theory, Harvard Business Review, September, pp.66-74.

Churchill, G.A., Iacobucci, D. (2002) Marketing Research: Methodological Foundations, South-Western, Thomson Learning, Mason, OH

Clayton, T. & Waldron, K. (2003) E-Commerce Adoption and Business Impact, A Progress Report, Economic Trends, Forthcoming (see OECD, 2003).

Coghlan, David, (1994), Research as a Process of Change: Action Science in Organisations, Irish Business and Administration Research (IBAR), Volume 15, pp.119-130

Collins, R. (2002 [1998]) The Sociology of Philosophies: A Global Theory of Intellectual Change, Belknap-Harvard University Press

Crowston, K. & Treacy, M.E. (1986) Assessing the Impact of Information Technology on Enterprise Level Performance, Proceedings of the International Conference on Information Systems, San Diego

Davis, C.R. (2002) Calculated Risk: A Framework for Evaluating Product Development, MIT Sloan Management Review, Summer, pp. 71-77

Deephouse, D.L. (1999) To be different, or to be the same? It's a question (and theory) of strategic balance, Strategic Management Journal, 20, pp.147-166

Easterby-Smith, M., Thorpe, R. & Lowe, A. (2002) Management Research – An Introductiion – 2nd Edition, Sage Series in Management Research, Sage Publications, London

Eisenhardt, K.M. (1989) Building theories from case study research. Academy of Management Review., 14 (4), 532-550.

Feeny, D.E., and Willcocks, L.P. (1998) Core IS Capabilities for Exploiting Information Technology, Sloan Management Review, Spring, pp.9-21

Feyerabend, P. (2002 [1975]) Against Method, Verso, 3rd edition

Ford, M. (2011), The mathematics of fish schools and flocks of humans, http://arstechnica.com/science/news/2011/02/the-mathematics-of-fish-schools-and-flocks-of-humans.ars, updated on February 22nd

Giddens, A. (1993) New Rules of Sociological Method, (2nd. Edition), Stanford, CA: Stanford University Press

Ginzberg, M.J. (1979) Improving MIS Project Selection Omega, Volume 7, Numer 6, pp.527-537

Glaser, B., & Strauss, A. (1967) The discovery of grounded theory: Strategies for Qualitative Research. Chicago: Aldine

Griffiths, P.D.R. & Remenyi, D. (2005) Theory-building in ICT evaluation through comparative analysis, Poceedings of the 12th European Conference on Information Technology Evaluation, Turku, pp.

Griffiths, P.D.R. & Remenyi, D. (2007) Using Knowledge for Competitive Advantage in Professional Services: A Case Study, Proceedings of the 4th International Conference on Intellectual Capital, Knowledge Management & Organisational Learning, University of Stellenbosch Business School, South Africa, 15-16 October, Edited by Dan Remenyi, pp.169-178.

Griffiths, P.D.R. (2005) A Framework to Analyse the Underlying Forces that Shape Strategies in a Banking System: The Chilean Case, Proceedings of the

British Academy of Management Conference 2005, Saïd School of Management, Oxford University, Paper No. 10387

Griffiths, P.D.R. (2005) The Application of Market Power Theory as a Value Driver for Information Technology Investment Decisions: A Study of Six Chilean Banks, Doctoral Thesis, Henley Management College/Brunel University.

Hair, J.F., Babin, B., Money, A.H., & Samuel, P. (2002) Essentials of Business Research, John Wiley & Sons: New York.

Hamel, J. (1993) Case Study Methods, Qualitative Research Methods Series No.32, SAGE Publications.

Haynes M and Thompson S (2000) 'The Productivity Impact of IT Deployment: An Empirical Evaluation of ATM Introduction' Oxford Bulletin of Economics and Statistics vol 62 (5), pp. 607-619

Heracleous, L. & Barrett, M. (2001) Organisational Change as discourse: communicative action and deep structures in the context of information technology implementation, Acadaemy of Management Journal, Vol. 44, No. 4, pp. 755-778.

Hitt, L. and Brynjolfsson, E. (1996) Productivity, Business Profitability, and Consumer Surplus: Three Different Measures of Information Technology Value, MIS Quarterly, (20:2), pp. 121-142

Howard, K. & Sharp, J.A. (1983) The Management of a Student Research Project. Gower, Aldershot.

Hunt, M.S. (1972) Competition in the Major Home Appliance Industry, Unpublished doctoral dissertation, Harvard University

Keen, P.G.W. (1991) Shaping the Future: Business Design Through Information Technology, Harvard Business Press, Cambridge, MA.

Keynes, J.M. (1936) The General Theory of Employment, Interest and Money, ch. 24, "Concluding Notes"

Kuzel, A.J. (!992) Sampling in qualitative inquiry, In B.F. Crabtree & V.L. Miller (Eds.) Doing qualitative research, (pp.31-44), (Research Methods for Primary Care Series, Vol.3), Newbury Park, CA: Sage

Layder, D. (1993) New Strategies in Social Research, Polity Press, Cambridge

Leonard, D. & McAdam, R. (2002) The Strategic Dynamics of Total Quality Management: A Grounded Theory Research Study, Quality Management Journal, Vol. 9, No. 1

Light et al., 1990, cited by Maxwell, 1996, p.71

Maurice, S.C. & Smithson, C.W. (1988) Managerial Economics: Applied Microeconomics for Decision Making, Irwin: Homewood, Illinois, Third edition.

Maxwell, J. (1996) Qualitative Research Design: An Interactive Approach, Applied Social Research Methods Series, Vol.41, SAGE Publications

McConnell, P. (1997) Risk Management Support Systems in International Banks, Henley Working Paper HWP 9706

McGrath, J.E. (1982) Dilemmatics :The Study of Research Choices and Dilemmas, In Judgement Calls in Research, by J.E.McGrath, Martin, J. & Kulka (eds.) Beverly Hills, California,: Sage Publications, 1982

McKeen, J.D. and Smith, H.A. (1996) Assessing the Value of Information Technology: A Focus on Banking and Insurance, Working Paper #94-27, Queens University.

Miles, M., & Huberman, A.M. (1984, 2nd Edition 1994) Qualitative data analysis: A Soucebook of New Methods, London: Sage Publications

Mintzberg, H. & McHugh, A. (1985) Strategy formation in an adhocracy. Administrative Science Quarterly, 30, pp.160-197

Mooney, J.G., Gurbaxani, V., and Kraemer, K.L. (1995) A Process Oriented Framework for Assessing the Business Value of Information Technology, in Proceedings of the Sixteenth International Conference on Information Systems, J.I. DeGross, G.Ariav, C.Beath, R.Hoyer, and C.Kemerer (eds.), Amsterdam, pp 17-27

Morse, J.M. (1989), (Ed.), Qualitative nursing research: A contemporary dialogue, Newbury Park, CA: Sage

Myers, M. (1997) Qualitative Research in Information Systems, MIS Quarterly, 21 (2) June: 241-2

Myers, M.D. & Avison, D. (2002) Qualitative Research in Information Systems: A Reader, Sage Publications Limited

OECD (2003) ICT and Economic Growth: Evidence from OECD countries, industries and firms, OECD Publications

Payne, A. & Holt, S. (2001) Diagnosing Customer Value: Integrating the Value Process and Relationship Marketing, British Journal of Management, Vol. 12, pp.159-182

Peppard, J. (2001) Bridging the gap between the IS organisation and the rest of the business: plotting a route, Information Systems Journal, Vol.11, pg. 249-270.

Popper, K. (1979 [1972]) Objective Knowledge: An Evolutionary Approach, Oxford University Press: Great Clarendon Street, Oxford

Potter, J. (1997) Discourse analysis as a way of analysing naturally occurring talk, in D.Silverman (ed.) Qulaitative Research, London: Sage.

Read, C., Ross, J., Dunleavy, J., Schulman, D., Bramante, J. (2001) eCFO: Sustaining Value in the New Corporation, John Wiley & Sons Ltd., Chichester, UK.

Remenyi, D. (2004) The Central Question in Academic Research: What is an Adequate Contribution, Presentation at the Research Techniques Workshop, Henley Management College, May (unpublished).

Remenyi, D. (2005) A Note on the Socratic Dialogue, forthcoming publication

Remenyi, D., Williams, B., Money, A. and Swartz, E. (1998) Doing research in Business and Management: An Introduction to Process and Method, Sage Publications, London

Roach, S.S. (1991), Services under siege – The restructuring imperative, Harvard Business Review, (Sep-Oct 1991), pp.82-92

Ross, J.W. & Beath, C.M. (2002), Beyond the Business Case: New Approaches to IT Investment, Sloan Management Review, Winter, pp. 51-59

Sanchez, O. & Albertin, A.L. (2004) Proposition of an Economic Theory Based Model (MAITEF) to Guide to Effective Firm-Level Information Systems Investment Decisions, AMCIS 2004

Santhanam, R. & Hartono, E. (2003) Issues in Linking Information Technology Capability to Firm Performance, MIS Quarterly, Vol. 27, No.1, pp. 125-153, March

Scholz, R.W. & Tietje, O. (2002) Embedded case study methods: integrating quantitative and qualitative knowledge/ Sage: Thousand Oaks, California

Strauss, A.L. & Corbin, J. (1990) Basics of Qualitative Research: Techniques and Procedures for Developing Grounded Theory, 2nd Edition, Newbury Park, Calif.: Sage

Taudes, A., Feurstein, M., Mild, A. (2000) Options Analysis of Software Platform Decisions: A Case Study, MIS Quarterly 24 (June), pp.:227-243.

Terry, R. (1987) Reflective Leadership: Seven Views of Leadership, Leadership in Public Policy Seminar, Hubert H. Humphrey Institute, University of Minnesota.

The Economist (2011) Follow my leader: Collective behaviour, February 26th, pp.87-8.

Treacy, M. & Wiersema, F. (1995) The Discipline of Market Leaders, Reading, Mass.: Addison-Wesley

Trice, A.W. & Treacy, M.E. (1986) Utilisation as a Dependent Variable in MIS Research, Proceedings of the Seventh International Conference on Information Systems, December.

Trochim, W.M.K (2001) The Research Methods Knowledge Base, Atomic Dog Publishing, Second Edition, Cincinnati, OH

Walsham, G. (1995) Interpretive case studies in IS research: nature and method, European Journal of Information Systems, 4 pp.74-81

Watkins, J. (1998) Information Technology, Organisation and People, Routledge Publishers, London

Weber, R. (2003) Editor's Comment: Theoretically Speaking, MIS Quarterly, Vol. 27, No.3, September, (pp.iii-xii).

Webster, J. & Watson, R.T. (2002) Analysing the Past to Prepare for the Future: Writing a Literature Review, MIS Quarterly, Vol. 26, No.2, pp. Xiii-xxiii(June)

Weill, P. and Broadbent, M. (1998) Leveraging the New Infrastructure: How Market Leaders Capitalise on Information Technology, Harvard Business School Press, Cambridge, MA

Yin, R. (1994), Case Study Research: Design and Methods, Sage Publications, Thousand Oaks, CA.

Index

www.ingramcontent.com/pod-product-compliance
Ingram Content Group UK Ltd.
Pitfield, Milton Keynes, MK11 3LW, UK
UKHW020144250726
13967UKWH00002B/862

9 781908 272119